The Authors :

Rita Dulci Rahman has 26 years of experience in international relations in different fields, among others in trade and investment, migration, conflict resolution, and development co-operation. She has been committee member or chair in several European and Dutch governmental and non-governmental bodies such as EECOD, CCME, ECLOF and Fondad. Born in the Dutch Antilles, she currently works as a diplomat for the Netherlands Government, and has been posted in Bangladesh, India and Tunisia. She obtained her Masters degree in Development Studies at the University of Leiden, Netherlands, and her Bachelors in Mathematics, University of Surinam. For three years (1988–1991) she taught at the University of Leiden. She has published more than 30 articles on international relations

Jose Miguel Andreu is Professor of Economics at the University of Sevilla, Spain. He has also taught Economics in the Basque Country University, in the University of Alcala de Henares, and in the Open University of Spain (UNED). For 30 years he has been delivering lectures on Introduction to Economics, Intermediate Macroeconomics, Superior Macroeconomics, Theory of Economic Growth, Money and Banking etc. He has published several textbooks for students, reports, and more than a hundred articles on Spanish and international economic matters. For two years (1981-1982) he was economic advisor to the Prime Minister of Spain. Recently (2000-2003) he served as a Spanish diplomat to India. Professor Andreu is currently working as an advisor to the African Development Bank in Tunis.

China and India

Towards Global Economic Supremacy?

Rita Dulci Rahman
Jose Miguel Andreu

Academic Foundation
NEW DELHI

NOTE FROM THE AUTHORS :

The opinions, view and recommendations expressed in this publication are strictly personal and do not reflect any official line of thought of the institutions to which the authors belong.

First Published in 2006 by

Academic Foundation
4772-73 / 23 Bharat Ram Road,
(23 Ansari Road), Darya Ganj,
New Delhi - 110 002 (INDIA).
Phones : 23245001 / 02 / 03 / 04.
Fax : +91-11-23245005.
E-mail : academic@vsnl.com
Www : academicfoundation.com

China and India: Towards Global Economic Supremacy?
by Rita Dulci Rahman and Jose Miguel Andreu

ISBN 81-7188-424-5

Designed and typeset by Italics India, New Delhi.
Printed and bound in India.

Contents

Author's Note

This is a book that contains three connected domains and one clear-cut message. The first domain is just an abstract of the main theories of Economic Growth and Development (Chapter 2). Although relevant, this Chapter may be overlooked by readers not interested in the scientific foundations of the growth of nations. Indeed, opting for passing over it will not impede the general understanding of the rest of the book, particularly, if the readers take note of the last item of Chapter 2.

The second field of our analysis is the history and evaluation of the economic policies and results achieved by China and India (Chapters 3, 4, and 5). To this respect we have to clarify that the analysis of China has been conditioned by the available statistical knowledge, scant, disputable and at times inconsistent, which has forced us to make choices among different statistical sources in order to make the most consistent judgement on the Chinese economy. We hope our choices have been right enough.

The third ground (Chapter 6), with its projections into the future, is somewhat speculative although based on solid foundations. In this Chapter, letting aside the *ceteris paribus* clause, typical of the conventional economic analysis, we have tried to introduce possible developments of China and India in a dynamic global political context. This is the reason why we have introduced different scenarios, which in any case are plausible.

Concerning the unequivocal message of the essay, we have to highlight that both text and conclusions on the future are tinged by the derivatives of the new rules that will dominate the economic and political game in the 21st Century. Democratisation in national and international political relations, declining political and economic control of ex-colonies by rich countries, progressive de-segmentation of world markets, easier access to full information and knowledge by communities, and adulthood of very populated and industrious Asian countries—such as China and India—are variables which, combined, will generate a rapid catching up of Asia and a slow but steady economic decline of the West in relative terms.

This future economic landscape will be the automatic result of the working of a non-neutral version of the neo-classical model that Western leadership, after having engineered it, should accept. As a consequence, new generations in the West will have to adjust to an existence more in accordance to their own merits and effort, and less in function of their economic and political heritage. Fortunately, the working of the mentioned economic model will induce a much less deprived life for a majority of the current poor dwellers of our planet.

Finally, and as usual, we will underline that our views, projections and conclusions, as expressed in this publication, are strictly personal and do not reflect any official line of thought of the institutions to which we belong.

— *Rita D. Rahman*
Jose M. Andreu

1

Introduction

"When India suffered two severe droughts in 1965 and 1966, the American President Lyndon Johnson, in order to teach a lesson to India, restricted food aid to a monthly basis under the P.L. 480 programme. This was done to force India not to condemn American aggression in Vietnam."

Datt and Sundharam. (2004:492). Indian Economy. Chand. New Delhi.

1.1. The Birth of Two Giants

At the edge of 1950, although in a very different way, two big countries entered or re-entered into the international political scene. In 1949, mainland China, with the creation of the People's Republic as a consequence of the victory of the communist revolutionaries over the Nationalists[1] who flew to Taiwan, experienced a radical political change. Since then, and during the entire Maoist age (1949-78),[2] the exerted control of the Chinese authorities on the political and economic activities was much deeper than that exercised at times of the last Emperor, the Kuomintang (KMT),[3] or even the Japanese.[4] Consequently, strict controls and instructions coming from the

1. When the former occupying Japanese surrendered in 1945 to the Americans, a civil war broke out in China, and the CCP army finally (1949) defeated the Nationalist one, which flew to Taiwan.

2. Although Mao Tse Dong died in 1976, political change, mainly tilted towards the economic reform, did not start until 1978, headed by the then Prime Minister Den Xiao Pin.

3. When the Empire collapsed in 1911, a nationalist party, the Kuomintang (KMT), succeeded to the last Emperor in the government of the new Republic of China. Nevertheless, long lasting efforts of the nationalists to gain complete control of the country failed. This was due to the fact that, from first moment onwards, the "nationalist" army was caught between two powerful enemies: the controlling Japanese, and the CCP army fighting in the interior.

4. In 1931 the Japanese conquered Manchuria, and in 1937 Japan launched a full invasion of coastal China, whose control lasted till 1945. The economic control of the Japanese was not so deep and extended as that exerted in the paramount period of the Maoism.

Chinese Communist Party (CCP) reached all the layers of the Republic, including the public firms, the labour world, the agricultural activities and even the familial life.

After the private property rights elimination at all levels, the Chinese economy became a copycat of the Soviet model, although more tilted towards agriculture and rural areas. Subsequent to a shameful century of partial occupation and surrendering[5] to foreign powers, and in order to fully defend own sovereignty, the new Chinese regime decided to castle the country, cutting off most of the former links with the rest of the world economy. Note that this decision was made in parallel with the US and allies commercial embargo decreed against the People's Republic of China, due to its intervention in the Korean war (1950-53).

This embargo lasted up to the early-70s.[6] At the end of this decade, after the death of Chairman Mao, a new style of economic policy more in accordance with the world's mainstream economics, although preserving the communist essentials, was initiated in China. Thus, a new economic age of opening up to trade and foreign capitals started its functioning.

Almost simultaneously (in 1947), led by the promoters of the motherland (Gandhi and Nehru), neighbouring India gained its independence from Britain, while suffering a traumatic Partition (with the appearance of Pakistan).[7] This Partition would condition the entire life of the new state up to our days (with the persistent Kashmir issue and the underlying communal Muslim-Hindu wrangling).

---

5. Let us remember that China was defeated by UK in the First Opium War of 1839-42, which resulted in the cession of Hong-Kong. This approach was followed by other "unequal treaties" that drove to the creation of a large number of foreign enclaves along the Chinese coast. These foreign enclaves and their corresponding profits obtained by foreign administrations were then considered as war compensation, generating a great "national humiliation" in China.
6. Note that some countries lifted the embargo just at the end of the Korean war. Observe additionally that after the visit of US President Nixon to China in 1971, the previous Western fiction whereby the Chinese nation was represented in all international institutions by the regime (of the KMT) installed in Taiwan, was progressively overturned.
7. Pakistan was then divided in two provinces, Western Pakistan (the current Pakistan) and Eastern Pakistan, which in 1971 emerged, after an independence war, as a new nation, the current Bangladesh.

Democratic from the very beginning and much more decentralised than China in economic decision-making, the Indian Union also opted for a planned economy, mainly for the development of a heavy industry till then almost inexistent. India did it in a framework of autarky concerning its external relations, in particular when in the late-50s the import substitution (IS) policy for promoting domestic industry gained ground in the developing world as a strategy for attaining higher levels of per capita income. Note that India not only adopted this strategy but also overdid it, becoming one of the most protective and autarkic states of the "free" world.

In the internal economic context, most of the Indian "formal" economic activity[8] had to be authorised[9] and submitted to different powers, those of Union and states, many a times under control of different political parties. This trait, a derivative of the Indian constitutional distribution of power,[10] based on the federalist political organisation of India, has often proven to be dysfunctional and little prone to economic change;[11] in particular when the Union government of India, seeking the unity of the internal market, has tried to introduce more rationality in indirect taxation.[12]

1.2. Common and Diverse Economic Traits of China and India

Along last 50 years China and India have shared several economic and political traits, while at the same time they have also shown relevant differences in their political organisation and developments,

8. Covering today not more than 8 per cent of the labour force. If the labour force was 470 million in 2002 (Table 3), the mentioned 8 per cent represents 37 million labourers working in the formal market.

9. For long, this was called the "Permit-Raj System".

10. In the Indian Constitution two lists of exclusive competencies of the Union and the states, and a list of "concurrent" competencies are specified.

11. Note that India is a Union of 28 states plus several Union Territories, which are constantly and in succession calling polls to their citizens. As a result, the country as a whole is almost in permanent electoral campaign. This is a feature that hampers and delays necessary consensus on relevant Union matters for economic progress.

12. In particular the process of introduction of the Value Added Tax (VAT) in substitution of the Sales Tax, administered by states, is taking too much time. After several attempts, its introduction, "currently expected" for 2005 according to a recent proposal (in July 2004) of the new Minister of Finance—Mr. Chidambaram—finally will generate one single market across India.

as well as in the evolution of the applied economic policies and results.

1.2.1. Similarities of the Two Asian Giants and Qualifications

Besides the almost simultaneous creation of these two countries (1947 and 1949) and the pervasive poverty they inherited from colonial times, a first common trait to be considered is the huge population they had at their inception, and the population explosion they suffered for decades; a population explosion that lasted less time in China than in India. This temporal divergence in choking off population explosion, jointly with other preceding political initiatives more tilted to market solutions, ensured that China would take meaningful advantage over India in the development process as it occurred in the last 25 years.[13]

A second common trait shared by these two big Asian countries is the economic model they initially chose for progress: socialism. Note however that whereas the Chinese socialist model was radical based on dictatorship of the proletariat and total public ownership of production assets, the Indian socialism was democratic and Fabian in which private property was constitutionally consecrated.[14] And this while the political and economic powers given to the different states were huge. The latter was, and is, in sharp contrast to the economic and political powers of Chinese "provinces" which were, and are, heavily dependent on the directives of CCP.[15]

A third shared feature of China and India is their initially chosen commercial strategy for growth: castling behind borders in the context of an "inward looking strategy". This was a consequence both of widespread reservations among their respective leadership towards former colonising powers, and over-confidence in the seize of their domestic markets for supporting healthy industrial development.

---

13. Observe that the per capita income of these two countries was similar in the late-70s, being today the double in China compared to India.
14. Due to this difference, the successive land reforms in China (although basically wrong) were quickly implemented, while in India the expected land reform is even today a pending subject always conditioned to compensations in exchange of confiscation.
15. China is a highly centralised country, having a "one law" system. All the provinces and municipalities share the same rules, and cannot change them or institute something for their own, without expressed permit of the Centre.

State as initial promoter of industrialisation is the fourth similarity amongst the two countries. Although differences between public Indian policies as formulated in 1948, 1956, 1977 and 1980, and those devised in China in times of the "Great Leap Forward" or the "Cultural Revolution" were huge, the public sector was in both cases the only visible head of the industrial thrust.

With some temporal differences and peculiarities, both countries also shared a fifth economic trait— the change in economic orientation, implemented at the end of the 70s and early-80s. Nevertheless, while the Chinese reorientation after 1978 was one of straightforward although partial opening of its economy to international trade, that of India was mainly directed towards a greater than before role played by the private sector,[16] delaying external opening until the critical 1991.

When through different models of industrialisation restated along 80s and 90s, a faster speed of economic progress became a reality in both countries, the distribution of the personal income worsened in China and India, although in consistency with a perceivable reduction of absolute poverty. Indeed, a sixth similarity of these countries that has to be corrected if Chinese and Indian governments want to guarantee the "social tenability" of their ways of growth.

Another initial priority, the seventh similarity of these two Asian giants, was the special consideration to agriculture and rural economic activity, looking for food security. Nonetheless, whereas in China a complete process of confiscation without compensation was initially implemented and different models of socialist agrarian

16. Vide Rodrick, D. and Subramaniam, A. (2004:18) "From Hindu Growth Rate to Productivity Surge: The Mystery of Indian Growth Transition" NBER Working Paper Series. WP 10376. These authors suggest that in the 80s the attained speedier growth in India was not only a consequence of the (Keynesian) deficit spending applied policy, but also the result of the stealthy reforms carried out in the 80s under Indira and Rajiv Gandhi Prime Ministerships. After an initial change of the "private" business climate performed under Indira, her son Rajiv made capital-goods imports easier, reduced taxes, subsidised exports, allowed some investments without a license and enabled the avoidance of the "a priory scrutiny" from the monopolies watchdog (set up by the Monopolistic, Restrictive and Fair Trade Practises Act). These stealthy policies improved Indian "joint productivity of factors" from 0.9 per cent in the 70s to 3.7 per cent along the 80s. Nevertheless, critics of Indira and Rajiv Gandhi's policies suggest that they did not supply new fresh air to Indian economy, just favouring incumbents rather than new entrants. It is also possible that these policies prejudiced the Indian income distribution.

production were successively essayed and scrapped, the implementation of priorities on Indian agriculture reform was more "conservatively" made, mainly through explicit or implicit subsidies[17] and the promotion of the "green revolution," while the reform of land would remain a pending issue.

As an eighth similarity, we have to underline the huge amounts of peasants even today stuck to agricultural activities. No other country in the world has such huge capacity for future transfers of human resources from agriculture to non-agricultural sectors, as China and India have. This is a trait that places these two countries in a privileged position for development in the next 30-40 years. A position which could even improve if China makes its labour markets more flexible to facilitate migration, and to de-segment the different sub-markets in the non-agricultural urban areas.[18] The same could be said about India in relation to its formal labour market,[19] many a time acting as a deterrent to domestic investment and FDI.

From a political point of view with adverse economic results, we find a ninth similarity among the two big Asian neighbours: their involvement in longstanding infighting and in external tensions or wars with neighbouring countries. While China was involved in armed confrontation with Korea and India, and in severe tensions with Soviet Union or Taiwan along the last 50 years, India lost a limited war against China and has been involved in three wars against Pakistan.[20]

On the other hand protracted infighting has also been an another common trait of these two countries. In particular the "Cultural Revolution" in China, and the frequent outbursts of violence between Hindu and Muslim communities in India, and several pro-

17. In a context of indirect support, the provision to Indian agriculture of certain inputs (energy, water, etc.) was for long very under-priced, and consequently faraway from healthy criteria for the allocation of resources.

18. Vide IMF (2004:88) World Economic Outlook Box 2.3. Can China sustain its rapid output growth?.

19. Labour laws in India make it hard to fire staff in big units without state-government's permission.

20. In the context of the Pakistan-India relations one could say that in the past 50 years these relations have never been totally normal.

independence initiatives in both countries, have all of them distracted human and financial efforts from more productive activities.

A tenth common set of problem in these countries is related to their public administrations. Deficiently organised public sectors supported by scant revenues, incipient Social Security systems, and a recent high propensity to incur in public deficit, are common traits to be modified in the near future by the central governments of these two countries.

Scant public revenues in GDP terms and significant deficits in both countries (particularly in India) are to some extent derivatives of their peculiar economic history. The pervasive poverty up to the 80s, which avoided gathering sufficient direct and indirect taxes, and the significant role of the profits of public firms in the total revenues of the Chinese and Indian central administrations, were consequences of the initially chosen model of development (based on public firms for industrial development).

When this model entered into crisis, the progressive dwindling of profits of public firms, as a result of progressive de-nationalisation and increasing competition, was conducive in both countries to a relative decline of total public revenues, not offset by new revenue sources, thus inducing deficits. And this on a base of low public expenditure of the central administrations in comparison to international standards.

Finally, as an eleventh common characteristic, one has to admit that the financial systems of both countries also require significant corrections, in particular that of China, which is in major delay.

1.2.2. Significant Differences between China and India

Although some differences have already been explained above, we will now explicit some additional ones. To start with, we have to stress that, as a derivative of their different political systems—dictatorship *versus* federal democracy—the decision-making process in India is enormously time consuming in comparison to that of China. In many economic reform issues, which at least partially fall under the constitutional competencies of the states, a rule of consensus is needed in India. This rule, as explained by the Public Choice theory, often paralyses the decision-making process, thus consequently placing India in a position of inferiority with respect to China in terms of the speed of structural reforms.[21]

A relevant economic difference between these two countries is that of their labour markets. Although both are mainly based in rural areas and activities, their behaviour has been and is different, being that of India almost completely flexible, except in formal activities,[22] while that of China has been almost entirely protected, segmented, and ruled by the public powers.

The strategies for industrialisation of these two countries have also been very different since their reforms initiation. The Chinese—from 1978 onwards—has been based on declining public sector firms, progressively substituted by rather small private ones and surging FDI, mainly located in some coastal areas and mostly tilted to exports. However, that of India has been based on slow and delayed privatisation and on new almost exclusively "private Indian" initiatives, thus resulting in moderate increases in relative exports. As a result, while the services sector in India represents (2002) 51 per cent of total output, and the contribution of the Indian industry to GDP is 27 per cent, the current contribution of the Chinese industry to GDP is 51 per cent, while the services in China only reach 34 per cent.

Although these two big countries have lastly played in favour of economic opening, with temporal advantage for China which started its aperture more than a decade before India, there is a great difference in the current importance and expansion of the international trade of these two countries. To the extent that whereas China keeps a rapid growing trade share, currently (2003) placed around 5.9 per cent[23] of total world exports,[24] India only keeps a

21. This is a similar problem to that currently experienced by the EU in comparison to the US. The time consuming and paralysing mechanisms in the EU for decision-making in relation to common issues, have additionally become compounded after the enlargement to 25. And this with or without the final ratification of the EU Constitution by EU citizens.

22. Note that the trade unions in India, mainly based in public sector and in big private firms (formal markets), use to behave extremely belligerent and in a counterproductive way for the rest of the country.

23. This figure has been taken from WTO (2004) Press/373, page 10.

24. If we add to the exports share of mainland China (5.9 per cent in 2003) that of Hong-Kong, which is also China, we would reach a figure of 8.9 per cent of total world exports. Note however that a significant part of the Hong-Kong exports are mere Chinese re-exports after coming from mainland.

quota of 0.7 per cent while its gaining share pace is slow. The same could be said in relation to the received FDI, which is enormous in China, around 4-5 per cent in terms of its GDP *versus* the scant figure of India of less than 1 per cent. This is a circumstance that has conditioned the recent Indian industrialisation and consequently has limited its export capacities.

As a result of its previous and successful economic opening, and its precedence in "solving" the problem of its population explosion (resulting in fast increases in internal savings rates), higher domestic investment rates of China have enabled this country to grow throughout more than two decades at almost a double digit annual rhythm. This annual figure of Chinese GDP growth rate, around 10 per cent as an average, has significantly surpassed that of India.[25]

A relevant difference, this time favourable to India, is that of the population structure. Doubtless, as a result of its more long-lasting population explosion, the present percentage of Indians under 15 by far outnumbers that of China, which is bracing itself to confront the economic derivatives of its ageing population.

With all the former data on the desk, we will finalise this quick comparison of the characteristics of China and India by saying that these two countries are nowadays differently considered by the international community. China, which until recently was considered only as a market with plenty of opportunities by western industrialised countries, has today become a source of concern, given the high speed of progression of its aggregated figures, particularly that of trade. However India, although gaining today (2004) certain attention from the economic powers (namely US and EU), is still not at the centre of considerations.

Notwithstanding that, optimistic projections over the economic future of these two countries, and the common political challenges they will have to confront in the future, have encouraged us to the realisation of the following economic and political analysis and comparisons of these two big countries.

---

25. In the last two decades there must have been a difference in the annual GDP growth rate of these two countries, of around 3.6-4 per cent points. This difference enables to explain why in 2002 China had a per capita income around the double of that of India, while at the end of the Maoist period both countries had an alike per capita income.

1.3. Initial Economic Under-Performance of China and India

Letting aside the practical economic stagnation (in terms of per capita income) of China and India in the first half of the 20th Century,[26] we have to say that for different reasons, the first three decades of the political life of these two new states was not easy, while their economic performance was poor and below their own expectations. And this although China achieved a significant development of its industry while incurring deep capital costs.

Since 1950 up to 1978-80,[27] while the world as a whole experienced its maximum historical annual economic growth rate in per capita terms (2.9 per cent),[28] China and India clearly underperformed. Specifically, the per capita GDP grew in China during this period at an average annual rate of 2.3 per cent while India at around 1.3-1.5 per cent. Note that, letting aside the spectacular case of Japan, and that of South Korea, Hong-Kong, Singapore and Taiwan, countries whose per capita GDP annually grew in these three decades above 5 per cent, China and India also under-performed in per capita terms in comparison to Malaysia (2.9 per cent), Thailand (3.6 per cent), Sri-Lanka (2.5 per cent) and other Asian countries.

Concerning the average evolution of their absolute real GDPs, China and India also under-performed in the mentioned period in comparison to total Asia (ex-Japan). Specifically, while Asia (ex-Japan) grew in the period 1950-73—the so-called "golden age of capitalism"—at an annual rate of around 5 per cent, China did it at

26. The per capita income of these two countries practically did not grow in the first half of 20th Century. This stagnation was caused in one of them (China) by the almost constant turmoil provoked by foreign incursions in its territory, lastly by the Japanese invasion; and in the other (India) by the continuation of the exploiting strategy deployed for centuries by the British. The per capita Indian growth rate in the period 1900-1948 has been recently estimated by Sivasubramanian (1998), who found a figure almost nil. Vide Y.V. Reddy, the present Governor of the Reserve Bank of India. RBI Bulletin. Dec. 07 2000.

27. From now onwards we will use the years 1978 and 1980 as moments in which for different reasons the speed of growth of China and India changed.

28. Vide Maddison, A. (2001:129). The World Economy. A Millennium Perspective. OECD. Paris. Note that the period considered by Maddison as the "Golden Age of Capitalism" covers the period 1950 to 1973.

4.4 per cent,[29] and India at an average around 3.5 per cent, the so-called "Indian growth rate".[30] If the real GDPs of China and India underperformed, and the rates of growth of their population moved around the average of Asia (ex-Japan), which was 2.2 per cent (2.0 per cent in China and a little higher figure in the case of India), the per capita GDPs of these countries had necessarily to under-perform, as mentioned above.

Note that the mentioned under-performance of these two countries in the period 1950-73 was mainly due to: 1) The internal economic instability generated in China by successive land reform experiments, the illogic of its forced industrialisation at time of the Great Leap Forward, and the political infighting unleashed in China in the 60s and early 70s in the days of the so-called "Cultural Revolution"; 2) The external political problems of India with neighbouring China and Pakistan, conducive to one lost (limited) war with the former and three successive wars fought with Pakistan, and permanent political border tensions in Kashmir; 3) The somewhat voluntary economic isolation of these two countries, although for different reasons, from the international division of labour; and 4) The selected model for internal economic progress (socialism, and extreme interventionism).

1.4. Brilliant Behaviour in Last Two Decades (1980-2002) and Current Economic Positions of China and India

Conversely, the economic behaviour in the last two decades of the 20th Century has been very different in China and India in comparison to their respective economic performances in the period 1950-1978 (80), particularly in the first mentioned country.

After 1978 the conception of the economic policy changed radically in China: the principle of supremacy of "collective agriculture production" was abandoned, the small-sized industrial and services activities were liberalised in a phased way (performing

29. Note that the figure of 4.4 per cent of average annual growth of China for the period 1952-78, has been taken from Maddison (1998:73). Book already mentioned.

30. This "Indian growth rate" (3.5 per cent), consistent with a contemporary per capita growth rate of around 1.3-1.5 per cent, is a well known expression original from Prof. Krishna.

then onwards better than public firms), and the Chinese economy progressively opened to external interchanges of goods and services, and to foreign investments.

This new economic orientation of China, born in 1978, was not followed either by the Soviet Union, whose economy was crumbling those days,[31] or by India, which instead of embracing in the 80s a new style of economic policy, just limited itself to some inward oriented "corrections", giving more chance to the corporate private sector in industrial development, while accelerating public expenditure.[32] This combination of policies in India generated, along higher average annual GDP growth rates (5.7 per cent), untenable inflation and public and external deficits. Finally, in 1991, to amend its then extremely difficult external situation, India had no remedy but to start its first period of significant reforms.

As a consequence of the undertaken pro-market reforms, initiated 13 years before in China (1978) than in India (1991), and with a greater and steady determination and velocity of progression in the former than in the latter, both countries began a new stage in their economic history. Needless to say that although the performance of India in the last two and half decades has been good, the registered new economic trend of China has simply been spectacular.

Specifically in relation with the period 1978-2002, China, helped by a downwards trend in the progression of its demography,[33] which moved from an annual growth rate of 2.0 per cent in the period 1952-78, to another of 1.1-1.2 per cent in 1978-2002,[34] experienced an astonishing per capita annual growth rate of 7.8-8.3 per cent. In

31. Note that in 1978 the per capita GDP of China was equivalent to 15 per cent of that of the Soviet Union, while in 2002 the Chinese per capita GDP represented around 50 per cent of that of Russia. Vide. Maddison, A. (1998:62) Book already mentioned; and World Bank (2004). World Development Indicators.

32. A common argument used to explain the unsustainable but rapid GDP growth rate of India in the 80s, mainly based on public deficit expending, has been clearly expressed by Ahluwalia, M. (2002) in "Economic Reforms in India since 1991: has gradualism work?" Journal of Economic Perspectives. Vol.16. Vide. also Srinivasan, T. and Tendulkar, S. (2003) in "Reintegrating India in the World Economy". Institute for International Economics. Washington D.C.

33. In China, from 1972 onwards, as we will comment it in Chapter 3, the "indirect" official pressure on families for reducing the family size was more than significant.

34. Vide figures of Maddison, A. (1998:66) Book already mentioned; and those of WB (2004) Book already mentioned.

the meantime India only marked a more modest figure of 3.8 per cent in its per capita income rise, a comparatively compressed rate partially stemming from the maintenance of a high population progression, placed in these two decades around 1.9-2 per cent.

Adding the figures of progression of population and per capita GDP, one may deduce that in the above considered period of two decades, the Chinese GDP grew annually at around 10 per cent, while that of India at around 5.8 per cent.

The combination of their huge and growing populations, their initial (in 1978-80) per capita GDPs,[35] and the two rough figures of 10 per cent and 6 per cent of GDP annual growth rates registered by China and India in the last 20-25 years, have nowadays (2002) placed these economies respectively in the 2nd and 4th places in the GDP-PPP world ranking.

Note however that the current disparities in terms of growth rates between China and India—to a great extent due to the earlier implementation of economic reforms in China, its faster industrialisation, and its prior population compression—could significantly be bridged in future, if the growth rate of the Indian population moves downwards and its so-called "second generation" economic reforms step up. All this would enable a significant increase of the domestic and external savings in India, which *ceteris paribus* would allow the achievement of greater domestic investment rates in physical (and human) resources, thus bringing the reduction of the current disparities between China and India in reach.

1.5. China and India: Two Countries with Great Economic Expectations

Although we cannot ignore the difficult economic position of the Chinese and Indian citizens who only count nowadays with limited per capita GDPs[36]—960 US dollars in China and 470 in India (2002)—and related shortage in the provision of many private and public goods and services, one should not undervalue the capacities

35. In the year 2002 the per capita GDP of China in PPP terms was around 4.520 US$, while that of India was 2.650 US$. Note that the per capita GDP (PPP) of the US—taken as a base for international comparisons—reached the figure of 35.400 US$ in 2002.

36. In terms of dollars at current exchange rate.

of progression of these two giants, assumedly called to become global powers.

Concerning predictions on the future of these two countries, one has to move in two tiers: the economic one and the political one. Specifically, the foundations of any economic prediction about the future of China and India have to rely on theories of economic development, applicable to those developing countries that experience rapid structural changes,[37] and on the conventional theory of economic growth.[38] This economic approach, with the help of econometric exercises, may show us a trend of China and India (less in the case of India) to quickly gain in world share, being this in GDP or in international trade or financing. In this pure economic and partial context, the recent exercise published by Goldman-Sachs[39] is illustrative.

Using the last available demographic projections, bringing in some "reasonable" assumptions on the evolution of internal saving rates, on the expectable external inflows of capital and on the trend of productivity, and playing with a capital accumulation model, the authors of the mentioned exercise have extrapolated the current economic trends of China and India year by year, from 2003 up to 2050. This exercise has been done also for the most relevant western countries, including the US. Logically, the longest the period of econometric prediction the lesser the credibility of the results, because the latter will become more and more contaminated with national and international political and economic changes, which currently cannot be envisaged accurately or cannot be foreseen at all.

According to the conclusions of the mentioned economic study, as early as 2009 a small group of four countries (China and India, plus Russia and Brazil) will have a joint absolute growth of their production (in US$ terms) greater than that of the six currently more advanced countries altogether: US, France, Germany, Italy, Japan and

37. Mainly based on the model of Lewis for rapid industrialisation, and on that of the opportunities from the backwardness, original from Gerschenkron. Vide. Todaro, M. (2003) Economic Development. 8th Ed. Pearson Education.

38. Mainly the neoclassical model with the complement of the endogenous growth perspective.

39. Vide Wilson, D. and Purushothaman, R. (2003) "Dreaming with BRICs. The Path to 2050". Goldman Sachs Global Economic website. Global Economics Paper No. 99. October.

the U.K.. This means that in 2009 the mentioned group of four will become the engine of economic growth of the world.

As suggested by the mentioned study, this catching up process of the four mentioned countries commanded by China and India will continue, which *ceteris paribus* would generate in 2050 a shocking picture in relation with the economic potentialities of the analysed countries. China, US and India, and by this order, would then be economically and politically the more powerful countries of the world. Behind them, but far away in the economic game, and consequently in the political one, would be Japan, Brazil and Russia. Finally in the last wagon, and by this order, we would find UK, Germany, France and Italy.[40]

In our view, the trend of the recent economic history may mark a future evolution for catching up not faraway from the mentioned one, and mainly in the cases of China and India.[41] These are two countries with pressing populations, mainly in the latter, with huge reserves of labour force with nil marginal productivity currently stuck to agricultural activities and with a great margin for technical improvement in their physical and human capital, and with a great capacity for generating internal savings, particularly in the case of China.[42]

Conversely to the successful 20th century cases of Japan,[43] Korea and some other Asian tigers, at the beginning of the 21st Century

40. Note that some of the mentioned Euro-Zone countries plus other current EU partners, long before 2050 may have become a EU Federation. In our opinion it is expectable that with the attainment of a voluntary Federation—probably out of the road map vaguely devised in the recently consented EU Constitution—the federated economy will reach significant economies of scale, reap economies of integration up to 2 per cent of its joint GDP, and significantly gather momentum, which could partially contradict the results of the commented Goldman-Sachs study.

41. In the first half of 2004, in the wake of the so-called "overheating" of the Chinese economy and the unexpected change of Government in India, which allegedly could derail the Indian reforms process (because Communist "could finally condition" the Government actions), some analysts have spread suggestions on the future lower growth rate of these two countries.

42. In the last years the gross internal saving of China has always ranged between 38-43.7 per cent in terms of its GDP. Although the gross internal saving of India has till now been more modest and placed around 21-22 per cent, there are few doubts that this parameter may easily increase when the Indian population growth rate recedes. In relation to predictions on decreasing population growth rates of India, Vide WB.(2004) World Development Indicators.

43. A common argument many a times listened in Western countries is that the current rapid economic progress of China may finish in a few years period, as it occurred with Japan in the 90s.

China and India seem to be very faraway from the typical positions of relative diminishing returns, suffered by some of the above mentioned countries just two or three decades after their "take off" processes. Indeed, China and India have started their new development processes in 1978(80) at significant lower economic levels in per capita GDP terms than many of their Asian competitors had, and with a delay of two decades. Hence, their current huge potentialities for transferring labour from their rural areas to the industrial and service sectors, may additionally last three or four decades as a minimum.

1.6. The Case of India as a Surprise

The previous comments on the long term future of the Indian economy, placing this country at the end of the first half of the 21st century side by side with the currently fashionable China and the mighty US, may come as a surprise for all those who, fully supporting comments and claims of western traders or foreign investors in India, have been or are pessimistic in relation to the future possibilities of the Indian economy.

Although acknowledging that in the last 20 years the way of doing business in India has not been easy for foreigners, it is likely that along the next ten years, many of the current problems of India will be overcome. Particularly, we are here referring to the achievement of the unity of market,[44] the simplification of the ex-asperatingly slow judicial machinery[45]—the slowest of the world according to some indicators—the establishment of limitations of Trade Union

44. Many a times, Westerners complain on the current lack of market unity in India (different indirect taxes in different states, different rates, etc.). Note however that while this unity of markets is sometimes bitterly demanded by the Western representations in Delhi, this unity is today far from being totally accomplished within the EU (in which there are different corporate taxes, withholding capital taxes, etc.).

45. As it is well known, the infuriatingly slow judicial machinery of India enables, among other things, that "assumed" criminals become MPs in successive parliaments. Former President of India, Mr. Narayanan, made in his last months in office a call to political parties to not include assumed criminals in the electoral lists. In current days, according to *Outlook*, an Indian weekly magazine, no fewer than 100 of the 542 MPs of the lower house face criminal charges. The fact that the "happening" of Ayodhya—an assumed illegal demolition of a Mosque by extremist *hindus* to build up a *hindu* temple in the same place—has not been solved after 12 years, is a paradigm of the annoying juridical system of India. Vide The Economist June, 19th, 2004, page 64.

actions in public sector, and the reduction of complexities in mutual relations among the different Indian administrations (Union and States). These modifications—together with that of the currently complicated electoral schedule and others—are urgent and would suppose a relevant change in the legal framework of India. Indeed, these changes, if implemented, could significantly accelerate by itself the rhythm of progress of the Indian economy.

On the other hand, one has to underline that India has a comparatively higher per cent of its population who speak English, and has a higher number of people involved in international relations, thus being better endowed for international business, which is an advantage in comparison to China. Finally, along the current and next decade, it is expectable that the infrastructure, energy, education and health deficiencies of India will be significantly reduced, while its population growth problem will be overcome, corrections that will place India in a position of steady growth at higher rates in comparison to other economic powers. And perhaps from 2013-2015 onwards[46] even at a higher rate than that of China.

1.7. Success of China and India and Likely Reactions of the West

Half a century—that is to say, perspectives up to 2050—is too long a period to keep untouched the *ceteris paribus* clause implicit in any economic exercise. Doubtless, if the current economic trend continues, it will naturally generate a larger international clout for China and India, which automatically could provoke international political reactions coming from those countries that would lose economic and political status and influence.

Along history of mankind, no hegemonic power (or group of hegemonic countries) has without any reaction given way to another more dynamic economic or demographic country (or group of them). Disturbing actions in economic matters, and more or less disguised or open battles, based on the "supremacy of own values" or on other *ad hoc* pretexts, but mainly rooted in the defence of own economic and political interests, have been common instruments for defending provisional privileged positions.

46. Vide. Goldman-Sachs (2003:21). Document already mentioned.

With the crumbling of the Soviet Union, the former international political equilibrium—which could have played in favour of China and India—has disappeared. This has given the US the opportunity of apparently[47] becoming a new hegemonic power in the world.[48] In the aftermath of the Twin Towers attack, a particular interpretation coming from its presumed hegemonic position has brought again to reality old and formerly abandoned doctrines, as those of pre-emptive actions and its justifications.[49]

In consistency with its new role as a hegemonic nation, and as expectable in absence of political countervailing powers, US international politics have become much more unilateral, in particular in the first years of the 21st century. This risky way of doing international politics has surprisingly gained ground in the West, even among some members of the EU. We understand that this political repositioning of some EU-partners, is an indicator of possible grouping in future, under the US leadership, for the defence of their common interests in front of a possible fundamental change in the gravity centre of the global economy.

In absence of a countervailing power, unilateralism and selected grouping of powerful minorities[50] could be conducive to economic or political abuse. In this a context, it is possible that any nation (or group of them) that may appear as a threat to the Western way of life, due to its comparative economic success, could become a target for economic or political action.

Note that these possible defensive actions of Western countries, would not only be unfair but also short-sighted. Unfair because, in

---

47. Although in possession of the most important pile of WMD and also having the highest-tech army, the amount of its human factor in the military service (personnel) is by no means sufficient to police the world on its own, as it has been proven in the case of the Iraq war. Additionally the American voters do not want to spend money in long wars.

48. We do consider that the existence of countervailing powers is a fundamental premise for democracy, be this national or international. In economics the absence of countervailing powers is conducive to abusive monopolies and in politics to authoritarian behaviour. We firmly believe that any *ad hoc* argument against this principle is pure demagogy.

49. For long abandoned, this doctrine has been at the core of the two pre-emptive wars recently launched by the US and allies. For an elemental consideration on the foundations of the pre-emptive actions, vide The Economist (2003:25) November 22nd.

50. Note that the US and EU only make up for around 10 per cent of the population of the planet.

this case, efforts of deprived citizens in China and India to improve their lives after long periods of colonial exploitation, would vanish. And short-sighted because, the expected rapid economic growth of China and India in the next decades, far for being negative for the collectively, would significantly improve the economic welfare of the world.

However, due to the fact that there are always losers in socio-economic changes, and being these losers the majority of citizens (workers) of richer countries, one has to expect defensive actions[51] from the West.

Consequently, we do believe that the economic future of China and India will also depend on their capacities to develop political strategies concerning actions in the global power play, mainly by means of promoting multilateralism—in the context of a renewed UN—in order to offset adverse actions of others of a bilateral character.

1.8. Content of the Book

In order to analyse in detail the possibilities of China and India to become successful economic global players, as some recent econometric projections have suggested, we will start (Chapter 2) with briefly presenting the foundations (theories) of Economic Development and Growth of nations. Once introduced these theories based on experience, we will rapidly identify the aggregated causes of the recent success and the current underlying problems of the Chinese economy. Likewise, we will also detect the current challenges that the Indian economy has to overcome in order to step up its growth rate, as desired by Indian government, to more rapidly alleviate the problem of its voluminous poverty.

After knowing the main theoretical traits of the process, we will successively enter (Chapters 3 and 4) in the description of the historically applied economic policies by China and India, glossing those incorrect and those successful. After that, we will refer to the recent economic performance of China and India (Chapter 5), with

51. Note that these actions would be supported internally in Western countries by their democratic institutions; decisions that, paradoxically would not be democratic at a global scale. In this regard and from now onwards, we do believe that the international community should discuss the future geographical dimension of democracy.

special reference to the evolution of their GDP, their demography, and their per capita GDP in a global context. We will also deal in this chapter with the evolution of the international trade of these countries and their hinterlands, with their labour markets, and with their internal and external financial figures, as restricting factors of their domestic investment processes; we will also review some political problems of these two countries. And all this will be followed by our reflections on some suggested ideas for internal corrections in different economic fields.

Later on (Chapter 6), we will make an academic exercise, trying to imagine the problems that China and India could face in the first two decades of the 21st century, in order to overcome the difficulties that external powers may put in front of them to limit or curve their velocity of economic growth.

In the wake of possible actions, we will describe possible strategies that China and India could adopt to move forward. Finally, the last chapter (Chapter 7) will deal with a summary of findings and conclusions, as well as with alternative scenarios that could become real.

2

Growth Theory and Development Policy

Before entering in explanations and due assessments of the economic policies applied in China and India in the last 50 years, it is convenient to provide the reader with some elements of the theory of economic growth plus some specific qualifications extracted from the theory of economic development.

As it is well known the ability of a country to improve the standards of living of its citizens depends crucially on its long run rate of economic growth. In this regard it is important to underline that, over a long period of time, even apparently small differences in the achieved annual growth rate by a specific country may generate significant differences in the standard of living of its citizens in comparison to those of other nations. Logically, if a country wants to initiate a manoeuvre for catching up, or to continue with it, as it is currently happening in the cases of China and India, the larger the attained growth rate the shorter will be the catching up period.

As it has recently been suggested, in strict economic terms *and ignoring international political variables*,[52] "no one understands completely why economies grow; and no one has a magic formula for inducing rapid growth. Indeed, if such a formula existed, there would be no poor nations. Despite of it, economists have gained useful insights about the growth process"[53] under the *ceteris paribus* clause, that's to say ignoring surrounding new political and economic events, capable of changing inertial trends.

Nonetheless, before entering in detailed considerations and assessments on past and future growth problems of China and India,

---

52. Note that to achieve the high economic standards of living as those historically attained by some western countries, (aggressive) defence efforts and its derivative of eventual political domination, have many a time been as important as technical corollaries stemming from the economic growth models.

53. Vide Abel, A. and Bernanke, B. (2001:206). Macroeconomics. Pearson Education.

and possible political reactions of the rich world, we will briefly explain in this chapter the basic economic forces that determine the growth rate of any country.

2.1. Non-strict Economic Factors as Pre-conditions of Growth and Development

Although many a time the non-economic factors are considered irrelevant for the analysis, the cases of China and India force us to take them into account more carefully. Indeed, it would be unwise to underrate the importance of the social organisation of certain big countries, and in particular the underlying psychological, sociological and cultural factors, that may condition their entire economic life. This is because some keys of the growth process lie in men's minds, and in the specific institutions in which their thinking finds expression. As the reader may imagine, the cases of China and India, are very different in these fields to the majority of the Western countries and, therefore their cultural factors should be beared in mind.

Consequently, most developing economies that want to start or to accelerate their growth process, not only must increase the level of their investments in comparison to their GDP, as we will clarify in next items, but also to gradually change some socio-cultural and political institutions, if they actually act as deterrent to a desirable economic progress, as this is today understood.

In this regard we should not forget that economic development cannot be upgraded unless people are minimally educated and healthy, the organisation of the state and related administrations is functional, the economic role of the public sector is clearly defined, the applicable law behaves as neutral and steady, and above all there is no infighting or violent conflicts with neighbouring countries. All these traits and conflicts use to inhibit or degrade the growth process, making the growth rates move under optima. The economic under-performance of China and India between 1950 and 1978(80) are clear proofs of the relevance of the statements above.

To the extent that deficient political organisation or non-organised markets exist in China and India, this dysfunction may place the production of these countries well under their "production possibilities frontiers." As a result, current standards of living of their citizens may remain relatively depressed in comparison to their respective potentials. Consequently, "mere" reshuffling of the economy and societal organisation—some times difficult to be implemented—may generate significant economic improvements for their collectives during a certain period, without spectacular changes in relative investments.

2.2. Sources of Economic Growth

Letting aside the above mentioned non-strict economic factors of development, and starting with a one-sector analysis of the macroeconomic evolution, as it is typically done in conventional handbooks on the issue, we have to say that the output of goods and services of an economy depends on the quantities of available inputs, such as capital and labour, and on the productivity of those inputs.

The relationship between output and inputs is described by professional economists who resort to the so-called aggregated production function, $Y=A.F(K,L)$, in which Y is the GDP, A is a factor related with the level of the joint productivity of factors, and K and L respectively are the available amounts of capital and labour.

For the quantity of output to grow, either the quantity of inputs must grow, or joint productivity must grow, or both of them. In any of these cases, the relationship between the output growth rate and the input and productivity growth rates[54] is:

$$\Delta Y/Y=\Delta A/A+a.\Delta K/K+ b.\Delta L/L \quad (1)$$

In this equation $\Delta Y/Y$ is the yearly growth rate of the output; $\Delta A/A$ is the annual growth rate of the joint productivity of factors; $\Delta K/K$ is the yearly growth rate of capital; $\Delta L/L$ is the annual growth rate of labour; "a" is the elasticity of output with respect to capital; and "b" is the elasticity of output with respect to labour.[55] The former

54. Differentiating the former equation $Y=A.F(K,L)$, we will arrive to the expression (1).

55. In this formula "a" is the percentage increase in output resulting from a 1 per cent increase in the capital stock, and "b" is the percentage increase in output resulting from a 1 per cent increase in the amount of used labour. These percentages are known in the macroeconomists jargon as elasticity's. Both elasticity's "a" and "b" are numbers normally ranged between 0 and 1 that must be estimated from historical data. If there are constant returns to scale in the production function, as frequently assumed, it will necessary occur that $a+b=1$.

expression (1) is the so-called "growth accounting equation," which enables reckoning the impact on GDP growth rate of an increase in capital, labour or joint productivity.[56]

As every variable of (1), except the variation of the productivity level, is observable, the evolution rate of the joint productivity of factors will be easily deducible from (1):

$$\Delta A/A=\Delta Y/Y-a.\Delta K/K-b\Delta L/L \quad (2)$$

Consequently the "growth accounting technique" will enable to reckon the portion of growth not explained by the registered increases in capital or labour. This is of special interest because it makes possible to analyse the causes of growth in every country[57] and in different periods within a specific country.[58]

---

56. For instance, if a new invention allows all firms to produce 10 per cent more output without increasing inputs of capital and labour, then the combined productivity of factors, A, will have risen 10 per cent, the same than the output. As a result, $\Delta A/A=\Delta Y/Y=10$ per cent.

    Conversely if both factors (K and L) increase by 10 per cent and productivity do not increase at all, the output will rise at 10 per cent. So in this case $\Delta Y/Y=\Delta K/K=\Delta L/L=10$ per cent.

    Finally, if firms invest making an increase of 10 per cent in K, and "a" has a value of 0.25, while volume of labour do not undergo any increase, the evolution of Y will be of 2.5 per cent. In this case the evolution of K will have been submitted to diminishing returns.

57. For instance, between 1966 and 1991, Hong-Kong grew more than 7 per cent per year, while between 1966 and 1990 Singapore, South Korea and Taiwan grew at more than 8 per cent. One could wonder for the causes of this almost miraculous growth, and if these high growth rates could continue for long. Precisely the "growth accounting equation" give us an accurate answer. Specifically, Prof. Young, using a variety of data sources which allowed him to know the growth rates of the GDP, capital and labour of all these countries, reached the conclusion that the rapid growth of these nations was due to the quick growth of the applied factors of capital and labour, and not so much to improvements in their joint productivity, A. This joint productivity did not grow more than 2.6 per cent (figure of Taiwan) in any of these countries, while the joint productivity of Singapore was almost nil (0.2 per cent). As a result, the spectacular growth rates of these countries during the mentioned periods were due to the rapid growth of the applied factors to the production, a growth that logically cannot continue for long unless their populations grow quickly (thus admitting migrants at high rates) and their saving rate continue being high. Conversely these countries could only continue their miraculous growth if their joint productivities grew at a much larger rate. Note however that the growth rates of the joint productivities of these countries in the same period were similar or lower to that of Italy, a country which did not enjoyed a "miraculous" growth. Vide. Young, A.(1995) "The tyranny of numbers: Confronting the statistical realities of the East-Asia growth experience". *Quarterly Journal of Economics*. August.

58. Note for instance that growth in China, despite its poor performance in the Maoist age was mainly due to the growth of factors (capital and labour) and not to the growth of its joint productivity. However its recent miraculous growth has been due not only because of its high rate of capitalisation but also due to the significant growth rate of the joint productivity of its factors, which has grown at around 2.5 per cent in the last two decades.

2.3. Growth Dynamics

Although the "growth accounting" provides indispensable information about the sources of growth, it does not explain the way of working of the economic engine of development. This is because the "growth accounting" takes as mere data the velocities of progression of factors and productivity, but does not explain the causes of the mentioned velocities.

From now onwards, we will introduce in the analysis the causes of the growth of the factor capital, initially considering (for simplifying) that the labour force grows at a constant rate, following the so-called neoclassical model of economic growth, original from the awarded Nobel Prize, Prof. Solow.[59] This model establishes the relationships between the growth rate of a country, the size of its savings rate, its labour force growth rate and the growth rate of its technical progress or joint productivity. The corollaries of this model also enable to formulate policies to accelerate the process of growth, while they will allow us to discuss the so-called problem of the "convergence" of the per capita GDP of the different countries, be these poor or rich.

2.3.1. The Neoclassical Model of Growth

In relation to the trajectory of the labour force, the neoclassical model assumes that its evolution moves at a constant rate, "n", precisely at the same rate as that of population. This implies that there is a fixed share of working population over total population.

This model also assumes that the capital of every year is larger than that of the previous one, because a new net investment ($\Delta K=I-dK$) is added to the previous capital.[60] Consequently, the production (Y) non-invested in gross terms is the consumption (C) of the period ($C=Y-I$).[61] If we divide all considered variables by L, we will arrive

---

59. Vide Solow, R. (1956). "A Contribution to the Theory of Economic Growth." *Quarterly Journal of Economics*. February.

60. Note that a part of the gross investment, I, normally a fraction "d" ($0<d<1$) of the accumulated capital, K, will necessarily be devoted to substitute the depreciated capital. Consequently the net investment, ΔK, will be equal to I (gross investment) less depreciation of existent capital, dK.

61. Note that in this model, just for simplifying purposes, are not included either the public sector or the external one.

at "y" (per worker production), "c" (per worker consumption), and "k" (available capital per worker).

Dividing the aggregate production function by L, it is also possible to formulate this production function in terms of production per worker, y=f(k), once having *provisionally* considered that A is a constant (which implies that joint productivity of factors does not grow). On the other hand, under the assumption of constant returns to scale, "y" will grow when "k" grows, but less than proportionally, due to diminishing returns of capital.

2.3.1.1. Equilibrium Steady State

One of the most relevant conclusions drawn from the neoclassical model is that in absence of productivity growth, any economy will reach in the long run an equilibrium steady state, characterised by constant values of "y", "c", and "k". This means that GDP, total capital, K, and consumption, C, will grow *pari passu* (at the same speed) with the volume of the working force, L.

In order that the available capital, K, grows at the steady rate, "n", to keep untouched the level of "k", this will require that gross investment, I, evolves at a level equivalent to (n+d)K. As a result, the steady state consumption, C=(Y-I), will be: C=Y-(n+d)K. This expression, taking into account all former considerations, could be restated in per worker terms as: c=f(k)-(n+d)k.

The last expression teaches us that the consumption per worker, being a function of "k" will have a maximum when f'(k)=(n+d), which is the condition that maximises the economic welfare of future generations.[62] This means that there always will be a value of k* that will maximise the value of "c", being the corresponding per capita GDP, y*=f(k*).

Having said that, one could wonder if policy-makers are in any case right when they recommend increasing the value of k=K/L, by stimulating savings and investment, in order to rise the value of "c" (the consumption per worker) of next generations. The reality is that in this regard the historical experience do not leave margins to doubt— the answer to the former question is "yes". Even for high saving and developed countries as Japan, further increases in capital

62. This condition is named by the growth literature as the Golden Rule of Growth.

per worker would lead to higher steady state consumption per worker.[63] The same could be said now-a-days about China and India, and with much more certainty, because their values of "c" (their per capita consumption) are well under those of Japan or US.

2.3.1.2. Path Towards the Steady State

The above achieved conclusions on the steady state equilibrium, has left two loose ends. The first is the proof of the convergence of any economy to the steady state equilibrium if joint productivity does not grow; and the second refers to what will be the situation reached by an economy in relation with "c" and "y" after a certain period of time, if productivity improves.

To explain the first conundrum, we will need an additional piece of information, the saving function, which is assumed by the neoclassical model as proportional to the GDP, (Y), that is to say, S=sY (being "s" < Λ, factor of proportionality). As a result, if in any period the equilibrium in the markets of goods and services of new production has to be fulfilled, the planned saving (S=sY) has to be equal to the required gross investment, I. This condition will imply in the steady state that S=sY=(n+d)K=I.

To determine the steady state equilibrium of k=k', we just need to divide the last expression by L. Doing so, we will arrive to the expression s.f(k)=(n+d)k. Logically, knowing the values of "s", "n" and "d", because they are parameters of the economy stemming and reckonable from current trends, the value of k' will be easily obtained.

Note that in a disequilibrium position, that is to say, if the volume of per worker savings (sy) is larger than the necessary per worker gross investment, (n+d).k, to keep the current value of "k", then the value of k will rise. Consequently, the expression that will describe the path of the economy towards the steady state equilibrium will be:

$$\Delta k = s.f(k) - (n+d)k \qquad (3)$$

This is an expression which proves that if s.f(k) is larger than (n+d)k, k will tend to grow; and if the opposite happens k will tend

63. Vide Abel, A., Mankiw, G., and others (1989) "Assesing Dynamic Efficiency: Theory and Evidence." *Review of Economic Studies*. January.

to diminish. Of course, as in equilibrium $\Delta k=0$, then the steady state equilibrium of the consumption per worker will be $c'=f(k')-(n+d)k'$.

Summarising, if we assume that there is no productivity growth, the economy in any case will reach the steady state equilibrium in the very long run. In this steady state output per worker and consumption per worker will remain constant over time, although the absolute value of the GDP (Y) and the consumption of the economy (C) will grow at a rate "n", which is the growth rate of the labour force coinciding with that of population.

This conclusion may seem gloomy because it implies that the living standards must eventually stop improving. However, that conclusion of the neoclassical model will be avoided if, as it has actually happened in last two centuries, productivity continually increases.[64] Consequently, if joint productivity of factors grows, it is perfectly possible to surpass the law of diminishing returns of capital. In this case, "y" and "c" will grow even in the long run at the rate $\Delta A/A$.

2.3.1.3. Determinants of Long Run Living Standards

As it is easy to prove, according to the neoclassical growth model depicted lines above, the levels of per worker income (y) and per worker consumption (c), will grow : 1) *when the saving rate(s) rise*, because this higher saving rate will enable to increase the volume of investments, which will make it possible for the value of per worker capitalisation to rise, thus increasing the per worker production (y); 2) *when the growth rate of the labour force falls,*[65] since the higher the growth rate of the labour force, the more output will have to be used to equip new workers with capital, leaving less output available for per worker consumption or to increase the per worker capital, and vice versa; and 3) *when joint productivity rise*, because higher productivity will directly increase the per worker production, and consequently the per worker savings and capital stock.

---

64. Vide Abel, A. and Bernanke, B. (2001:223) "Macroeconomics." Book already mentioned.

65. Or when the growth rate of the population falls. Remember that the model assumes that the labour force and the total population grow at the same rate.

2.3.1.4. Policies to Step-up Living Standards Stemming from the Neoclassical Model

Of the factors affecting long run living standards, the growth rate of productivity is the most significant in the neoclassical model of growth. There are several ways through which governments may positively affect the level of the productivity factor, A.

Improving infrastructure[66] could be in general terms[67] a clear mechanism for raising the joint productivity of factors in LDC. Indeed lack of sufficient infrastructure use to choke their development processes. *Building up human capital* is another source of productivity growth. To increase expenditure in primary and secondary schooling are investments in human capital with maximum social return rates from a perspective of long run growth. Working training, labour reallocation and health programmes implementation may also significantly increase the joint productivity of the factors. *Removing barriers (red tape) to entrepreneurial activity* could also increase productivity by encouraging new initiatives. Finally encouraging "research & development" (R&D) will also significantly increase the joint productivity of factors.[68]

2.3.2. The Neoclassical Model and the Problem of Convergence

The corollaries of the neoclassical model of growth may also help us to describe the possibility of the per worker or per capita incomes of the different countries, developed or developing, to converge. Although the reality does not seem to point in the direction of convergence,[69] we will here discuss the corollaries of the neoclassical model on this issue.

---

66. Namely, highways, bridges, dams, airports and utilities.

67. Note that not always an additional increase of infrastructures raises productivity. It has been said that some times additional infrastructure may be a consequence of having a high average productivity in the economic system, and not vice versa. This has probably been the case of Japan in the 90s, a country that in the context of a juncture—but micro-economically inefficient—Keynesian policy, may have invested in infrastructures more than necessary as to increase productivity.

68. Political claims for increasing the percentage of GDP devoted to basic research, in small countries, are many a time a mistake because the positive results of the basic research are a rather direct function of the absolute value of the devoted funds and not of the high relative ones possibly applied in a small country. This last strategy would just be a money squandering one.

69. Vide to this respect, Rahman R. and Andreu J.M. (2004) *Responsible Global Governance: A Programme for World Stability and Institutional Reform*. Academic Foundation. New Delhi. In particular Chapter 3, titled "On Economic Results of Globalisation and the Role of Multilateral Institutions."

There are at least three possible scenarios for the evolution of living standards throughout the world: unconditional convergence, conditional convergence, and no convergence at all. Following Abel and Bernanke,[70] "by unconditional convergence we mean that the poor counties eventually will catch up with the rich countries so that in the long run living standards around the world become more or less the same. (In this regard) the (neoclassical) model predicts unconditional convergence (only) under certain special conditions".

Effectively, if the different world economies currently diverge mainly in terms of their per worker (or per person) capital ratios, k—being as a result the level of "y" and "c" of the developing countries lower than those of the developed ones—an *unconditional convergence* only would take place if the saving rates, population growth rates, technological process, and production functions[71] were the same.[72]

As a consequence, if countries differ in the mentioned traits and there is no mobility of factors, the developing countries only may opt for a *conditional convergence,* according to the neoclassical model. This means that the living standards of these countries only will be able to converge within groups of countries having similar "relevant traits". As a result it could be conceivable, that if the access to the newest technologies is free, a poor country with a low saving (and investment) rate could catch up in due time to a richer country only if the latter has also a low saving rate, and the labour and population growth rates of both of them are coincident. Of course, this catching up would be impossible, or very slow, if the technology access is not totally free, or the population growth rate is higher in the described poor country.

2.3.2.1. Do LDC Open Economies Actually Converge?

Note that till now our discussion on the neoclassical model of growth has been based on closed economies. Consequently if, conversely, the economies are open, and the international flows of

70. Vide Abel, A. and Bernake, B. (2001: 228). Book already mentioned.

71. Last two conditions imply free accessibility by all countries to the same technology.

72. Remember that till the moment we are assuming that every country is isolated and that there are no international relations among them.

capital are free, some additional forces—not all[73]—would support an unconditional convergence. Specifically, as poor countries use to have lower saving rates and less capital per worker, and thus a higher marginal productivity of their capital factor, if newest technologies are accessible, it could be expectable—in a world without economic barriers and economic failures[74]—that savers of rich countries transfer flows of capital to the poorest ones, thus increasing in the latter the rate of total available savings (internal plus external) and their domestic investment rate. Mentioned transfers—basically under the form of FDI as currently recommended by mainstream economic policy[75]—would increase steadily the level of "k" in poor countries up to levels of "unconditional convergence".[76] Even more, if the international movements of workers was free, the migration processes would additionally deactivate the initial differences in the value of "k", thus accelerating unconditional convergence.

Finally, there is another possibility: *no convergence at all,* or even divergence. Although reconciling the non-convergence scenario with the neoclassical model corollaries is conceivable, this outcome would be inconsistent with the spirit of that model, which is one of perfect competition.[77] Note however that competition, although very heralded by international economic institutions and Western countries, is almost always practiced in an asymmetric way at international level.

---

73. If international movements of people are not free, and the poorer countries have a larger growth rate of population than the rich countries, the unconditional convergence is theoretically impossible.
74. Nevertheless, the economic failures exist, as well as different costs of transports and transactional costs.
75. We deeply disagree with that possibility, because the behaviour of the West in many related matters is just against former considerations. Currently as well as in the past, free access to newest technologies is difficult, while free movements of people is a chimera. And this without mentioning the asymmetries in international trade negotiations, or the non-consideration of the relevance of the required public transfer of resources to promote infrastructures, health and education to surpass negative externalities, as we have explained in another essay. Vide Rahman, R. and Andreu, J.M. (2004:38) Book already mentioned.
76. Note that although in this case the production per worker of poor countries could converge with that of the richest ones, the consumption per worker would remain at a lower level because part of the output (of poor countries) should be devoted to pay to foreign investors.
77. Consequently, isolated LDC with special characteristics, high value of "n" (population explosion), low value of "s", or without access to the newest technologies—which move upwards the joint productivity of factors in rich countries—may be *ceteris paribus* condemned to "diverge".

2.3.2.2. Disputed Evidence on Convergence

As we have mentioned before, only the existence of a totally free mobility of goods, services and *factors* (capital and *human*) may induce unconditional convergence. Consequently, till the current circumstances do not significantly change in relation with relevant markets, such unconditional convergence is not expectable.

Unfortunately for the poor countries of the world, there is hardly any empirical support for the so-called unconditional convergence. Most of the realised studies have found little tendency of poor countries to catch up with the rich ones. For instance, in a study of 72 countries over the period 1950-1985, Prof. Baumol, of the Princeton University,[78] found no overall tendency towards unconditional convergence.

However, this same author using data since 1870 found some convergence among a small group of 16 major free market economies. Three years later, Bradford DeLong[79] criticised the last finding of Baumol because the latter, by exclusively focusing on rich countries in 1980, implicitly rejected others that having been rich a century ago had economically failed, thus introducing a bias that invalidated the analysis. DeLong suggested that if Baumol had introduced the cases of Argentina, Chile, the former East-Germany, Ireland, New Zealand, Portugal and Spain—countries that were relative rich in 1870—the Baumol's evidence for unconditional convergence would disappear.

The case of *conditional convergence* seems however to be more plausible. For instance, Mankiw *et al.*[80] examined 98 countries over the period 1960-1985, and concluded that poor countries had failed to catch up because they had low rates of savings and high population growth rates. However these authors found a strong tendency to the relative convergence among countries with similar parameters.

Conversely to former findings, Sala-i-Martin has recently found some evidence on unconditional but slow convergence by analysing

---

78. Vide Baumol, W. (1986). "Productivity Growth, Convergence and Welfare: What the Long Run Data Show." *American Economic Review*. December.
79. Vide DeLong, B. (1988). "Productivity Growth, Convergence, and Welfare: Comment." *American Economic Review*. December.
80. Vide Mankiw *et al.*, (1992) "A Contribution to Empirics in Economic Growth." *Quarterly Journal of Economics*. May.

a large group of countries of the world. By playing with average incomes of each of these countries, Sala-i-Martin has tried to prove that the current process of globalisation has reduced the relative income gap among nations.

Note however that in many countries of the world the internal income distribution has clearly worsened. In particular, we could here mention the cases of China and India, which are substantial in the Sala-i-Martin analysis, whose "converging" results are allegedly based on the recent creation of significant middle classes in these Asian countries.

Even more, if one takes into account the analysis and figures of Maddison,[81] one has to agree on the case *of no unconditional convergence*. The regional income disparity in the world has almost monotonically grown from 1870—when it was 5:1—to a figure of 19:1 in 1998. And in the last two-three decades of the 20th Century nothing lesser than 168 "shaking countries" have experienced a per capita GDP slumping or stagnant.[82]

The former disappointing empirical results on convergence, does not mean that the neoclassical model is constructed badly. On the contrary, what the empirical evidence suggests is that the economic world does not follow the core of assumptions of the model. International economic competition, although heralded, does not exist in pure terms. Factors—especially the labour—cannot freely move, goods and services find limitations to free interchange, and negative externalities suffered by poor countries are difficult to be removed without significant public transfers coming from the rich ones.

2.3.3. *Endogenous Growth Theory*

According to the neoclassical model, the productivity growth is the only source of the per-worker (or per capita) GDP growth in the long run.[83] Let us insist that if productivity growth would not exist,

81. Vide Maddison, A. (2001:126). Book already mentioned.

82. Vide Madisson, A. (2001:129). Book already mentioned.

83. Note however that, in the short run there are fluctuations in the value of the residual factor (A), motivated by the different degrees of under-use of the capital and labour factors. Vide Bernanke, B. and Rottemberg, J. Edt. (1995) "Capital Utilisation and Returns to Scale." NBER Macroeconomics Annual.

the per-worker production and consumption will have a non surpassable limit. Consequently, a full explanation of the causes of the economic growth will also require the knowledge of the long run determinants of the "joint productivity of the factors." Note that the neoclassical model simply takes the productivity growth as a deducible datum, which is reckonable with the help of the "growth accounting equation" (expression 2), but it does not explain at all its foundations.

Mainly to cover this lacuna of the neoclassical model, the "endogenous growth theory" has recently appeared. This is a theory that tries to explain the foundations of the evolution of the "joint productivity of factors," but *endogenously,* that is to say from within the model.[84]

The most important implication of this theory is that in the long term, the per worker growth rate of a country will depend on its rates of saving and investment, and not vaguely on exogenous productivity growth, as deducible from the neoclassical model.

To simplify the exposition of this model, one could imagine that the number of workers remains constant, which implies that the growth rate of GDP per worker is equal to the growth rate of the GDP. Consequently, in this case the aggregate production function would be:

$$Y=AK \tag{4}$$

In this expression, A is a positive constant. As a result there will not be diminishing returns of capital, as it has for long been observed from empirical evidence.

One could conceive two main reasons for this keeping up in the capital return: 1) *The role of the human capital growth*[85] as a countervailing mechanism that, duly combined with the growing capital, will avert the diminishing returns of the latter; and 2) *The research and development activities,* which make that increases in capital

---

84. Vide Romer, P. (1986) "Increasing Returns and Long Run Growth." *Journal of Political Economy*. October. Vide also Lucas, R. (1988) "On the Mechanics of Economic Development." *Journal of Monetary Economics*. July. A more simple description of the endogenous growth theory can be found in Romer, P. (1994) "The Origins of Endogenous Growth." *Journal of Economic Perspectives*. Winter.

85. This human capital is composed by knowledge, skills and training of individuals.

and output tend to generate increases in technical know-how, thus offsetting any tendency to the decline of marginal productivity of capital.

Once justified the shape of the new production function (Y=A.K), we may continue considering in this model that the aggregate saving (S) is a constant fraction of Y=AK, so S=s.AK. If now, to simplify, we just consider a closed economy, the goods and services markets equilibrium will need that S=I.[86] Consequently, the equilibrium condition will now be: $I=\Delta K+dK=sAK=sY$.

After an immediate process of substitution and doing simple transformations, we easily will arrive to:

$$\Delta K/K=sA-d \quad (5) \qquad \text{or} \qquad \Delta Y/Y=sA-d \quad (6)$$

Equation (6) proves that, in the endogenous growth model, the growth rate of the GDP, as well as the per worker growth rate,[87] depends on the saving rate, "s". Note that this is a significant contribution per comparison to the results of the neoclassical model, which established the irrelevance of the value of "s" in the long term growth rate of countries (although not in the steady state equilibrium values of "y" and "c").

In effect, the saving rate "s" affects the long run GDP growth—according to endogenous growth theorists—because higher rates of saving and capital formation stimulate greater investment in human capital and research & development activities. Consequently any public policy that affects positively the domestic saving rate "s", and consequently the investment rate, will additionally accelerate the economic growth. In this regard policies that fiscally encourage private (personal or corporate) saving should be most welcome. Complementary, policies devoted to raise public savings in the developing countries, by means of implementing fiscal reforms seeking budgetary efficiency in a context of microeconomic neutrality, would also be desirable.[88]

---

86. Let us remember that I is the gross investment, composed by ΔK plus depreciation d.K.
87. This is because we have assumed that the number of workers is constant.
88. We have to mention here that, the private saving being little elastic to interest rates, the effects of a tax reduction on private savings returns—thus increasing the after tax net interest rate—would be little effective to push aggregate savings.

2.4. The Problem of Population in the Developing Countries

Although, the growth rates of labour and population are equal and constant under the premises of the neoclassical model, this assumption is clearly unrealistic when analysing developing countries. This is because they are in general involved in a downwards trend of their population growth.

2.4.1. Demography in Traditional Societies

The theory of the "demographic transition" is a theory that explains the causes of the so-called "population explosion" as a middle in the way phenomenon which appears when the population moves from a traditional society to a developed one. According to this theory, birth and death rates were high in the traditional societies. Poor diets, primitive or almost nil hygiene and sanitation, and scant medical aid generated high death rates. Birth rates were also high in these societies as a consequence of widespread illiteracy, early marriages, and other social considerations about the size of the family as a mechanism to produce security for the elder. As a result of these death and birth high growth rates, the population growth rates of these societies were low, while the expectancy of life was short.[89]

2.4.2. The Stage of the Population Explosion

Along economic development, growing income levels enable the people to improve their diets, and to progress in hygiene, sanitation, and medical aid. At the same time better transport and trade systems avoids famines when harvests are insufficient. All these factors logically reduce, normally very quickly, the death rate. Conversely, and due to the existence of some social inertia mechanisms, birth rates behave more inflexible downwards, thus temporary remaining high, and igniting the population explosion phenomenon.

To the extent that the population pyramid remains young, when government takes initiatives to reduce the birth rate, positive results concerning reduction of population growth rate will delay, due to the so-called "demographic momentum." This is a phenomenon that will

89. As an ancient British philosopher (Hobbes) could have said today, "the current life in some LDC, in particular in countryside, continues being dirty, brutal and short".

avert for a while a fast reduction of population growth, although the birth rates have meaningfully moved downwards before.[90]

2.4.3. The Final Stage of the Demographic Transition

As it is well known, the process of economic growth and development changes the traits of the economy. It becomes more industrialised and more urban. In this new context, with the new role of women outside home and with the new feelings on familial security motivated by larger incomes and expectancy of life, the traditional extended families start changing into dysfunctional. In this new frame "numerous children become more a burden than an asset"[91], a sentiment that induces the reduction of the fertility rate, moving the birth rate downwards. Consequently the typical traits of this third demographic stage are low death rates, low birth rates, smaller family sizes, longer expectancy of life, and low or almost nil population growth, combined with a steeper population pyramid.

Nevertheless, till the achievement of a new demographic equilibrium significant changes will appear within the population pyramid. The population will start ageing, thus creating in coming years financial problems to the incipient Social Security systems. These financial tensions will be larger, the faster the reduction process of birth rates. Finally a new balance as already depicted will be reached. In this new population context, the age of retirement of workers and their pensions will depend on Social Security institutions, and workers (and employers) contributions.

2.4.4. The Growth of Labour Supply

Quantitative changes in the population growth rate and mutations in the shape of the demographic pyramid—all generated by the "demographic transition"— plus ongoing changes in the

---

90. Nations with high birth rates have a large proportion of children and adolescents in their population. In such a high fertile population, young people greatly outnumber their parents, and when this generation reaches adulthood the number of potential parents will inevitably be larger than at present. Even if these new parents have only enough children to replace them (2.1 per couple), due to the fact that the total number of couples having 2 children will still be much more than the number of couples who previously had more children, the total population would still increase substantially before levelling off.

91. Vide Coale, A. and Hoover, E. (1959: 10). *Population Growth and Economic Development in Low Income Countries*. Oxford University Press.

education period of children and youngsters and diverse velocities of embodiment of women to the labour market, may significantly alter the rate of evolution of the labour force and the rate of activity of the population. As a result, the growth rate of the labour supply in the second and third stages of the demographic transition will in general be larger than that of the population growth, which by no means will be constant until the arrival to a final balance.

This divergence between the growth rate of population and the growth rate of the labour force is something that should be taken into account. This is because it may have an enormous influence in, or may condition, all the economic policy to be implemented in a developing country.

There is a possibility that while population annually grows for instance at a rate of around 1 per cent after years of population control[92]—as it is the current case of China—the total labour supply grows well over that figure. This is because in the supply of labour there are additional variables that have an extraordinary influence on it. In particular we have to mention the evolution of the share of the labour force in the population (activity rate) that normally grows along development when the opportunities in the non-agricultural sector (industry and services) grow.

Consequently, in the developing countries and for decades, the labour supply may keep annual growth rates well over those of the rhythm of population progression. And this use to happen irrespective of whether the population growth rate is low or high, as it currently happens in the case of India (a country in which the population control policy has not successfully worked).[93]

2.5. Growth and Structural Change

Till now, with the neoclassical model of growth and with the endogenous growth theory, we have reached some interesting conclusions. Nevertheless, we have worked in these cases with a very

92. The population policy applied in China (one family one child) has resulted "successful" by means of offering incentives to the families, such as an increase in the salary by 12.5 per cent, priority in housing, preference in school and job admissions, etc., or by introducing tax disincentives, surcharges, etc.

93. Note that the soft turning point of the population explosion in India started working basically by the endogenous forces of development. These endogenous forces, which have mainly worked in urban areas, have to do with the new social attitudes towards women, children, sexuality, and family relations.

simplified model of one sector—ignoring the implications for growth of the relations of agriculture, industry and services—thus hiding a big chunk of the development conundrum.

The development process is not only one in which the GDP growth rate experiences a leap forward. Besides this, and to accelerate that GDP growth rate, it is necessary to reallocate resources more efficiently, moving them from the traditional sector (agriculture) to the modern ones (industry and services). This is a process that, involving relevant shifts of resources, in particular the human one, is impossible to be analysed with the uni-sectoral models presented above.

There are two basic reasons that will induce mentioned shift. First, the so-called "Engel Law", according to which the more the per-worker (or per capita) income grows, the less will be the income fraction devoted by families to food expenditure. Consequently, given that the main function of agriculture is to provide food, the demand for food and its production will grow proportionally less than the production in other sectors; as a result, the primary sector will progressively lose importance in the production structure. A second reason reinforces the first: because the joint productivity of factors in agriculture has in the last century tended to progress quicker than those of the rest of the sectors, the number of workers required by agriculture has additionally tended to move downwards.

Accordingly, the relative share of the production of the non-agricultural sectors has pervasively tended to grow. The same has occurred with non-agricultural workers, who have tended to concentrate in growing cities or towns. This process of urban agglomeration has induced a meaningful growing participation of the construction and housing industries in the total production of the developing countries. This trend, as it has been proven, has been constant and universal.[94]

2.5.1. A Two Sectors Model: The Agriculture-Industry Relation

Long before the definition of the GDP by western professional economists in the 20th Century, the relative evolution of the different productive sectors had already been studied by classical economists.

94. Vide Chenery, H. *et al.*, (1975). *Patterns of Development*, 1950-1970. London. Oxford University Press.

Particularly by Ricardo,[95] who included in his economic approach two basic assumptions that since then have played a relevant role in the explanation of the (bi-sectoral) development of countries: 1) The diminishing returns to scale,[96] to which the agricultural sector was doubtless prone; and 2) The labour excess initially existing in the primary sector; an excess that could be transferred to the incipient urban industry and services, without increasing the real urban or rural wages.

This concept of labour excess in agriculture coined by Ricardo is tightly linked to what we define today as "hidden rural unemployment" in the primary sector. This is a phenomenon that exists because traditional agriculture does not generate sufficient activities to keep all the available potential labour force living in the rural areas, full time at work. As a result, if this vacant force in rural areas was transferred to the industrial sector, the agriculture production would not diminish, the average occupancy (in hours) of remaining peasants would grow, while migrants from countryside to cities and towns could work full-time with additional gains for all.

2.5.1.1. The Growth Model with "unlimited" Supply of Labour

The analysis of some of the inter-relations between agriculture-industry in a context of economic growth was precisely the object of the Lewis model.[97] This is a model of two sectors with a significant labour excess in one of them, the agriculture.

According to Lewis, a big part of the human factor in the agricultural sector of developing countries has a nil[98] marginal productivity, thus positioning this variable well under the "minimum wage of subsistence".[99] Even under these considerations, peasants will

95. Vide Ricardo, D. (1817). Principles of Political Economy and Taxation.
96. We should not forget that the factor "land", remaining fix in the classical model while the number of workers increases, will provoke the diminishing returns of the labour.
97. Vide Lewis, A. (1955). The Theory of Economic Growth. Homewood. Illinois. Irwin.
98. When marginal productivity of labour in agriculture is nil, all workers with this nil productivity can be transferred to industry without any reduction in the agricultural production.
99. To understand the "subsistence wage" in agriculture we have to analyse the familiar behaviour of the individuals. In this regard, the notional real wage "perceived" in kind by any individual (materialised in his or her own consumption) will be equivalent to the average productivity per person of his or her family. This wage is "paid" at familiar level in a context of solidarity. This means that if the family may produce the same output for instance with two individuals less, these two individuals have a nil marginal productivity and therefore are economically transferable to other sectors.

not abandon the familial plot unless they may obtain in other activities higher wages than those they "receive" ("subsistence wages") in their current "jobs".

This mentioned abundant human factor with nil marginal productivity ensures that the supply of industrial labour behaves as perfectly elastic to wages, in a relevant segment of its complete schedule. Consequently, if the industrial wages are placed sufficiently over the "subsistence wage" in agriculture, the industrial sector will be able (in first stages of development) of contracting a growing number of workers, coming from the countryside, without paying growing wages.

Note however that, after a period—the length of which will depend on the initial volume of peasants in situation of nil marginal productivity and on the velocity of its absorption—the traits of the economy will change into a situation in which the previously nil marginal productivity of agricultural workers will disappear. From then onwards, prices of agricultural goods will rise and agricultural production will fall if additional peasants abandon the sector. As a result the industrial wages will also rise and the unitary industrial returns will start a process towards reduction.

Observe also that during the period in which new workers coming from the countryside are contracted at low and constant wages, absolute and relative profits will grow, thus enabling firms to have larger savings and reinvestments. These increased profits will also enable a progressive rise in the internal saving rate of the country,[100] which according to previously explained theories (neoclassical model and endogenous growth theory) will reinforce the development process.

Logically, when the agricultural labour wages start rising, the labour contracts in industry will become more expensive than before, the unitary industrial profits will start their reduction, and *ceteris paribus* the internal private saving rate will tend to decline.

---

100. As in the first stages of the development proccess, the very scant capital factor will rise while maintaining increasing returns, it is expectable that the profits obtained by this factor grow more than proportionally, thus enabling the mentioned increase of the average internal savings rate. If, at the same time, ownership of capital-resources is concentrated, a worsening in the distribution of the per capita income is also expectable.

The former elemental explanation of the growth process in an economy with two sectors, in which one of them has initially a lot of nil marginal productivity workers, enables also to explain the initial propensity to worsen the income distribution in the first stages of economic growth. This initial worsening in the internal distribution, according to available information, is something that, as expectable, has occurred in China as well as in India in the last two decades, precisely the decades in which their accelerated development began.[101] This seems to be a new confirmation of the working of the so-called Kuznets curve[102] in the context of capitalist societies.

2.5.1.2. Implications of the Population Growth in the Lewis Model

Once the former considerations are made, additional details will clarify some implications of population growth on the development process, and on the evolution of agricultural marginal productivity of labour. In relation with the first issue, it could be said that, since there is a long-run tight relation between population growth and available supply of labour, an increase of the population will make a larger employment in the non-agricultural sectors possible, as well as the lengthening of the period of absorption of rural workers at the same (initial) industrial real wages. Consequently, higher population growth rates, of course inconvenient in the short run, will make possible *ceteris paribus* a larger and longer growth capacity, and will enable high industrial profits over a longer period.[103]

---

101. Observe that the worsening of the individual distribution of income may be initially consistent with a contemporary reduction of the number of people situated under the poverty line. This consistency has also been perceivable in the last two decades in China as well as in India.

102. Vide Kuznets, S. (1955). "Economic Growth and Income Distribution." *American Economic Review*. In his reflection, Kuznets suggested that the temporal relation between the per capita income and the degree of economic unevenness would adopt a trajectory U-shaped. This means that after the initiation of the process the individual income distribution will worsen, although after a while, when real industrial wages start meaningfully their run up, the personal income distribution would quickly improve, thus reversing its previous negative trend.

103. In this regard the cases of China and India are paradigmatic. These two countries have undergone high growth rates of population, but they now, particularly India, have an enormous amount of transferable manpower in countryside, the transfer of which may last 3-4 decades, as a minimum.

2.5.1.3. Progressive Disappearance of Unlimited Labour Supply and Consequences

Logically, if we ignore some of the assumptions introduced in the Lewis model—as for instance that of the existence of a certain volume of agricultural labour in excess—we could draw some additional and alternative implications to those previously extracted from the Lewis model.

In this regard, one may easily imagine that in the last stage of the industrialisation model of Lewis, there will be no agricultural labour excesses. As a consequence, the agricultural wage will further depend on normal curves of supply and demand of labour, thus generating an agricultural wage that will be placed well over the "minimum subsistence wage." In this case any explanation of the inter-relation between the two considered sectors should be analysed in the context of a bi-sectoral neoclassical model.

To begin with, we have to say that the implications of population growth on the main variables of the model will now be significantly different to those drawn from the Lewis model. Alternatively, in the neoclassical model, a population-labour growth in the agricultural sector will generate some additional agricultural output.[104] In this case however, if the differential of wages between the sectors is significant, the shift of workers to the non-agricultural sector will continue, although in a general context of growing industrial wages, lower industrial profits, lower private saving rates and lower growth rate of the industrial sector.

Note additionally, that in this neoclassical context, a certain shift of workers from agriculture to industry or services sectors without enough population growth will *ceteris paribus* reduce the food production, and will quickly increase the industrial wages, thus additionally decelerating the industrialisation progress.

Therefore, if in the context of a bisectorial neoclassical model, the public powers want to develop the non-agricultural sectors, they should do parallel efforts to increase the agriculture production in order to provide additional food to the industrial-services workers (and families), as well as to those remaining in the primary sector.

104. This occurs because in the bi-sectoral neoclassical model, the assumption that in agriculture there are workers with nil marginal productivity, does not work.

In this frame, the only way for delaying the slowdown of the accumulation process in the non-agricultural sectors would be either a continuous raise of the number of people and workers in the primary sector—a not very desirable solution at short-mid term—or a better one, to increase the joint productivity of agricultural factors,[105] by means of meaningful investment in rural areas.

2.6. Backwardness and Opportunities for Growth in an Open Multi-sectoral Economy

Till now, we have described the economic growth—always understood as a way of continuously rising the per worker or per capita output—as a very aggregated process, that mainly depends on the "joint productivity of factors" growth rate, ($\Delta A/A$), coming from exogenous or endogenous causes, and from the value of the saving rate, "s".

Note, however, that the development process may come, in certain contexts already depicted, from the mere reallocation of resources among sectors. Nevertheless, reality is much more complex than that, because, besides the existence of the two above mentioned sectors, there are different industries or activities within the non-agricultural one, capable of growing at different speeds. And these different velocities, if bad coordinated, could decelerate the aggregate process of growth, thus placing it under optimum.

On the other hand, since any country, even the developing ones or LDC, may "potentially" use the last available technology,[106] or may profit from the general accumulated knowledge by human kind, in general at affordable cost, their backwardness may today be quickly overcome mainly due to the following expectable phenomena: 1) A more rapid impulse of domestic investment, as a consequence of the current accessibility to modern financial systems—a mechanism which may enable the increase of the internal and external funding—and, as a result, a more rapid appearance of

105. This would happen if additional investments or progressive technical changes were introduced in the agricultural sector. Mentioned additional investments could be done either directly by the public sector in some specific matters related with spill-over effects, or by the private sector through implementation of some stimuli (tax sops, subsidies, etc.)

106. Note that last available technology was not so easily available to the current developed countries in the first stages of their development.

large, modern and updated industrial firms; and 2) A larger investment domestically financed not only by agriculture profits and savings—as it historically happened in the today industrialised countries—but also by that of all sectors of the economy. As a result, a faster industrialisation process with powerful growth rates in the non-agricultural sectors could be expectable.

Consequently, a backward country has nowadays far more opportunities than in the past for achieving a fast, complex, and rich in structural changes, industrialisation. Nonetheless, this does not mean that a very poor country, lacking certain necessary preconditions to start the process, can easily do it. Hindrances as low domestic saving rate, "s", low education and health levels, lack of infrastructures, or significant population explosion can significantly delay the process or even to arrest it.

2.6.1. Balanced and Unbalanced Economic Growth

At the start of the de-colonisation process, in the 50s-60s of last century, the growth strategy of many developing countries was based on the acceleration of physical investments in a context of an economic "inward looking" approach, the so-called "import substitution strategy" (IS).

This almost globally followed strategy was in many cases a serious mistake because many small developing countries had then no possibility of achieving a healthy growth, given the small size of their markets. Even some of the largest developing countries committed mistakes when they indiscriminately practised castling policies concerning external commercial and financial interchanges (as China and India did).

Nevertheless, the then selected strategy was not completely wrong, nor was it fully their fault. The almost generalised lack of sufficient internal financing, difficult to be complemented with the external one,[107] and the hurdles posed by the West to their possible massive agricultural and allied exports (with comparative advantage), were obstacles for the implementation of an industrialisation process prone to external freer interchanges.

---

107. The ODA and the FDI movements were for long very scant, and when these flows increased, their direction was mainly towards a very selected number of developing countries, forgetting most of them.

Even more, internally focussed investments in economic activities with comparative advantage (mainly in the primary sector and allied), which would have brought developing countries into a very unbalanced and fragile economic structure, could have been a wrong strategy too.[108] Possibly, with this pro-market strategy, the industrialisation process of many developing countries, that today have accumulated relevant industrial assets, could not have taken place.

In the context of the mentioned IS strategy, the ideas of a group of economists[109] that advocated for a "balanced" or relatively proportional growth rate of the different domestic industries, were at times taken into consideration.

Nonetheless this proportional growth contained severe technical (existence of non-divisible projects) and financial problems that most of the developing countries could not cope with. Consequently, in order to overcome their financial problems, other economists[110] suggested the convenience of the public support to a sectorial unbalanced development, thus concentrating the development policies and their scant financing possibilities in a few industries with relevant "backward links" or "forward links" with other activities. That is to say in those industries with more powerful capacities of growth induction in related activities.

2.6.2. Commercial Growth Strategies

Although the "import substitution" strategy was the mainstream approach for industrial development after the independence wave of the post-Second World War, in the 60s and 70s some developing countries opted for an "outward oriented" industrialisation. This implied that the industrialisation process should be stimulated and directed to the production of exportable goods and services—those which enjoy comparative advantage—while necessary imports should be facilitated and trade barriers abated at different speeds. Examples

---

108. The reality is that historically no one of the current developed countries chose initially the model of free trade, and when they started practising it, they did it in an asymmetric way.

109. Vide Nurkse, R. (1953). Problems of capital formation in underdeveloped countries. Oxford University Press. Vide also, Rosenstein-Rodan, P. (1943). Problems of industrialisation of Eastern and South Eastern Europe. Economic Journal.

110. Vide Hischman, O. (1958). The strategy of economic growth. N. Haven. Yale University Press.

frequently quoted of this export oriented strategy are those of South Korea, Taiwan, Hong-Kong and Singapore, as well as neighbouring countries such as Thailand, Malaysia and Indonesia. Note however, that many of these countries received, as part of the geo-politics of the West, important external support for their "outward oriented" industrialisation.

As a consequence of the relative success of the last strategy and the significant failure of the "inward looking approach," from late-60s onwards the "import substitution" strategy came under rigorous and generalised scrutiny. Former defensive arguments in favour of this policy, such as those of "nascent industries," fluctuation of prices and quantities of traditional raw materials and agricultural exports, or the so-called "elasticity's pessimism," were reassessed. Some years later, when the relative prices of the most relevant internationally exchanged raw materials, mainly oil, went up, and thus the economic mainstream veered to microeconomic efficiency, the import substitution tide finally ebbed.

2.7. Fundamental Variables for Inducing Economic Growth: Application to the Cases of China and India

As a guide for the right evaluation of the economic facts, as they happened in China and India in the last 50 years, as well as to asses what could be the economic development of these two countries in the coming decades, we have reviewed in this chapter the central approaches for economic growth.

First of all, we have mentioned certain non-economic factors that could condition the start or the strengthening of the economic development process. We have underlined that the most important of them is political stability. This means that a serious variable that conditions development, refers to the necessity of absence of sustained infighting—as those occurred in China in the era of the Cultural Revolution, or in India with the so-called communal problems—or long standing violent conflicts with neighbouring countries, as it has been the case of India in relation to Pakistan,[111]

111. The case of the Indian-Chinese war cannot be considered as a sustained conflict. This is because the current aspiration of the Indians to the then disputed territory is today practically nil, as well as the Chinese former interests in Sikkim, a northern Indian State.

or the tensions of China with the passed away Soviet Union, and with Taiwan.

Besides the required political stability, we have to insist that according to conventional wisdom, the level of the total saving rate, "s" (the internal plus the external one), equivalent in a balanced economy to the domestic investment rate, is simply crucial according to the neoclassical model and the endogenous theory of growth. In this regard, it has been observed that a clear correlation between the level of the saving (and investment) rates of the nations and the speed of the progression of their GDP exists (this correlation has been specially clear in the cases of China and India in the last 25 years).

Additionally, one should not overlook the evolution of the joint productivity of the factors, a variable that clearly explains the long run evolution of the per capita GDP, this being the best available indicator of the reached living standards of the citizens as an average. Note in this regard the remarkable acceleration of the joint productivity of factors in China in the period 1978-1998, which reached a figure of 2.5 per cent in comparison to that obtained in the Maoist period (0.5 per cent). The same could be said in the case of India, whose joint productivity of factors reached a figure of 3.7 per cent during the 80s.

We have also considered the relevance of the evolution of population in the economic growth process, especially in the case of the developing countries. After analysing the model of Lewis—one with initial almost unlimited labour availability stockpiled in the primary sector—and its implications on rapid industrialisation, we have found that, what is inconvenient at the beginning of the process—the population explosion—may result in an advantage in the long run. This is because the initial "non-desirable" population explosion—which delays the per capita income growth—may protract, after the taking off, the length of the period of a "high growth rate" of the GDP, induced by the rapid sectorial shift of cheap labour.

Finally, we have discussed two strategies for growth from the perspective of the economic opening: 1) the internal oriented one (import substitution strategy), susceptible of a double industrial interpretation, either proportional or unbalanced (mainly depending on financing capabilities of the states); and 2) the one related with the outward looking approach (export oriented growth). Although the outward looking strategy is more recommendable at long run, we have underlined that almost all developing countries have firstly used the inward looking strategy.

Using the models, as described in this chapter, on the cases of China and India, one has to acknowledge that in Economics there are no miracles. China and India are nowadays growing at high but different speeds, being the growth disparity between them rather well explained by the different rates of available financial resources ("s") in these two countries.

Note that in the successful economic progress of these two countries over the past 25 years, the different evolution of their populations and labour forces have also played a relevant role. The same could be said about the observed changes in the total productivity factor rates, induced by the reorganisation of their respective economies. A reorganisation that, stirring up a rapid shift of human resources from agriculture towards industry (mainly in China) and services (basically in India), has helped to speed up the GDP growth rates of these two countries.

Finally, as a last conclusion of the chapter, we have to underline that, given the current huge volume of workers with nil marginal productivity in the primary sector in China as well as in India, and due to the annual limited absorption capacity of workers by the two countries non-agricultural sectors, the additional duration of their high speed growth process will be around 3-4 supplementary decades.

3

Brief History of the Economy of China Since 1949

3.1. Applied Policies in China in the Last Five Decades

As we have mentioned in the first Chapter, the political and economic changes undergone by the People's Republic of China in the so-called Maoist-era (1949-1978) were simply dramatic. Even more dramatic than those undergone by the Soviet Union in the first stages of its construction. In this regard, we have to underline that the Chinese version of "total socialism," put to practise by the then CCP government, implied a very risky bet, rather inconsistent with the proven egoistic human behaviour in front of pervasive economic de-stimuli.

Indeed, besides the initial confiscation of land, the de-stimulant effects generated by the two big political shifts devised in the Maoist period—the Great Leap Forward (1958-1960) and the so-called Cultural Revolution (1966-1976)—generated economic under-performance[112] and political infighting and chaos, as well as serious famines.

Despite mentioned political and economic misconceptions and subsequent under-performance, the Chinese GDP more or less three folded between 1952 and 1978, its per capita GDP rose around 80 per cent, and the labour productivity did it by more than 60 per cent.[113] In particular, the production of industry, which in 1952 had

112. This economic under-performance must be understood more as a squandering of the capital resources involved in the industrialisation process of China in the Maoist period—which imposed an extraordinary effort (under-consumption) on Chinese citizens—than as a lack of GDP and industrial growth results. These results in GDP terms were just slightly under those of the world average in the period 1950-1973.

113. Vide Maddison, A. (1998:61). Book already mentioned.

an importance equivalent to 1/6th of that of the agriculture, surpassed it in 1978. Although the economic experience of China in the Maoist period was a fascinating one for some analysts, and an awful occurrence for many others, we have to underline that it has always been difficult to assess, mainly by lack of reliable data.[114]

Along this period—as suggested by Maddison—China pursued four main economic targets: 1) Radical reform of property rights; 2) Achievement of sufficient public revenues to finance not only the necessary accumulation process, but also the consolidation of the new red army and the omnipresent administration; 3) Substitution of the formerly existent prices system by a complicated set of administrative rules, directed to allocate the investments according to the "new Chinese conception" of the economy, in order to generate "convenient" wages and prices for goods and services in consistency with the official desired targets; and 4) Monopolisation by the State of all external economic relations of China.

The abolition of the property rights was initially directed against three main groups of owners: the rural landlords, the urban *bourgeoisie* (mainly traders and bankers) when they did not adjusted, and the foreigners doing business in China. On the other hand, the pursued new fiscal sufficiency had to enable the authorities to focus on investments in the heavy industry, while superfluous consumption had to be severely restricted, thus the Government giving priority to elemental food production and to the provision of health and basic education. The new authorities were also extremely interested in the price, stability in order to avert the internal discredit reaped by the previous KMT regime, being the full employment another fundamental target of the new state.

A central mechanism for planning was rapidly set up in order to reduce the rural consumption and to meet compulsory food quotas to be delivered in urban areas. This was done to keep urban wages at low level,[115] and to facilitate the reallocation of resources (investments) towards the heavy industry and other priority activities.

114. Many of them were intentionally manipulated for political reasons, and even the Official Bureau of Statistics was closed between 1968 and 1972, in times of the Cultural Revolution.

115. Note that even before the presentation of the Lewis model in 1955, for its application to free capitalistic economies, its corollaries were essayed in China (and before it in the Soviet Union), although in a compulsory way.

Note however that, despite the existence of this central planning, at national, provincial and firm levels autonomy in management was unavoidable, given the poor level of the infrastructure, communications and transport systems. Notwithstanding that, firms had by no means autonomy to recruit or dismiss workers in a general context of segmentation of the labour market in rural and urban sectors. In particular rural workers were not authorised to move to cities or simply to change their jobs.

3.1.1 Agriculture Policy in the Maoist and the Reforms Periods

Although the new regime did put special emphasis and rhetoric's on the alleged inherited feudal situation of the land to radically transform it, the initial movements—although essential—were not so spectacular as the following ones.

In order to properly evaluate the first undertaken strategy of land confiscations, one should note that, in 1933[116] there hardly existed in China typical big properties (*latifundios*) with a lot of landless dependent workers. Conversely, the overwhelming majority of peasants were owners, tenants, or share-croppers, although this does not mean that the land was then well distributed. Specifically 10 per cent of rural families had no access to land at all.

3.1.1.1. Successive Reforms and the Failure of the Communes

Despite the mentioned tenure-distribution of land, in the first moments (1949-50) of the Maoist regime, a radical agriculture reform drove to the confiscation of almost half of the cultivated land. As a result, around a 4 per cent of the population was deprived of their lands,[117] while 60 per cent of peasants profited from the process. Consequently, the initially implemented reforms were directed to the creation of an egalitarian system of agricultural exploitation for more than a hundred million families.

---

116. Vide Buck. (1937). The comment has been taken from Maddison, A. (1998:77). Book already mentioned.

117. This figure of 4 per cent of expropriated owners and that of 50 per cent of expropriated cultivable land gives a more clear idea of the distribution of property before the revolution. Property concentration which was consistent with significant fragmentation of the plots.

Soon after, the land reform process entered in a second phase. In this stage the public powers encouraged the peasants to put in common their human and material capacities (animals, tools, etc.) in order to create incipient voluntary cooperatives. Already in 1955 around 2/3rd of peasants worked in these common exploitations, which numbered an average of 26 families.

In 1956-57 the land reform process deepened even more and the so-called "advanced cooperatives" were created. The peasants were then forced to participate in them, losing their former mutual property rights and control, except in small reserved plots in which they could grow something for themselves.[118]

In the second half of 1958, the most important and paradigmatic reform of the Maoist period took place: the creation of the "communes." According to this paramount reform carried out in 1958, around 553,000 former "advanced cooperatives" in which 123 million families worked, were forced to gather in 20,000 communes. With this reform, all private properties disappeared, including the previously reserved small plots for familiar purposes, and the small monetary revenues obtained by families. In consistency with the absence of these monetary revenues, rural markets were also closed.[119]

Note that these Communes, which were created in the era of the "Great Leap Forward," had under their own aegis the local administration and taxation, the provision of health and education, the supervision of agriculture production, as well as the construction of industrial plants and the provision of other services.

There is today a consensus that the role then assigned to the Communes was excessive, even with commitments in industrial targets in the context of the Great Leap Forward policy. The underlying "rationale" of this policy was the extreme political isolation of China in those days, and the alleged convenience of setting up a totally de-centralised economic system capable of surviving a nuclear fallout.

---

118. These "reserved plots" amounted around 5 per cent of the collective land, and the average size of the "advanced co-operatives" was around 160 families.

119. As an average, a commune was formed by 4,600 families and 6,700 workers, which meant that these communes were 30 times larger than the collective soviet farms created at the birth of the Soviet Union.

As a result of this new economic reorganisation-commotion, around 30 million Chinese workers of the communes were shifted to the new industrial activities (iron, cement, housing, irrigation networks, etc.).[120] The fast reallocation of manpower, added to the de-stimulant effects of the elimination of the "reserved plots", made that, in 1961, the agricultural per capita production experienced a fall of 30 per cent in comparison to that of the 1957. As a result the ghost of famine reappeared.

When in few years time this enormous economic misconception became crystal-clear, the new decentralised and "rural industrialisation experiment" was officially abandoned.[121] Although these communes continued their existence up to the 80s, already in 1962, the economic policy, went back to pre-last reform positions.[122]

3.1.1.2. New Agricultural Policy

Once Chairman Mao passed away (1976), with the arrival to power of a new breed of politicians, the agricultural policy decidedly started a new, pragmatic, and step-by-step change of orientation. The redistribution of land to families re-started, although in a reversed sense. The reserved plots of cooperatives at private disposal rose up to 15 per cent of the total, the agricultural prices became more flexible and grew quickly, and the "communist" system of equal payment to the peasants irrespective of whether their productivity was high or not, was abandoned and substituted with "responsibility" contracts with the families.

Although nowadays the state continues playing a fundamental role in the determination of agricultural prices and commercialisation of agricultural products, while rural land is still not tradeable, because it continues being "public domain," the new individual stimulant effects brought in by the last reforms are indisputable.

---

120. As it has been commented, a good part of this new production had no value, or was non-usable at all.

121. Note for instance that, according to official figures, the industrial employment in China during 1957 was 23 million people. It reached the figure of 62 million in 1959, but in 1963 the volume of industrial employment had returned towards its initial position, or perhaps towards a lower one.

122. Progressively the management of the agricultural exploitations was given back to units of around 30 families, the small familiar exploited plots were also given back, the rural markets were re-opened, and then onwards significant quantities of inputs were bought outside the "co-operatives".

3.1.2. Industrial Policy in China Along the Last 50 Years

Fast industrialisation of the country was probably the first economic priority of the CCP at its coming into power. Logically this desired rapid industrialisation would enable in due time the production of intermediate and final goods, necessary for the programmed quick rise of investment in heavy industry, as well as to meet the weaponry and transport needs of the national defence. In order to fulfil these aims, the authorities needed to compress the domestic level of consumption, in such a way that previously committed factors in the agriculture and services sectors were transferred to the industry.

As a whole, disregarding huge sacrifices (under-consumption) beared by citizens in the Maoist age, and further significant modifications mainly introduced since 1978, this initially selected strategy resulted "nominally" positive: the volume of industrial production multiplied by 43 between 1952 and 1995 (the volume of the heavy industry production multiplied by 100), while in the meantime, the agriculture output only multiplied by four.

In the 90s in which a global acceleration took place in the industrial sector of China in connection with successful gathering of FDI installed in SEZ' and soaring Chinese exports, the manufacturing sector grew annually in real terms around 10-12 per cent as an average. In the same period, given the size of the country, and its road and rail network deficiencies, the construction of infrastructure was also relevant and supported by public budgets.[123]

Beside this, the investment-demand of real-estate also shot up in the 90s, particularly in the larger cities (Shanghai, Beijing and others). Although recently there has been some indicators on the possible existence of a speculative bubble in housing (hotels, offices, etc.), the reality is that, after individuals gained for the first time the right to buy own homes in the late-90s, a great part of the current housing boom seems to be robustly founded.[124]

---

123. This has been a partial consequence of the governmental attempts for supporting the high speed of the GDP growth rate of the economy of China.

124. Note that previously, most of urban shelters were provided against a rent by government institutions or by public firms.

As a consequence, China became in the 90s one of the most industrialised countries of the world in terms of the weight of this sector in the total economy (around 51 per cent in 2002).[125] Nevertheless, the volume of employment in the Chinese industrial sector did not grow, but continued being comparatively low along the 90s, given the relatively high and growing productivity of labour in the industry. Nowadays, the current level of absolute employment in the industry continues being stable[126] as it also happens in agriculture, while the services sector has significantly incremented its volume of employment.

Paradoxically after 1978, when reforms started, the industrial growth rate entered into a period of relative deceleration while other sectors initiated a more pronounced booming period. Specifically, transports, communications, domestic trade, and construction registered growth rates that surpassed those of industry.

Before starting the reforms, the industrial process and its investments were completely controlled by the State. After 1978 the state control began to diminish in such a way that between 1978 and 1996 the number of public industrial firms outside the state monitoring, multiplied by 6, reaching a figure of 1.6 million. It is also convenient to underline that the number of private industrial firms moved in the same period from nil to 6.2 million.[127] These private firms are nowadays more efficient than the public ones, profiting from the cheapness of contracted labour, although they certainly are less capitalised in per worker terms than those of the public sector.

---

125. In 1995, when the Chinese industry represented a 41 per cent of its GDP, in the UK and US the industry generated 22 per cent of their GDP, in India 25 per cent, in Japan and Germany 28 per cent, in South Korea 29 per cent, and in Taiwan 36 per cent. Today (2002) the Chinese industry has reached a figure of 51 per cent of its GDP, while in India this figure represents 27 per cent. This disparity is an additional indicator of the relative economic delay of the Indian economy.

126. The currently constant level of employment in the Chinese Industry is due to the drop of jobs in the State owned industries, which went down for around 18 million in the period 1998-2002, while the jobs in the private enterprises increased in the same period by 10 million, and in the so-called "limited liability corporations" by around 6 million (the "foreign funded units" only increased the volume of jobs created in the period by one million).

127. Most of these so-called private firms are small sized, placed in rural areas, and managed by individuals (families) or local collectives.

Concerning average size of the industrial firms in China it is clear that it has dramatically diminished,[128] although not in the public sector in which they have kept their former dimension.[129] Note however that the size of the industrial public firms in China has always been smaller than those in other planned economies, as well as in many Western countries.[130]

3.1.2.1. Two Stages of Industrial Policy in the Maoist Period

From the very beginning up to 1958, and in a very different way to what had happened in agriculture, the communist regime, adopted to some extent, a restrained policy of taking over private Chinese firms. However, most foreign firms or with foreign capital were quickly confiscated.[131] Consequently, between 1949 and 1957 there was a period of co-existence of remaining foreign firms with Chinese private and public firms, although of course, all private firms (national and foreign) were forced to co-operate with the state.

Nevertheless, from 1958 onwards, in the context of the new industrial policy—the so-called "Great Leap Forward"—the industrial private firms completely disappeared from the People's Republic, and a new breed of small rural based industrial firms proliferated (in particular those devoted to the production of iron, cement, machine-tools, etc.).

As previously mentioned, this was an attempt to accelerate the industrial production by means of transferring to these small-rural industrial firms around 30 million unskilled workers. However soon after, it became evident that this irrational and forced industrialisation policy could not succeed due to its bad or useless industrial outputs. Consequently this policy was hastily abandoned, giving back to agriculture the formerly transferred workers for this "industrial experiment."

---

128. The average industrial dimension has moved from 175 to 14 employees.

129. As an average, their dimension in labour terms has continued being of around 375 employees.

130. While in 1987 the average number of workers in industrial firms in China was of 14, this figure was 49 in US, 30 in Germany and UK, 19 in France, and 16 in Japan.

131. Half of these firms were Japanese and were nationalised at the end of the revolution. Note additionally that many private Chinese firms that had co-operated with the Japanese invaders had time before been expropriated by the KMT regime.

A similar and noisy failure was also reaped by the almost contemporary Third Front Industrialisation policy, consisting of setting up industrial firms in remote areas, to preserve part of the Chinese industry from the then assumed imminent nuclear fallout. Difficulties with the transport of raw materials and workers to factories, and problems of accessibility to markets of generated products, made that this outlandish geographical approach for industrialisation had to be abandoned in the 70s in favour of the easier promotion of the coastal areas.

As a consequence of all these utopian policies put into practise between 1957 and 1978 the squandering of resources was huge. Undeniably, as suggested above, the industrialisation process was fast, but its cost in terms of involved capital was enormous. Consequently, although the productivity per industrial worker grew in this period at a significant annual rate of 3.1 per cent (4.8 per cent in the period 1978-95), the joint productivity of factors grew only at an annual rate of 0.5 per cent. As a result, one should conclude that the rapid growth of the Chinese industry up to 1978 was not at all brilliant in terms of implicated factors, in particular in terms of the huge amount of capital involved in the process.

3.1.2.2. The Reforms Period and the Industrial Policy

After 1978 the total (controlled or not by the state) number of industrial public firms in China continued growing, but their importance in the total industrial production decreased to 28 per cent in 1996 from more than 75 per cent in 1978.[132] The same could be said in relation to the relative added value and the relative employment of these public firms. Particularly, we will mention that in the period 1998-2002 the number of jobs depending on state-owned units decreased by around 18 million.

Logically, after the "de-nationalisation-liberalisation" process implemented in the wake of reforms, the communal and individual industrial firms based in rural areas gained ground as a result of the lower wages paid. Nonetheless, the bulk of industrial competition

---

132. Vide Maddison, A. (1998:92). Book already mentioned.

came from the so-called "special economic zones"[133] and other areas of industrial promotion based in coastal regions.

These new sources of domestic competition, combined with the relaxation of the control in state-public firms, not only reduced the profits of many of them, thus plummeting the State revenues coming from public undertakings, but also forced the State to maintain non-profitable and inefficient public firms with subsidies, in order to keep at mid-term their level of employment.[134]

This paying for time manoeuvre was additionally in need of enormous supportive credit advances (many of them non-performing) taken from the official (public) banking system. Note furthermore that this financial strategy for public firms support, also carried out in countries such as India, could in future crowd out private financing from banks,[135] or prejudice the stability of prices (if government monetisises the outstanding debts of these firms by means of provision of fresh money to banks, in order to partially write off their non-performing credits).

Despite this inconvenient financial situation, a rush process of privatisation of public firms—following the Russian experience forced by IMF (International Monetary Fund) after the crumbling of the Soviet Union—is not expectable in China. This is mainly because in absence of a sufficient Social Security system, capable of paying dole-compensations, it would be reckless to hastily close a higher number of inefficient public firms, which would inconveniently increase the unemployment in urban areas, thus triggering political problems.

Note on the other hand, that current China has a huge volume of foreign reserves (more than 650 bn. US dollars), which enables the country to practise unconditioned (also industrial) policies, far from

133. These Special Economic Zones have been recently copied by Indian authorities although with a significant delay and unknown results. To avoid observed dysfunction of incipient SEZ, the Indian Government has promised in 2004 to promulgate a specific Act for reorganising the issue.

134. Note that the industrial output of many of these firms had and has weak demands, or simply was or is difficult to be sold, reason why these firms have a lot of accumulated stocks.

135. Note that, conversely to what has been mentioned by some authors, the maintenance of inefficient Chinese public firms and the "non-performing" credits granted to them, is not at all necessarily conducive to banks default, because the latter count with the "protection net" of the State.

the typical requirements of the international financial institutions at times of serious unbalances in the external sector of the countries.

As a consequence, the official adopted strategy to get rid of part of the payrolls of these inefficient public firms seems to have been a rather balanced process, implemented by means of either retirement, or transfer of redundant workers to private industrial firms. Note however that this process has geared up in the second half of the 90s and first years of 2000, due to the improvement of the economic situation.

3.1.3. Policy for the Service Sector After 1978

3.1.3.1. The Internal Commerce Activity

We will here refer mainly to the internal commerce activity. This is a sector in which the official policy has enormously changed after 1978. Note that during the Maoist period the distribution channel was strictly controlled by the State, thus limiting its capacity of progression. Soon after, in 1978, retailing and restaurants were liberalised and the development of these private activities grew at high speed. Note that the development of these activities does not need important capitals, neither special skills, nor does it have meaningful technical barriers to entrance.

As a result, in the middle of the 90s, more than 90 per cent of the Chinese retail activity, more than 95 per cent of restaurants, and more than 50 per cent of the wholesale commerce were in private hands. Consequently it is possible to say that most of these commercial activities are currently exerted in China in a conventional capitalistic way.

3.1.3.2. Special Consideration of the Financial System in China

During the Maoist period, there was practically no other relevant bank in Continental China than the People's Bank of China. This Bank controlled most financial transactions of the country, including those related to the insurance sector. Some years after the start of the reforms period, the People's Bank changed into a Central Bank, while several commercial banks were created or transformed,[136] as well as

136. This explanation will be complemented in Chapter 5, item 5.6.2.3.

an important number of investment banks, insurance companies and urban and rural credit cooperatives.

As early as 1981 the first bonds were issued, and in 1988 a secondary market for the interchange of these titles was initiated. In 1990 the Shanghai Stock Exchange set up a secondary market for shares, and in the next year the same was done in Shenzen. Of course almost all the public financial institutions created after 1978 belongs to the State, although they work in a decentralised way.

With the setting up after 1978 of this entire financial framework, and also as a result of the demographic change introduced by authorities in the 70s, the State successfully introduced a strong dynamic component into the internal savings, whose evolution will be extensively commented lines below. Nonetheless, despite the huge increase in the domestic savings rate experienced by the Chinese economy in the last 25 years, one has to admit that the state has missused a huge amount of funds by supporting sick public firms.

One has also to agree that this way of supporting public firms is neither efficient nor convenient in the long run. Consequently, a significant effort could be made in the future by authorities to make the industrial labour market more flexible—by making hiring and firing easier—and to rise taxes in order to finance the re-floating or privatisation of these firms during an officially defined period of transition, as well as to correct other additional sources of public deficit. Otherwise the country could be confronted at mid-term with problems of inflation acceleration.

In this regard, one has to admit that the Chinese centre fiscal revenues of the tune of 7-8 per cent[137] in GDP terms (around 17-18 per cent of the GDP for all public sector), even below those of India, not to mention those corresponding to EU countries of around 35 per cent, or those of around 20 per cent of US or Japan, is a simple misconception of what public finances of a modern state should be.

137. Note however that this small comparative figure—taken from World Bank (2004) must be tributary of the peculiarities of the economic organisation of China, an almost full socialist country but very decentralised. On the other hand this mentioned figure of 7-8 per cent is consistent with the total expenditure of the Chinese Central government which in 2001 was around 11 per cent in GDP terms. Vide World Bank (2004).

Observe that the structural change in public finance of the last 25 years (with total public revenues changing from 31 per cent to 17-18 per cent) has forced the government to reduce relevant public expenditures, f.i. the relative public expenditure in education for the weakest segments of the population, whereas the expenditures in infrastructure have not grown at the desired rhythm. An adequate social system of protection has not been developed either.[138] As a result the State will have no other remedy in the medium term than to implement an effective rise in the level of taxation, while a system of quotations to finance social protection will have to be extended and re-enforced notably.[139]

3.2. Demography and Labour Market in China

As it is well known, the Chinese official policy has successfully encouraged the reduction of the birth rate, mainly since the 70s, which has induced a significant reduction of the annual population growth rate. This rate, that was 2.0 per cent in the period 1950-78, in the last two decades has moved downwards to a more manageable one of 1.1-1.2 per cent, while an additional declining movement to 0.6 per cent growth rate along the period 2002-2015 is expected.[140] Note that this rapid fall in the growth rate of the population in China has induced a significant ageing, that is going to produce economic problems to the country.

---

138. Observe that the current Pensions system is a mess, and the government only has a few years time to sort it out before a fast ageing population turns the current problem of insufficiency into a full-blown crisis. Aware of the problem, China began trying to set up a mix new system seven years ago. The idea was to change from a pay-as-you-go system, whereby retirees are paid out of the contributions made by those still working, to a partially funded system. The new planed system consists of paying basic pensions to retirees, who additionally will receive a complement depending on their previous personal contributions to personal accounts. Unfortunately, the new system is not working. There is a rampant evasion of the exorbitant contributions required, while nearly half of urban employees and almost all farmers and migrant workers are not covered. The main current problem is that the new pension system has taken on the liabilities of the old one. So to pay current retirees from the old system, local governments often use the money that should be going into the personal accounts, thus making the new mix system non-tenable. Out of 31 provincial governments only six or seven have pension funds in the black, while central government has scaled back its contributions dramatically. Vide *The Economist*. May, 22nd 2004. page 62.

139. Note for instance that the pension contributors in China in 1994, reached only a figure of the 17.6 per cent of the total labour force. Vide World Bank (2004:42), *World Development Indicators*.

140. Vide World Bank (2004) *World Development Indicators*.

As we have explained in Chapter 2, this strategy had to induce a change in the population pyramid, thus initially increasing the proportion of potential active population over the total population. Even more, given the massive embodiment of women to the active population, the level of employment has grown to a higher rhythm than that of the potential active population, particularly in the agriculture sector.[141]

Before 1978, China did not efficiently allocate its labour force to economic activities at all. Rural families could not freely migrate to urban areas (this continues to be the case), or change their activity in countryside. In general, in the Maoist period, rural workers were paid in kind or with points changeable for money at the end of the year. But these restrictive working conditions in the countryside significantly improved after 1978.

During the Maoist period (1950-78), public firms placed in the urban sector could hardly recruit or dismiss workers, since their employment quota was authorised by the Ministry of Labour, which also established the different levels of wages on their payrolls. The movement of workers among firms was practically impossible, while the volume of workers of public firms was in general excessive.

Although these strong restrictions in the public sector remained until recently, the fast emergence of the private sector since 1978 has introduced a certain flexibility in the labour market as a whole, particularly in the cities and in the services sector, which has improved the allocation of human resources to different activities. To the extent that a necessary condition for a maximum exploitation of the economic potentialities of China is the additional flexibilisation-reorganisation of its industrial labour market, a further liberalisation of it is currently expected.

As to the quality of the human factor, one has to underline that its improvement along the last half a century has also been spectacular[142] although non-steady. Nonetheless, the education efforts

---

141. Note that in the 30s of the 20th Century, the women working in the agriculture were a 20 per cent of the total, while in the 90s this share reached the figure of 50 per cent.

142. Between 1952 and 1995 the average period of instruction of the 15 years old population has moved from 1.7 years of schooling to a figure of near nine.

of the government in the last 50 years have resulted in a low adult illiteracy rate in 2002 (7 per cent in China in comparison to 31 per cent in India).

In 1995 the number of students in secondary schooling in China[143] was 2/3rd of the population slab between 15-19 years, while at the same time a 6 per cent of the slab population between 20-24 was embodied into the higher education, and a significant number of youngsters studied abroad.[144]

The mentioned improvement in schooling has been accompanied by a parallel one in the field of health, that to a great extent is currently paid privately when it implies high costs (hospital assistance). All this has finally induced a longer expectancy of life which has moved from 38 years in 1950 up to 70 in 2001.[145]

3.3. The Evolution of the Income Distribution in China

As we have mentioned in Chapter 2, the process of accelerated growth in capitalist economies with a major part of the population initially attached to agriculture, use to generate negative distribution of individual incomes along the first stages of their industrialisation (let us remember the so-called Kuznets curve[146]). Although China is not *strictu sensu* a capitalist economy, the implemented pro-capitalistic reforms since 1978 have also been conducive to this phenomenon of temporary negative income distribution.

This theoretical expectation towards a negative distribution of the personal income in China has become a reality in the post-reforms period. Specifically, the Chinese income inequality, as measured by

143. Since 1978, China adopted a "nine year compulsory schooling system" which means that all children are required to attend school at least for 9 courses.

144. Note that in the Cultural Revolution period, the higher education suffered a significant blow. Many professors and students were sent to countryside for re-education, most of the higher education centres were closed, and the number of higher education students fell from near one million in 1960 to only 50 thousand in 1970.

145. The main factors that have contributed to the rise of the expectancy of life in last 50 years have been: the improvement of hygiene and feeding, and the easier access to medicines by Chinese citizens.

146. On Prof. Kuznets curve, Vide for instance, Ahluwalia, M. (1976). "Inequality, poverty and Development." This paper may be found in Meier, G. *et al.*, (2000:387) *Leading Issues in Economic Development*. 7th Ed. Oxford University Press.

the Gini index,[147] has risen in China to 0.45 in 2001 from a figure of 0.40-0.41 in 1996, which may be a clear pointer of the negative evolution of the individual income distribution in China in the post-reform period. Note additionally that the last known Chinese Gini (2001), is astonishingly superior to that of the US (which was of 0.41 in 1997).

Actually this is not good news for the CCP, although there are other countries as Brazil, Malaysia or the Russian Federation, whose personal income distribution is worst than that of China (note that the Gini index is significantly lower in India, whose personal income distribution is similar to that of the EU countries).

Developing of inequality within and between different urban areas have had to do with the structural changes registered in the post-reform period. Standards of living in areas or cities with surging private (foreign or Chinese) firms have relatively improved, while those in areas or regions formerly or currently dominated by public firms have experienced a relative fall.

Inequality has also developed between urban and rural areas. According to available information, the average income disparity between cities and countryside has increased from 1.8 in 1995 to 2.4 in 2002. Finally, we have to underline that the disparity of personal incomes has also grown between coastal and inner areas, due to their different degrees of infrastructure (transport and communication) development.

3.4. The Evolution of Domestic Investment in China

As it is well acknowledged by economic theory (Chapter 2), the domestic investment rate, materialised in physical or human factors, is one of the main explanatory variables of the development process. This domestic investment has to be financed by domestic savings or by external ones, as to guarantee macroeconomic equilibrium.

In the field of domestic investment, the success of China has simply been overwhelming. Specifically, the non-residential gross

147. The range of this index moves from a value of nil (which represents an equal income distribution for all people) to another of one (which would result from a situation of extreme bad distribution).

investment rate has moved from 4 per cent (in GDP terms) registered before the revolution, up to levels of 11 per cent in the 50s, 18 per cent during the Maoist period, and 20 per cent or more after the reforms period.[148] Note that in the Maoist-era the bulk of investment was financed by the public sector, which to increase the public saving to finance the accumulation process, kept the wages subdued, thus compressing the average personal consumption. Later on, after starting the reforms process and while achieving a significant reduction of the demography growth rate, the private saving (mainly coming from families) began to grow significantly, which enabled to finance more profitable and forerunner industries mainly through the banking system.

If one reviews the last available figures (2002) of the Gross Capital Formation of China, one has to conclude that today this country has the highest rate in the world (40 per cent),[149] even over the one South Korea had in 1990. Besides this, given the long lasting assumed capacity of this country to transfer human resources to non-agricultural sectors (for 3-4 decades in the future), no wonder that an outlook of continuous and relative high growth of China in the future is expected by many Western observes.

3.4.1. The Apparent Puzzle of External Chinese Financing

Entering now into the explanation of the recent financing of the huge domestic investments of China, one has necessarily to refer to the high current levels of internal and external savings gathered by this country, and to the figures of Gross Domestic Investment, trying to make each other consistent.

---

148. Note that the Chinese levels of investment are significantly higher than those of the capitalist advanced countries. Note additionally that in the investment process of China the "variations of stocks" have for long played a special role. This variable represented between 1978 and 1994 a figure of 7.1 per cent in GDP terms, while this ratio hardly reached 1 per cent in the Western countries. Although this phenomenon is typical in developing countries in which the service sector has a minor relevance, the Chinese case is rather exceptional, proving the inefficiency of the public production and the transport system. Vide Maddison, A. (1998:71) Book already mentioned.

149. Note that this figure of 40 per cent in 2002 is clearly superior to that of India, which in 2002 only reached 23 per cent (These figures are taken from World Bank (2004), World Development Indicators). Observe that this difference in Gross Capital Formation is narrowly correlated with the current disparities in growth rates of China and India, as simple models of economic growth suggest.

To begin with, it is surprising that the recent figure of internal savings—Gross National Savings—provided by the WB referring to 2002, reaches an amount of 43.7 per cent in GDP terms. This is a figure that is at the top of all the internal saving rates registered in the recent history of Development Economics in relation to large countries.

Note additionally that according to the last figures provided by the World Bank, the internal saving rate of this country (43.7 per cent) has been (in 2002) larger than its domestic investments (40 per cent). This means that, contrary to what one could expect from a country with a high velocity of GDP growth, but with low per capita GDP, China behaves as a net lender. Of course this net external position is consistent with the current account surplus of China and with its rapid accumulation of foreign reserves (that nowadays reach a figure over 650 billion US dollars).[150]

It is also well known that the Chinese economy receives significant external flows of capital, to a great extent in the form of FDI (Foreign Direct Investment). Specifically, in the second half of the 90s and first years of the current decade, China has annually received FDI amounting up to 4-5 per cent in GDP terms (3.9 per cent in 2002). This means that in order to square the figures, if these are accurate, China would be nowadays lending to the rest of the world more than 6 points of its GDP as a whole.[151]

Summing up, although with a rather unusual internal and external saving composition, the funds devoted by China to internal investments (40 per cent) are relatively alike, or superior in magnitude, to those enjoyed by Japan and South Korea in their paramount historical moments. The big difference in our opinion is

---

150. Note that the amount of foreign reserves accumulated by China in 2002 represented around 11 months of imports (more than 12 months in 2003). Although this high relation is alien to the habits of the Western Industrialised countries, and allegedly a bad business for China, which partly invests those reserves in bonds of the American Treasure at low interest rates, it could be considered as convenient for the Chinese economy, from a special point of view. With this huge volume of kept reserves, China may relatively decouple its economy from the western business cycle. In the context of a future Western economic slump the Chinese economy could continue growing despite a reduction of its exports, if simultaneously it is capable of stoking its internal demand to partially substitute the external one.

151. Note that in 2003 the volume of external reserves of China grew by an amount of around 10 per cent of its GDP.

that China (as well as India) will count with a larger period than those of the above mentioned countries without reaching significant diminishing returns.[152] Consequently 30, 40, or more years of comparative fast growth are *ceteris paribus* practically guaranteed in China (as well as in India).

3.5. China and the Development of International Economic Relations

After the revolution and during the beginning of the 50s, China only had commercial relations with the Soviet Union and other communist countries. In particular the Soviet Union provided China with significant equipment-goods and technological assistance.[153] These almost exclusive commercial relations with communist countries were reinforced at the time of the commercial embargo with China, imposed in the early-50s by Western allies, as a result of the Chinese participation in the Korea war. This embargo by US and others meaningfully affected the trade of the country.[154]

During the 50s the foreign trade of China was a monopoly of the State, who basically imported tool-machines for industry and agriculture, inputs for the oil and electricity industries, trucks, fighters, submarines, experimental nuclear reactors[155] and so on. Due to political conflicts with the Soviet Union, mutual commercial relations suddenly broke in 1960 and many of the underway projects had to stop. Note that this break up overlapped with the inconvenient industrial policy implemented in those years (The Great Leap Forward).

---

152. As recently stated by "The Economist" (March, 20th 2004) in relation to China, "whereas in the 80s and 90s it took $2-3 of new investment to produce $1 of additional output, now it needs more than $4. Even India, often compared unfavourably with China, is now more efficient on that measure". Note however that the observed rise in this incremental capital-output relation is not a good measure of the evolution of joint productivity of factors, but rather a rough approximation to the marginal productivity of capital. A capital productivity that always is (apparently) lower when the domestic investment process is deeply tilted to infrastructure, health and education, activities of long-lasting periods of gestation and output recovering.

153. In 1950, Soviet Union agreed with China on an initial loan of US$ 300 million for the financing of equipment and technical assistance.

154. UK, Japan and most of the rest of the allies, lifted the embargo at the end of the war, but the US kept it up to 1971.

155. This special trade gave China the opportunity of early (1964) becoming a nuclear power.

Note additionally that in those days China was significantly indebted to the Soviet Union, till reimbursement in 1965. At the same time, China was a donor of other Asian countries, while the received remittances from Chinese abroad were under minima. As a result, the external financial situation of China in the late-60s became chaotic, and much more uncomfortable than that of other neighbouring Asian countries. In particular we could here quote the case of South Korea, which in the 50s and 60s received foreign savings that, as an average, reached the figure of the 7.8 per cent of its GDP, while Taiwan received foreign funds around 2.5 per cent of its GDP.[156]

3.5.1. *China and Multilateral Institutions*

In the 70s the Chinese position in global relations began to improve. In 1971 the People's Republic of China substituted current Taiwan in the UN and the Security Council, thus ending the previous fiction whereby the small (and also non-democratic) pro-Western Taiwan represented all the Chinese citizens in the UN. In 1972 the Chinese relations with Japan and the US significantly changed and, formally or informally, these countries initiated their diplomatic relations with China, while the US lifted its commercial embargo and gave China the status of "most favoured nation" concerning import facilitation. In 1980, China became a member of the WB and IMF, and in 1982 a member of the Asian Development Bank (ADB). In the same year (1982) China entered as an observer in the GATT, and finally in 2003 reached membership in the WTO, thus becoming internationally a completely homologated country.

3.5.2. *Chinese Policy for Attracting FDI and Commercial Success*

At the end of the Maoist-era in 1978, the Chinese authorities decided to abandon the autarky, thus progressively opening the mainland economy to international commercial and financial relations. The exchange rate of the Yuan (against the US dollar), which had artificially been kept fix between 1955 and 1970, suffered in the following years (up to 1996) five devaluations. As a result, rigid disparities among internal and external prices progressively

---

156. A relevant part of these foreign flows were ODA directed to plug political leaks at the frontiers of communism.

dwindled, thus step by step enabling China to recover its comparative advantages.

The creation of the so-called "Special Economic Zones" (SEZ) by Chinese authorities was the star instrument of the new economic international policy. These SEZ are geographical enclaves in which imports of raw materials and intermediate goods, and exports of manufactures are duty free, the paid wages to workers are comparatively low in terms of international standards, and the profits of the *ex-novo* foreign installed firms have significant and temporary tax reductions. Four zones were initially created in the 80s. One of them, the most important, was placed in the surroundings of Hong-Kong, another in the neighbourhood of Macao, one in front of Taiwan and the last one in Shantou at Kuang-tung.

In 1984, 14 coastal cities were also opened to economic activities focused on international trade. In particular the cities of the Yang-Tse delta and Shanghai were integrated in the process. Finally an additional SEZ was created at the island of Hainan.

Once implemented, the very favourable results of the new policy overcame expectations. Although the volume of exports had already doubled between 1970 and 1978, they multiplied by more than eight in the period 1980-1996, while it now doubles every 4-5 years as an average. Consequently, while in 1978 the Chinese exports represented a figure equivalent to 4.6 per cent of its GDP, this relation reached a level of 29 per cent in 2002.

Concerning the evolution of the export share of China in total international exports, one has to certify again that the success of China has been spectacular. Thus, from a figure of 0.8 per cent of the total world exports in 1978, China moved to another of 2.9 per cent in 1995, and in our days (2003) this figure is 5.9 per cent, with a recent trend to annually gain quota equivalent to 0.5-0.6 per cent points.

Given the fact that China is a country very dynamic and highly populated, its more than significant current share in global trade (5.9 per cent), although rapidly growing, has not at all reached its equilibrium position. As a result it is not risky to state that this country could be the first exporter of the world around 2010-2012 (if we consider in *net terms* the joint export figures of mainland China and Hong Kong).

3.5.3. *Trade Composition After 1978 and Problems Stemming from Commercial Success*

During the first years of the new People´s Republic, the Chinese exports focused on food, raw materials and textile items. By and by, the industrial exports started gaining importance and, at the end of the Maoist period the industrial exports reached a rough figure of 50 per cent of total Chinese exports. Later on, in the 80s China started exporting oil and, finally in the middle-90s the Chinese exports were highly diversified, being the volume of exported manufactures around 85 per cent of the total (90 per cent in 2002).

In relation to the Chinese imports, these were also well diversified at middle of the 90s. Equipment and intermediate goods predominated, but China also imported manufactured consumption-goods in order to technically improve, via competition, the domestic production of these items. Recently, as a consequence of its rapid growth, the Chinese economy, which formerly had been an oil exporter, has become significantly dependent on oil imports (although not so much as India). Today (in 2002) 80 per cent of the Chinese imports are manufactures.

Note additionally that along the last years, the international trade of China has reflected surplus with a lot of Western countries, in particular with US[157] and many EU partners.[158] Nonetheless, trade account balances of China with several East-Asian countries have reflected deficit, in particular with Japan.

The recent success of the exports of China, whose current speed of growth is simply spectacular, has nowadays unleashed fears across the Western hemisphere. This success has been based on the relative cheapness of the industrial labour in China, and on the alleged under-valuation of the Yuan. Concerning these issues, Western countries have recently suggested that China should either increase its industrial labour wages—something that China cannot rationally do with its enormous hidden unemployment in agriculture—or alternatively, to re-value the Yuan.

157. Note that the US official evaluation of the Chinese imports uses to include those that come from Hong-Kong, as mere Chinese re-exports.

158. Nevertheless, Germany has recently obtained successive current account surpluses in its economic relations with China.

Nevertheless the Chinese authorities continue to keep the Yuan pegged to the dollar, because an operation of putting the Yuan into flotation for a progressive revaluation, could generate adverse movements of capital, thus additionally disturbing the current fragile situation of the Chinese banks, overloaded with non-performing credits advanced to sick public firms, as we have already mentioned.

3.5.4. Peculiarities of FDI in China and SEZ Problems

In 1978, after having repaid in 1965 the remaining balance due to the Soviet Union, and in consistency with the autarkic economic policy practised in the Maoist age, China had no international debts while the received Foreign Direct Investment (FDI) was practically nil. Nevertheless, after 1978 it was thought that FDI should be promoted, not only to complement the interior savings—then not so high as they currently are—but also to profit the Chinese industrial activity with the annex transfers of technology, which typically occurs when FDI flows in.

Although between 1979 and 1991 the flows of FDI steadily grew, during the 90s these flows significantly multiplied, thus siphoning potential FDI that could have gone to other destinations if circumstances had been different (for instance to India). But the Chinese FDI phenomenon had only started: in the last years of the past decade up to 2002 China received figures of FDI equivalent, as an average, up to 4-5 per cent of its GDP (around 30-35 per cent of all the FDI received by all developing countries).

Despite former comments made in lines above, it is important to insist that the geographical origin of this FDI in China is peculiar and politically entangled, intertwining neighbouring countries and own citizens living in the mainland. In 1996 for instance almost 65 per cent of the total received FDI came from Hong-Kong, Taiwan and Singapore, places where many Chinese live. Even more, a substantial part of the received FDI may be re-sent by own Chinese citizens who, living in the mainland and after illegally transferring funds to Hong-Kong, re-direct them to the mainland as FDI, to profit from the fiscal privileges attainable through investing in SEZ.

Of course these fiscal paradises (SEZ) have also distorted the internal allocation of resources, siphoning funds that otherwise could have gone to other geographical spaces of China, thus generating a process of geographically unbalanced development.[159] Note additionally that the existence of SEZ has promoted smuggling to the rest of the country of consumption goods that arrive to the SEZ without paying tariff duties.

All this unfavourable facts have been the economic cost of attracting the massive FDI that China has successfully gathered. Note though that, despite the mentioned problems generated by these SEZ, other countries, including India, are also essaying the promotion of these special fiscal enclaves (although we have to underline that the speed of their effective promotion in India is rather slow and mutually competitive among different states).

3.5.5. Other Sources of International Financing and External Solvency of China

Besides FDI, China also receives funds from the WB and the ADB, from bilateral official creditors, and from private creditors (credits from external banks or gathered by means of issuing bonds). At the end of 2002 the total external debt of China reached a figure of US-$ 168 billions, of which US-$ 125 billions was long term debt. Note that in 2002 the total outstanding external debt of China was equivalent to 14 per cent of the Chinese GDP—a very moderate figure—whose short term component was only of around 25 per cent of the total.

The long term maturity composition of these debts, plus the moderate external indebtedness of China, plus above all, the enormous quantity of accumulated foreign reserves China, have changed this country into an armoured one against any international speculative movement on the Yuan, thus significantly de-coupling the internal development process of China from the western economic business cycles.

Finally we have to mention that although the international economic solvency of China is beyond any doubt, there are some misgivings on the future property rights of foreigners.[160] In this

159. This propensity to the generation of additional geographical unbalance, will also occur in India, if finally the Indian SEZ system become successful.

160. Along the 90s the Chinese government clearly recognised that the private firms and the property rights are essential parts of a healthy economy. Of course, in many areas—like TV, broadcasting, main transportation, telecommunications, etc.—private access is not allowed in China. Recently, in March, 2004, the CCP has initiated an additional movement in relation of thawing former private property bans, ruling from the beginning of the Revolution.

regard one frequently hears in Asia that it is very easy to invest money in China but not so easy to repatriate its proceedings and principal.

3.6. Some Traits of the Macroeconomic Performance in China

Although in Chapter 5 we will enter into details explaining the current macroeconomic positions of China and India in comparison to those of many relevant countries of the world, particularly to those of the western ones, we will here mention some general aspects of the macroeconomic performance of this country along the last half century.

3.6.1. Performance up to 1978

As we have mentioned before, between 1949 and 1978, along with dangerous collectivist experiments in rural areas, and application of hazardous industrial policies—which made possible that the testing of "total socialism" reached its heydays with the "Great Leap Forward" and the "Cultural Revolution"—the Chinese economy became a micro-macro ultra-controlled one, doomed to squandering of resources and relative under-performance.

In the Chinese economy of those days, the State decided the amount of total public funding and distributed the available funds among the different sectors and activities. The production assets were property of the state or collectives; the prices of goods, services, and factors were politically defined; and the consumption goods were rationed and many of them subsidised. The financial system was clearly underdeveloped—and relatively continues being so—and submitted to official financial targets for every line of economic activity. Finally, the State had the monopoly of the control of exchange rates, and FDI was practically inexistent.

In relation to public finances, the budgetary system of China and its planning process were completely integrated. The main item of the expenditures of the State was the so-called "Economic Construction" of the country, which included investments (all of them public) and the administration of the main sectors of the economy. Note however that in those days, collective farms, public firms and cooperatives overwhelmingly had to finance their own investments, while borrowing from banks and issues of financial assets for financing non-planned investments were practically inexistent.

From the side of the revenues of the Centre, a significant part of them came from the profits of public firms owned by the state. With the exception of the years of the "Great Leap Forward" and those of the beginning of the "Cultural Revolution," the budgetary behaviour of the state was prudent and the state normally generated surpluses.

Finally note that the annual average inflation between 1949 and 1978 was around 2 per cent, thus fulfilling one of the main targets of the revolutionaries.

3.6.2. Macroeconomic Performance After the Start of the Reforms

Logically, after 1978, the nature of the Chinese economy radically changed. In this regard, the role of the state in the direction and financing of the development process was played down. As a result of the progressive liberalisation of the economy, the revenues of the state (in good part coming from owned public firms) started a degrading process in GDP terms, reaching finally figures well under 10 per cent. To the extent that from 1978 onwards, the state continuously spent more than its decreasing revenues, it necessarily had to incur in public deficits. These successive deficits of the state generated a significant increase of the public internal outstanding debt, that in 1995 reached an amount of near 30 per cent in GDP terms. Needless to say that this unbalance was partially covered by the Chinese financial system, particularly by official banks.

Changing the focus, it is necessary to mention that from 1978 onwards, the Chinese economy, rather homogeneous before the reforms, split into a two velocities economic system. The first could be defined as a "fast track economy", which being external to the official plans, grew at high rhythms. This is an economy that uses less capital per worker, whose wages are lower, and that lacks significant Social Security for the protection of workers. Hiring and firing is free (for private firms), and consequently its flexibility is almost total. Note that this economy is mainly formed by units of production focused on labour-intensive activities, mainly located in SEZ and other privileged coastal areas.

Soon after the start of the reforms, this "fast track economy" entered in competition with the "slow track economy" (public firms), with a clear advantage for the former. As a result, the revenues of public firms decreased meaningfully, which induced lesser transfers of profits to the state. Even more, in many cases the previous transfers of profits changed into receiving subsidies from the state, to offset accumulated losses and keep employment levels. All this explains the downward trend of the state revenues and the growing deficits.

Despite the arrival to a budgetary crisis, the inflation rate did not alarmingly stepped up, although it was much higher than that of the Maoist period. Between 1978–1994 the inflation rate reached an average of around 10-11 per cent. However, in the first years of 2000 it dropped to 1-2 per cent, although with a trend to grow (in mid-2004 it peaked around 5 per cent). In the meantime, as a consequence of the Chinese success in its population limitation policy and in its higher attained growth rates, the internal saving rate shot up reaching almost unimaginable figures, as mentioned lines above (around 43.7 per cent in GDP terms).

As a result of the high speed growth of private saving rates, huge amounts of money has been channelled to the official banks, which have accumulated funds that, in part, have been used for financing the public sector. If we add to this public financing from banks, the process of direct or indirect monetisation undertaken by the People's Bank of China, to cover part of the deficit of the total public sector (including public firms in red), we may conclude that the internal seigniorage rights,[161] stemming from issuing of new money, has helped the state to cover its deficits without incurring in more hazardous operations.

3.6.3. *On the Over-heating of the Chinese Economy*

Although the trajectory of the Chinese economy has been spectacular in the last two decades, and in particular in the last 10

161. These "seigniorage rights" obtained by the state, via People's Bank of China, are proportional to the increase of the new printed money put into circulation. Although different in conception, note that the so-called M1 (monetary supply) was in 1978 equivalent to less than one third of the GDP, whereas this ratio was of the tune of 1:1 in 1995. This increase of the circulating money may have generated a significant margin for obtaining seigniorage rights (stemming from expansion of the monetary base) without unleashing meaningful inflation.

years, this does not mean that some juncture problems may not appear as a consequence of the registered rapid growth process.

To the extent that in any decentralised economy a lot of economic agents intervene making independent decisions, investment over-reactions to brilliant and hopeful expectations can not be ruled out, and this may be the case in current China. Let us not forget that on this sort of aggregated mistakes, most of the theories of the economic cycle are founded. Consequently, to assume that the Chinese economy cannot enter into a cyclical correction, induced by private agents or imposed by the government as a result of patent short-term unbalances, is simply not realistic.

On the other hand, appearance of disequilibria in the development process—as for instance negative distribution of the incomes (personal, regional or sectorial), bottlenecks in infrastructure or energy, or even inflation—when this is moving in a partially decentralised framework and at high speed, are expectable phenomena.

In relation to the recently observed inflation resumption in China[162] and its causes, we should not forget that an excessive investment,[163] with its sequels of low profitability,[164] could be at the core of the problem. Mentioned dysfunction in public firms and financial system, insufficiency of tax revenues in the public sector (both phenomena forcing injection of fresh money into the system), and the construction of an excessively export oriented economy in demerit of the internal production of consumption goods, are also drawbacks to be corrected to curb inflation. In particular if—as we will hypothetically assume (Vide. Chapter 6)—Western countries take initiatives for protecting internal production and jobs, which

162. Note that in March 2004, the Industrial prices moved at an annual rhythm of almost 4 per cent.

163. The investment in fix assets rose in 2003 at a rate of 28 per cent, when the GDP increased at 9.1 per cent. Nevertheless, during the first quarter of 2004 the former rate significantly accelerated its velocity of progress as to reach a figure of 47 per cent, in comparison to the first quarter of 2003. Certainly a figure out of any rationality, even in the context of the Chinese economy.

164. We have already mentioned this problem in lines above, which in due time could result in diverting FDI currently directed to China to other areas, with advantage to India (of course if India behaves better in future after due implementation of so-called second generation reforms).

would force Chinese authorities to encourage internal consumption to avoid slowdown.[165]

Note that the Chinese economy is frequently criticised for being too much tilted to an ever growing industrial production in relative terms. This is considered by some commentators as another flaw of the Chinese economy,[166] although they should not forget that the accessibility of the Chinese (and Indian) services to the industrialised countries is much more difficult than that of industrial goods. This lack of sufficient accessibility may have been the cause of the industrial stressing of the Chinese economy.

Anyway we have to mention the recently adopted monetary and regulatory measures by Chinese authorities to curb inflation. The first has been implemented by means of rising the required reserves ratio of the banks, in order to sterilise part of the huge volume of liquidity—at nil cost for the state[167]—partially injected through the external sector, as a result of its successful exports and received FDI. This measure accompanied by others, realised "at hand" to curb monetary and credit growth, could be sufficient to reach smaller growth rates in relation to the evolution of the monetary supply and consumer prices.[168] In relation to regulatory measures we have to mention the establishing of moratoria for new investments in certain critical sectors (steel, textile and auto-motion) whose recent investments have been considered as overdone.

Although these corrections to the current juncture may soften the landing of the Chinese economy, taking it to a more moderate growth rate figures, as for instance 8 per cent, we consider as practically guaranteed the continuation of the high cruise speed of the Chinese

---

165. Figures of annual GDP growth rates under 7 per cent, would be catastrophic for the Chinese expectations, as it has happened in India when the growth rate has moved under 4 per cent.

166. Prof. Xu Xiaionian, research director of the CICC, has suggested that "it is absurd that a country as China, intensive in labour but with scant raw materials, focuses its production in raw materials intensive goods". Notwithstanding this suggestion, we do believe that if China had done as mentioned, it would have collided with problems of accessibility of agriculture and services in industrialised countries.

167. This sterilisation could alternatively have been made more efficiently by means of issuing additional internal public debt. However, given the development stage of the domestic financial system and the Chinese economy, the rising of the reserves-coefficient seems acceptable.

168. The Chinese consumer prices growth rate in April 2005 was just 1.8 per cent.

economy which, after an adjustment period, will *ceteris paribus* continue exhibiting high growth rates.

Nevertheless, we have to underline that a reduction of the GDP growth rate, from near 10 per cent to 8 per cent during a period of 1-2 years, could significantly increase the level of unemployment in the cities, which currently could be placed at around 8-10 per cent.[169] This figure jointly with that of the deficient personal distribution of income, and the appearance of a two speeds China, would be the long term costs of the reforms undertaken in 1978.

3.6.4. Troubles and Opportunities Induced by Rapid Growth

Indeed, one has to acknowledge that along the development and industrialisation process, the economies have to overcome the difficulties generated by the necessary reallocation of resources, mainly the human ones. A reallocation of human resources that has to move workers either from the agriculture to non-agricultural sectors or from an inflexible and at times overloaded industrial public sector towards the private one; or simultaneously in both directions, as it is now happening in China.

Specifically, we have to mention that between 1998 and 2002 around 18-20 million workers of the industrial public sector, or around 10 per cent of the urban labour force became unemployed. As a result, it is said that the current unemployment rate in the five main cities of China may be fluctuating between 7 per cent and 13 per cent, while other local disparities of the unemployment rates may be much more pronounced, reaching in some cases—as for instance in some old mining places—up to 40 per cent.

As the reader may imagine, the appearance of the mentioned urban unemployment rates, although unavoidable in the process, poses a real challenge to the Chinese government which has to quickly reallocate these workers to avert political problems in the most important cities.[170] And this while it has to lead the

---

169. Although the government does not consider as unemployed those who have been recently laid off from state-owned enterprises, because they get a basic stipend for three years after losing their jobs, many Chinese analysts put the figure of 8-10 per cent as the probable figure of unemployed in urban areas. Vide *The Economist*. September 11th 2004. Page 55.

170. Observe that this unemployment problem also forces the Chinese authorities to peg the Yuan to the US-dollar in order to continue with the Chinese model of rapid GDP growth rate based on quickly rising exports.

urbanisation, development and industrialisation of the countryside, being the latter a long scope process that has barely started.

Note additionally that in the last years, after the relative saturation of the coastal areas, a geographical spreading of industrial economic activity towards inland China has started. In particular the hinterlands of Shanghai and Guandong—including Hong-Kong and Macau—are progressively spreading towards inner China, thus significantly improving the situation of many workers formerly attached to agricultural activities. And all this while a parallel and general process of urbanisation has taken a non-expected speed, doubling in 25 years the relative figure of the Chinese population living in cities, a percentage that has today reached a figure of around 40 per cent. Note that this phenomenon of doubling urban population took 50 years in America in the 19th Century.

4

Brief History of the Economy of India Since 1947

4.1. The Biased Treatment of the Economy of India under the British Rule

As it occurred in China at the moment of taking over by the revolutionaries (1949), when India gained its independence in 1947, it also inherited a crippled economy with a scant industry, a stagnant agriculture and a peasantry immersed in poverty.

According to many Indian historians, the history of the "British Rule" of India was a long story of political neglect and systematic economic exploitation of a people whom they had shrewdly enslaved through a typical policy of "divide and rule".[171]

As prominent Indians have repeatedly said, as a consequence of the asymmetric and non-neutral applied policies by the colonial power, the benefits of the British rule (for Indians) were rather incidental. This happened because the main motive of almost all British applied policies in India was to serve the interest of Britain, disguised as those of the "empire".[172]

4.1.1. The British Rule and the Indian Economy before Independence

Parallel to the slow and lengthy process for the achievement of power in India, which protracted along one century up to 1852,[173] England witnessed at home its most critical but brilliant economic

---

171. We believe that this comment could be applied to almost any process of colonisation in the World History.

172. Vide Datt, R. and Sundharam, K. (2004:29) *Indian Economy*. 49th Edition. New Delhi. Chand.

173. Note that the British conquest of India took about 100 years, from 1757 (battle of Plessey) to 1858 (the so-called Rebellion or Mutiny).

period, the so-called "Industrial Revolution." This Industrial Revolution heavily reduced the unitary cost of the machine-made goods in Britain; goods that everywhere had previously been handcrafted. This temporary synchronisation of the Industrial Revolution in England with the colonisation of India gave the Brits the opportunity of selling machine-made goods to India, thus placing this country in a clear manufactured-goods disadvantage, in particular in textile handicrafts, the then most relevant "industrial" activity in India.

Paradoxically—although in historical consistency with the asymmetric way of doing international politics by Western powers—while the British emphasised the convenience for India of a bi-directional free trade system, which could have meant that the latter exports raw materials and imports machine-made goods[174] and also *machinery*, the British did not allow the imports of equipment coming from Britain, thus averting the industrial modernisation of India. This asymmetric and obstructionist commercial behaviour of the British not only generated a decline of the contemporary scant Indian industry but also induced a progressive ruralisation of the Indian economy.[175]

Indeed, the British rulers of India mainly focused on the commercialisation of primary Indian products, thus stimulating the Indian exports of raw materials. After 1850, as it occurred everywhere, a railways network was constructed in India by the British, with the aim of linking the interior of the country with ports and urban marketing centres in order to make the export activity easier.

As a result, the Indian agriculture started to work for world markets, while the village's production of handicrafts meaningfully declined across all India. Even worse, in some years of bad crops, the enforced fulfilment of the export quotas established by the British rulers, compounded the contemporary problems of rising prices and famines, typical phenomena of years of bad monsoon and short agricultural productions.

---

174. This process enabled the swamping of the Indian textile market with British textile manufactures.

175. The opening of the Suez channel in 1869 significantly reduced the transports costs, thus facilitating the mutual but biased British-Indian trade.

4.1.2. Process of Industrial Transition in India

India set up its first "modern" industrial factories in the period 1850-55, parallel in time with the construction and working of its first line of railways. Since those years till the end of the 19th century, the number of cotton, jute, and coal production factories increased significantly. Note however, that the British, who obviously pioneered and managed the process, refused to get involved in heavy industrial developments through further utilisation of coal and iron mineral reserves, for intermediate industrial goods or for manufacturing production, in order to increase the Indian added value. Conversely, they mainly promoted the export of these goods just as raw materials.

In the second half of the 19th century, although selected Indians joined the ranks of the local-British industrialists and their industrial role progressively gained ground, they mostly performed the same abusive "managing agency system",[176] thus emulating the British. Only in 1905 a *swadeshi* movement for Indian industrialisation by Indians started. As a result around a hundred factories were opened up to 1914.

The First World War could have been a good opportunity to industrialise India. Note that along this war Indian imports from Britain fell, whereas exports to Britain shot up, in particular those of iron and steel, jute, leather goods, cotton and textiles; goods which were sent to Britain to collaborate in the war effort. Nevertheless, as a result of the absence of significant heavy industrial factories, and particularly those of machine-tools, the Indian industrial production could not take off.

Well after the war, in the period 1929 to 1939, several domestic Indian industries received protection from the (British) government of India, in particular iron and steel, jute, sugar, paper and pulp industries. As a consequence, these industries grew more rapidly in the mentioned epoch. Of course the outbreak of the Second World War created a very intensive and urgent demand for manufactured Indian goods, and as a result the industrial production of India experienced again a significant push forward. Afterwards, as a

---

176. The so-called "managing agency system," will be explained below.

derivative of the underway independence process, the Indian industrial production almost stalled.

4.1.2.1. Colonial Mistreatment of Indian Commerce and Consequences

According to many Indian authors, the constant and major form through which the colonial exploitation of India was performed—note that this sort of exploitation was not very different to those implemented by other colonial powers in their "protectorates"—was through the setting up of asymmetric international trade conditions. Of course, this does not mean that there had not been other forms of exploitation and abuse.[177] No wonder that current Indian officials, as it also happens with the current Chinese administration, are so distrustful and cautious in present international negotiations, in which the West often try to maintain the traditional and asymmetric commercial state of affairs.[178]

Although for long Britain proclaimed and continues doing so, to be a follower of the free trade doctrines, its trade relations with India (and other colonies) never were symmetrical. Note that before the full British take-over of India, Indian cotton and silk cloths had a clear comparative advantage in international markets. Nevertheless, in that age the then "mercantilist" Britain banned cotton and silk cloths imports coming from India.

After taking over, heavy import duties were imposed in Britain on all Indian goods other than foodstuffs and raw materials. Conversely, the British exports to India of machine-made goods were promoted, while paradoxically the exports of machinery to India were practically banned.

When at the beginning of the 20th century, a strong demand by the Indian national movement (*swadeshi*) to protect interests of Indian industries developed, the colonial government decided "to

177. For instance, by encouraging British direct investors to take up only consumer good industries, by allowing financing systems "of agency" doing their own way while conveniently turning a blind eye to major appropriation of profits through malpractices, by forcing Indians to pay for the colonial administration of India, as well as by forcing Indian taxpayers to finance British wars against neighbouring countries.

178. Vide Rahman, R. and Andreu, J.M. (2004:74). Book already mentioned.

support" this defensive initiative. Even so, this protection was granted exclusively against countries alien to Britain, thus practically remaining the previous advantageous situation of the British exporters.[179] To get this special treatment, Britain forced India to introduce in its legal commercial framework, a clause of "most favoured nation" applicable to Britain; certainly a reverse approach to that undertaken by GATT many decades later, which only favoured the developing countries (and not the developed ones).

In relation with other matters, relevant lobbies in Britain also exerted their influence in favour of themselves, while "supported the interest of the Empire." Consequently, tariff duties for around 3/4th of the Indian import items were low or nil, thus negatively affecting not only the promotion of Indian industry but also the Indian Exchequer.

4.1.2.2. Financial Mistreatment of India

The mentioned mistreatment in the commercial field was complemented with other forms of irritating manoeuvres in the financial one. Note that from 1857 onwards, a systematic economic exploitation of India (directly or through subsidiaries) was undertaken by many British international firms. To reach their purpose, the setting up and control of indispensable utilities (mainly generation of electricity and water supply) as well as railways and road systems was initially dealt with. Besides these fundamental infrastructure-activities, investments in coal mining, metallurgical industries, agricultural commercialisation, banking, insurance and trade, were also promoted or taken over. However, investments in heavy Indian industries were not authorised by the colonial government.

The "agency system"[180] was a frequent exploitation procedure, implicit many a time in the private financial transactions between England and India. In a context of scant competition and funding, the

179. In the cases of woollen, chemicals, and cement, demanded protection of Indian firms was denied.

180. The "managing agency system" may be described as a partnership formed by a group of individuals with strong financial resources and business experience, directed to manage Indian companies. These managing agencies were entitled to the management of the whole affairs of the managed company. Vide Datt *et al.*, (2004:26). Book already mentioned.

managing agents forced the invested companies to pay minimum remunerations (12-14 per cent on investments as profits), disregarding the economic evolution of the company. And this after, at times, charging figures equivalent up to 50 per cent of gross profits, as managing agency fees.

Summarising, the systematic drain of wealth performed by the British significantly prevented the process of capital formation in India. Nonetheless, part of this drained capital used to come back to India under the garb of British investment to continue with economic abuse, supported by the colonial administration (paradoxically paid by own Indians). Of course, although the British build up a lot of administrative buildings, a roads net, a railways network, monuments, etc., which after independence have been useful for Indians (and tourists), one may agree that under the British rule "India was modernised but (conveniently kept) underdeveloped".[181]

4.2. Evolution of Agriculture Since Independence

The Indian agriculture today, as well as that of the colonial times, might be considered as the backbone of the Indian economy. Being the largest single economic activity, it currently gives occupancy to 65 per cent of the national labour force, and generates around 23 per cent of the Indian GDP. However this has not always been the case: in 1950 agriculture generated 55 per cent of the Indian GDP, and 70 per cent of the Indian population was attached to this activity.

Note that the contribution of agriculture to GDP has meaningfully moved downwards in the last 50 years, whereas the population attached to this activity has only mildly decreased. This last phenomenon could not be explained if India had not undergone a significant population explosion mainly in the period 1950-1980. This is, and has been, an inconvenient trait of the Indian economy in the last 50 years, that paradoxically may change into a huge advantage for India in next decades.[182]

181. Vide Chandra, B. (1970:3). Colonialism and Modernisation. Presidential Address. Indian History Congress.

182. Remember to this respect, the already mentioned model of development with two sectors, in which one of them, the agriculture, contains an almost unlimited supply of labour for the industry (Lewis model).

4.2.1. Relevance of Agriculture in the Development Process of India

Agriculture in India, as it happens in other developing countries, is a basic source of raw materials for a significant part of the Indian industrial sector.[183] It also plays a relevant role in the international trade of the country,[184] mitigates poverty when monsoon behaves, and generates a significant additional fraction of manufactures and transportation demand, engendering prosperity to the rest of the sectors, when harvest results a bounty.

Nonetheless, in India (as well as in China) it is necessary to rapidly shift agricultural resources (mainly human) to the non-agricultural sectors, because the continued maintenance of 65 per cent of total workers depending on agriculture is a clear squandering of human resources without advantage for the country.

Note additionally that to reach a balanced growth in the country it will be necessary to transfer—through well organised markets—agricultural goods surpluses to the new non-agricultural workers; and this in exchange of a greater demand of industrial products and services by the remaining peasants in the agriculture sector.

4.2.2. Development of Agriculture Since Independence

According to figures of Bhattacharjee,[185] whereas in the first half of the 20th century the Indian population rose 38 per cent,[186] the cultivated land only increased by 18 per cent, while the land productivity grew around 13 per cent only. These last figures clearly suggest that the population growth rate surpassed that of agriculture production by a great extent, thus making impossible the Indian economic take off and the poverty alleviation.

---

183. Cotton and jute textile industries directly depend on agriculture; the same occurs with the sugar industry, etc. Note that other industries depend indirectly on agriculture, as it is the case of many cottage and small scale industries, handloom weaving, oil crushing, rice husking, etc.

184. Agricultural products as tea, sugar, oilseeds, tobacco, etc. are relevant items of the Indian exports. If we add to these exports the figures of the industrial exports with some agricultural content (as manufactured jute, cloths, etc.), the total contribution of Indian agriculture to its exports would be well over 50 per cent.

185. Vide Bhattacharjee. (2004:482). *Studies in Indian Agricultural Economics*. Quoted in Datt, R. *et al.*, Book already mentioned.

186. In the second half of the 20th century, Indian population multiplied by 3, reaching a figure of around 1,050 million people at the end of 2002.

However years later, since independence up to 1965, the former figures meaningfully changed. There was a significant growth of the land surface under cultivation, and from 1965 onwards, the per ha. productivity of agriculture quickly jumped as a consequence of the implementation of the so-called "green revolution." This technical revolution induced a higher than before growth rate of agriculture production that, as an average, more than matched the population growth rate.

Note that the annually registered figures of agriculture production of India are highly fluctuating, as a consequence of the variability of the rainfalls regime (monsoon) and weather conditions. On the other hand, we will mention that after the initiation of the "green revolution" in 1965, the surface of cultivated land almost stagnated, thus substituting previous constant increases of cultivated land by increases in land productivity on an almost non-growing cultivated space.

Although in the context of the Green Revolution in India, the agricultural productivity of land significantly grew, this productivity continued lagging in relation to that of other countries.[187] This means that although positive, the introduction of the Green Revolution in India has been less successful than in other nations. This gap proves that, despite the hindrances generated by the fluctuating climate of India, there is a significant margin for improving future results of the Indian Agriculture.

There are several general factors that explain the lower productivity of Indian agriculture: 1) its human overcrowded situation in certain productions and regions, with too many workers and people—not absorbed by non-agricultural sectors—depending on the primary sector as a consequence of the undergone population explosion;[188] 2) the negative social framework in the rural areas, with

---

187. For instance in the case of rice, the per ha. productivity of India is currently around 1/2 of that of China, in wheat around 6/10th of that of its great neighbour, and in cotton around 1/4th of the Chinese productivity (these are figures of Datt, *et al.*). Besides the former figures, we have to mention that in 2000-02, according to data of the World Bank (2004), World Development Indicators, the added value per worker in India was 401 US-dollars, while in China this figure was 338 (all in dollars of 1995). Note that if these two figures are consistent, the number of workers per cultivated ha. in China has to be significantly higher than that of India.

188. This last phenomenon, added to inheritance practises, has led to an excessive fragmentation of cultivated land and to the nil marginal productivity of many peasants.

most of farmers poor, illiterate, superstitious, etc. and embedded in cast and extended family systems, circumstances that generate an adverse situation for modernisation; 3) the non-existence of an adequate and complementary non-farm services system such as financing and marketing; and 4) the existence of a poor infrastructure which has for long limited the marketing possibilities of the Indian agriculture.

To these general limitative factors of progress, the so-called institutional and technological hurdles for development of the agriculture should also be added. A very important factor, which forces the low productivity of agriculture is the pattern of "land tenure". Although the old *"zamindari"*[189] system has been ruled out and the new legislation protects the tenants better than before, their current position remains far from satisfactory because ultimately the latter may be deprived whenever the landlord wants. Under these circumstances the tenant cannot significantly invest in the plot, and so productivity of land cannot rise. Poor techniques of production and inadequate irrigation facilities[190] do the rest in a country characterised by its warm climate.

Summing up, although Indian agriculture has taken a leap forward in the last half a century, the huge growth rate of the Indian population and the insufficient increase of agriculture productivity, has kept the agricultural surpluses of India well under potentialities, although well over food-insecurity.[191]

Notwithstanding that, to meet future needs of its growing population and to increase exports of agricultural and allied manufactured goods, India will have to achieve significant increases in the productivity of the cultivated land. These rises probably could only be attained by means of a more generalised multiple cropping system, which will require the introduction of new selected seeds and

---

189. Lines below this system of land tenure will be outlined.

190. Note that before Independence only 18 per cent of cultivated land was irrigated. Nowadays, 57 years later, only a 33 per cent of the cultivated plots are irrigated.

191. Officially, India achieved food self sufficiency in 1976. Since then, Indian imports of cereals have remained negligible, and the likelihood of famine appearance have become almost nil. Note additionally that the applied policies in the last two decades have enabled a significant accumulation of grain (around 40-50 million tonnes as an average), sufficient to avert famines. However, problems of geographical distribution have some times turned away the disappearance of hunger pockets.

a thrust to irrigation. Of course all this means larger investments directed to the sector.

4.2.3. Agriculture and Subsidies

In the 60s, a Public Distribution System (PDS) was introduced in India, the aim of which was to establish a price support programme for consumers during the periods of shortage. Then onwards, this system has mainly acted as a countervailing force against those private traders who used to hoard agricultural commodities to obtain large profits, thus exploiting the more pressing needs of the poor. Consequently, the target of the PDS was, and is, to provide essential commodities to the Indian population, such as rice, sugar, edible oil, kerosene, etc. at subsidised prices.[192]

With the fast progression of the Indian GDP in the last two and a half decades, one could have expected a reduction of these subsidies in terms of GDP or Government Expenditure. Far from that, the volume of subsidies in terms of Total Public Expenditure has moved to 5.2 per cent in the Union Budget 2002-03 from under 3 per cent in the fiscal year 1980-81. This growing trend has been rightly criticised, as well as the internal structure of the subsidies, tilted to sugar (35 per cent of the total granted subsidies) and kerosene, commodities that are largely consumed by relatively richer layers of the population.

4.2.4. The Pending Land Reforms

Besides larger investments in machinery or in better seeds or fertilisers, to increase the land productivity of Indian agriculture, it is also crucial to "reform" the land. Of course, this reform would imply some redistribution of land ownership, but mainly to increase the average farm sizes, and to improve the current regulation on hiring and rents.

There is consensus among Indian economists that without these reforms it is not possible to give sufficient stimuli to farmers for increasing land productivity. A full concept of land reform should also include the reorganisation of the intermediation, in such a way that speculators, while doing business, pursue the interest of the

192. This system covers today the needs of protected food of around 160 million families. This is a figure that may be equivalent to 800 million people across India.

many, thus scrapping monopolistic behaviour in their mediation on agricultural products.

Against the old Indian categories of "*zamindaries,*[193] *mahalwari,*[194] *and ryotwari,*[195] abusive tenure systems little prone to increase productivity of cultivated land, early after Independence (in 1948) some partial steps were undertaken to correct mentioned abuses. Nevertheless, whereas in the old Soviet Union or more contemporary in China—the abolition of land ownership "to improve" the tenure was done without paying "compensation", this approach was not followed in India.

In order to redistribute or reorganise the land in some regions, and according to the nature and productivity of the plots, "ceiling limits" (between 4 ha. and 22 ha.) to family land holdings were established in different states of the Union. Consequently, the addition of surfaces which surpassed the defined ceilings for individuals or families—who many a time dodged their obligations throughout "*malafide*" transfers of property—made up the calculated volume of "surplus lands" to be reorganised. These surplus lands were then allocated among allottees in exchange of a price payable in instalments, which would not be larger than a reasonable rent.

Despite the good intentions of rulers and the setting up of the above mentioned legal machinery, the reality has stubbornly proven that the redistribution of land has not performed adequately, having been very short in its scope. Since the inception of the land reform policy till 2001 only a "surplus area" equivalent to 2 per cent of the total Indian cultivated land[196] has been declared transferable.

---

193. The "*zamindari*" system was introduced by East India Company to create vested interests in countryside through the creation of a privileged and loyal class. The land was divided by British. Revenue collectors of land taxes were appointed by the Company, and raised to a landlord status. *Sine die*, or for long term periods, the appointed new owners, who rented plots, were finally responsible of paying taxes. When population and consequently, land demand grew, rents increased. As a result, the *zamindari* system, purportedly erected to improve agriculture production, changed into a pure landlord-absentism system, thus enabling growing exploitation of landless labourers, who besides had no clear right to remain in plots by means of automatic renewal of their tenures.

194. The "*mahalwari*" tenure system, of Muslim roots, consisted on communal property of land of villages, the members of which being able of hiring plots, were responsible to pay the land revenue tax. This system finally changed in the same sense than that of *zamindari*: higher and higher rents paid by tenants and no innovation at all.

195. The *ryotwari* system generated the same effects than the two other systems.

196. Vide Datt, R. *et al.*, (2004:558). Book already mentioned.

Legal claims of owners against the declaration of land surpluses, due to significant loopholes in legislation, proliferated. Accordingly, the intentions of the land reformers resulted watered down, as typically happens in India with plenty of reforms undertaken by Union Government. Additionally, the Supreme Court, reading the Constitution in an "over-conservative view," significantly overturned the intentions of legislators on land reform. Note as well that the legislation on "ceilings" provided a significant number of exceptions[197] that were conveniently used by owners to dodge their "surpluses" obligations.

Definitely, in the last 50 years the implementation of land reform has failed in India due to the lack of political will, tepid attitude of bureaucracy, lack of accurate data on real estate situation, and last but not least existence of legal hurdles: in particular, the constitutional inviolability of private property and the protracted litigation system inherited from the British.

4.2.5. Rural Financing in India

Another additional problem for the agricultural development in India, as it happens almost in every developing country, is the lack of sufficient and adequate financing of the primary sector activities. In general farmers only have access to two main sources of financing: 1) the private financing source, including the so-called money-lenders,[198] traders and commission agents,[199] relatives, and landlords; and 2) the institutional financing which includes funding from government, cooperatives, and commercial banking (including Regional Rural Banks of India).

---

197. For instance for sugarcane farmers, mango coppices, gracing lands, lands for charity and religious trusts, cattle breeding farms, etc.

198. Moneylenders use to commit some malpractices, very well known by farmers: 1) They use to force the farmers to sign bonds and notes, whose nominal are well above the quantity lent to them; and 2) they charge higher interests than those charged in the institutional sector, frequently surpassing 20 per cent. Moneylenders are well known (normally rich) people of the area that, knowing the potential borrowers and their individual risks, can lend to poor farmers who have no access to the banking system or to other institutional financing, due to lack of collaterals.

199. Traders and commission agents supply funds to farmers well in advance of their harvests. These advances give the agents the opportunity to force the farmers to sell their crops at low prices, while the former additionally charge high fees for their mediation activity.

Needless to say that conditions and interests of private lenders to farmers are exigent and many a time monopolistic and abusive (if the repayment process fails, farmers may lose their plots), and consequently contrary to an appropriate development of the agriculture. This is because over-exigent borrowing conditions act as a deterrent to the necessary investments for improving land productivity.

Although private financing of agriculture in India had significantly declined from 90 per cent of the total received funds in 1952 to 37 per cent in 1981 (moneylenders counted in that year 16 per cent), and this may have continued its downward trend in last two decades, there is still much to do for substituting this financing source by the institutional one.

Nonetheless, one should not forget that despite significant improvements in institutional financing of agriculture in the last 20 years, the rapid growth of this rural financing has been mainly directed to middle and affluent members of the rural world (who have collaterals), and not to the poorest (the 70 per cent of total). Consequently, landless labourers, casts, and tribes—who are around 30 per cent of rural population continue being exploited by money-lenders and landlords. This has to change in India if this country wants to increase the land productivity of its agriculture.

4.3. Indian Industrial Policy and Industrial Public Sector

In the pre-independence period there was practically no public firms sector in the Indian economy. Perhaps the sole cases to mention were those of the Railways, the Post and the Telegraphs, the Port Trusts and some other undertakings (salt, quinine..) managed by the colonial power. Nevertheless, in the post-independence period, a rapid expansion of the public industrial sector was undertaken as an integral part of the industrial policy followed by successive Indian governments.[200]

As we have already mentioned, at time of independence, the country was a backward one, typically agrarian and without a significant industrial base. The level of internal savings and domestic

200. Vide Datt, R. *et al.*, (2004:187). Book already mentioned.

investments was low, and consequently the Indian growth capabilities were almost nil in per capita GDP terms.

As a result of the urgent need for investing in projects of long gestation (mainly in energy, infrastructure and heavy industries), it was then thought that the government intervention was essential and indispensable. In relation to this selected pro-public approach two traits should be underlined: 1) the Indian government was then a (Fabians) socialist one, so hardly anyone could have expected another approach to accelerate the development process since Independence; and 2) this consideration in favour of public impulse to the industry by government was then highly pervasive all over the world (including developing and developed countries) with some few exceptions.

4.3.1. Industrial Policy of 1956

After the implementation of the First Five Years Plan[201] (1951-56), which was tinted by the special problems of those days, such as the economic consequences of the Second World War and the Partition—two phenomena that generated meaningful influx of refugees, severe food scarcity, and growing inflation—the Second Plan (1956-61) radically changed its focus.

At the beginning of this Second Plan period, in 1956, the government announced a new Industrial Policy on the basis of a (Fabians) socialist conception of economic life. Accordingly, the new industrial policy was aiming at a quick industrialisation, with a strong emphasis on the development by the state of basic and heavy industries.[202]

Consequently all the basic and strategic industries, as well as public utilities, should necessarily be developed under the aegis of the public sector. Additionally, following the ideas of the then Planning Commission, the public sector not only had to initiate those industrial projects that the private one was not prone to undertake,

201. As an inheritance of other times, India continues with the successive elaboration of the so-called "Five year plans," the last of which, the "Tenth Five Year Plan" (2002-2007), is currently ruling.

202. In particular those of iron and steel, heavy chemicals, fertilisers, heavy engineering, and machine-building industry.

but also to necessarily play a dominant role in the exploitation of natural resources. In this context, although accepting the mixed economy of market, it was officially expected that the public sector would significantly contribute to the stepping up of the GDP growth. Of course, these ideas, after the protracted and exploitative colonisation period, were easily accepted by a society that, at the same time, observed that the private capacity for thrusting industrialisation was very low.

The Industrial Policy of 1956, which developed and complemented the urgent one formulated in 1948, rescheduled the formerly ruling four lists of activities (three of them defined as a field of action of public undertakings), and their different public-private treatment.[203] As a result, three categories of industrial firms were re-defined in 1956. Again, as it had occurred in 1948, in the last category that acted as a residual, were placed the activities accessible to the private sector.

Although a certain relation (via inputs, outputs, etc.) among the different categories of industries was then allowed, one should note that, conversely to what then happened in western European countries—in which public sector mainly acted in substitution of the private one— the private sector in India had no legal capabilities to play a significant role in the industrialisation process of India. This incapability protracted for decades till the stealthy reforms of the 80s and, mainly, till the initiation of the more open reforms in 1991.

In the context of the typical mix of aims and means in public firms—ruling also in Europe—the Industrial Policy of 1956 also guaranteed "a fair and not discriminatory treatment of the private sector," while it encouraged Small Scale Industries (SSI).[204] This Industrial Policy also tried to remove the regional disparities of per

---

203. The Industrial Resolution of 1948 beheld a mixed economy, reserving some fields of the industrial activity to the private sector, but most of them to the public one. So, the industrial activities were divided in four categories. 1) those defined as belonging to the exclusive monopoly of the state (atomic energy, railways...); 2) A series of activities that could henceforth be undertaken by the State (coal, iron, steel, aircraft construction, shipbuilding, telephone manufacturing...); 3) others that government would consider as convenient to place them in the public sector; and 4) a last category comprising the remainder of activities, which was defined as accessible to the private sector.

204. Then onwards, the State supported and "encouraged" the cottage and villa and Small Scale Industries (SSI). Specifically, a complete set of activities exclusively reserved to the SSI was listed. These SSI would also enjoy a complete privileged fiscal treatment.

capita income by means of stressing investments in public undertakings in the most backward regions or states of India.

As a consequence of the suffered industrial exploitation by the colonising power in the past, the attitude of the Industrial Policy of 1956 was a very pro-Indian one. In this regard although acknowledging the need of counting with foreign savings and capitals to additionally impulse the urgent industrialisation of the country, the government embraced the idea of a progressive nationalisation-indianisation of the then existing private foreign firms (becoming more and more controlled by Indians).

4.3.2. The Negative Industrial Policy of 1977: Restatement in 1980

During a short period of the 70s in which the BJP[205] was in power, a new and even less friendly-market industrial policy was proposed. Taking into account "some dysfunctions" of the previous approach (lack of enough jobs creation, growing rural-urban income disparities and stagnation of industrial investment), the BJP made proposals that further stressed the former (also "*swadeshi*") industrial approach of the Congress Party.

First of all it was suggested to further support the development of the SSI sector, reserving much more activities than before to the small and medium sized industrial firms.[206] Secondly, the areas for economic action of the large scale sector (heavy industry and manufactures) were also redefined. As a complement and in synchrony with the new industrial policy, a new financial policy accompanied it. In this regard it was proclaimed that in future the big industrial conglomerates could not have access to an almost unlimited private and public funding, as it had occurred in the past. Instead of that a significant part of the banking financing, previously

205. The Bharatiya Janata Party (BJP) is a nationalist pro-Hindu party that, after governing the country for 7 years, has recently (2004) lost the power in India in benefit of the Congress Party. In the 70s, after the so-called period of Emergency, in which the Congress Party and Mrs. Gandhi overused their power, the BJP politically dislodged the Congress Party for a short period. Note that the Congress Party has practically ruled India since the Independence up to 1997. Note also that the BJP has always supported the so-called "*swadeshi*" policy.

206. As against 180 economic activities reserved before to the SSI, the BJP government expanded the list up to 807 items.

received by big industrial firms, should be redirected to the SSI sector.

Thirdly, the role of the public sector was then enlarged, while it was suggested—against the then extensively recommended policy of growth—that the contribution of FDI to the capitalisation of the country should dwindle, thus proclaiming the supremacy of India in safeguarding industrial ownership. Finally, although to some extent in contradiction with former targets, the new policy suggested the convenience of removing indiscriminate protection of the sick industrial units.

Note that this Industrial Policy of 1977 was a rather extemporary and counterproductive one, given the fact that in China for instance, as well as in many places of the world,[207] the winds were already blowing in the opposite direction. Specifically the idea—paradoxically supported by successors of Chairman Mao in the CCP—that the development process should hinge on more national and international market freedom, on progressive de-nationalisation and liberalisation of a significant part of the industrial tissue, and on (conditioned) facilitation of FDI entrance inside the country, started gaining ground in China.

Broadly speaking, the industrial policy devised by the BJP in 1977 was a deepening of the industrial policy of 1956. But a deepening in the wrong direction (less market freedom). Fortunately for India this more radical industrial policy was hardly applied, because soon after its formulation, the BJP fall, thus giving the opportunity to the Congress Party for formulating a new industrial policy.

Note that instead of trying to control internal monopolies with a relative opening of the borders, by means of adequately inducing foreign products or capital to enter, the main intentions of the proposed industrial policy in 1977 was to encourage the promotion of the SSI sector and to establish additional hindrances to FDI.

Conscious of these problems, the Congress Party, again in power in 1980, announced a new industrial policy, which tried to improve the managing of the public sector and to redefine the SSI sector (authorising higher limits of the capitalisation of these small firms). This policy of 1980 also blessed the automatic expansion of large

207. In US, Western Europe, and South East Asia.

scale firms, which till then were in need of permits for increasing production.

As recently suggested,[208] this industrial policy resulted in an effective promotion of the private corporate sector. Mrs. Gandhi abandoned earlier populism (against capitalists), and looked for political support in the Indian entrepreneurial tissue. This shift in attitude, sent a powerful signal to the Indian businessmen till then intimidated by omnipresent government. As a result, private formal manufacturing sector started flourishing and was the most benefited by the new Gandhi manners, specially in states allied with the Union government of the Congress Party. After Indira (1984), her son Rajiv Gandhi continued with cautious reforms favourable to the private sector.[209]

Accordingly, Indian "joint productivity of factors"[210] significantly jumped in the 80s to 3.7 per cent from that registered in the 70s (less than 0.9 per cent). Note, as suggested by Roddick and Subramanian, that the productivity leap initiated in early-80s preceded some years the also partial and piecemeal reforms of Rajiv Gandhi. As a whole, these silent policies of the Gandhis proved that in the mid-term, a simple unleashing of the "internal" market forces may result highly productive for the economy growth.

Of course this internal and partial pro-private sector move (against former pervasive and suffocating pro-public legal framework) mainly directed to favour corporations was not sufficient; and badly accompanied in late-80s by overdone deficit spending policies, changed the macroeconomic unbalances into untenable ones.

4.3.3. The Industrial Licensing Since 1951

As it has been mentioned before, the Indians who inherited from colonisers a strong command of the (then small) industrial system,[211]

208. Vide Roddick, D. and Subramanian, A. (2004) "From 'Hindu Growth' to Productivity Surge," article already mentioned in Chapter 1, Note 16.

209. On these reforms, vide. Note 16.

210. Remember the value of $\Delta A/A$ explained in Chapter 2.

211. Note that the industrial control of India exerted by the British in colonial times was then realised with a very different purpose: to delay the creation of an industrial system that time ahead could compete with their own.

not only kept former widespread control, but also expanded it as a consequence of the socialist approach given to the economy by Prime Minister Nehru and successors.[212] As a result, the industrialisation process, clearly tilted towards public sector, was submitted to a strict regime of authorisations: authorisation to start a factory, to expand the gamut of its production, to locate it in a certain place, to reach a given size, to overcome it, etc.

The authorisation regime—the so-called license-permit-Raj—also implied that government could take over any undertaking which failed to carry out power instructions, or ruling policies. The authorisation regime also empowered the administration to prescribe prices, methods of production, volume of output, channels of distribution, etc.

Two decades after the establishment of the pervasive license regime, relevant critics emerged within the country.[213] Multiple and constant applications by the same industrial group for the same or different products, significant advantage of the big industrial groups—which had permanent offices in Delhi for lobbing—in comparison to the minor ones, regional unbalances allegedly induced by the licensing system, and lack of follow up actions to survey if licenses were in fact used, and not just kept for future undertakings, were the main points of criticism.

After some liberalising attempts in 1970, the Industrial Policy of 1980 introduced major changes in this issue, in particular in favour of the so-called large business houses (big industrial private groups). Freedom for increasing capacity to gain economies of scale up to 49 per cent of the previously authorised size, a broad banding

---

212. Prime Minister Nehru was in power from the Independence to his death, in 1964. After a short period under Shastry, Indira Gandhi—daughter of Nehru—took over Prime Minister-ship in 1966 and she was in power until she was dislodged by the BJP in 1977. Indira Gandhi recovered the power in 1980, and in 1984 she was murdered by two personal guards (Sikhs), as a consequence of the Amristar happening (armed assault to the Golden Temple by the Indian army). Rajiv Gandhi, son of Indira, got his first Prime Minister-ship automatically after the death of Indira. Rajiv, being in power up to 1991, was also murdered being Prime Minister. After him, Narasimha Rao took power. Note that Indira Gandhi was surnamed Mrs. Gandhi due to her marriage with Feroze Gandhi, a member of the Congress Party, who was not at all a relative of Mahatma Gandhi.

213. Vide Hazari, R.K. (1967). "Industrial Planning and Licensing Policy." Final Report. Taken from Datt, R. *et al.*, (2004:179). Book already mentioned.

concept,[214] as well as other relaxations were then introduced, thus serving the expansion of the private corporate sector.

4.3.4. New Industrial Policy Since 1991

In the summertime of 1991, the Indian government then headed by Narasimha Rao and Manmohan Singh (as Finance Minister),[215] proclaimed a new industrial policy, whose main traits were: 1) To unshackle the Indian industry from the then existent cobweb of bureaucratic controls; 2) To liberalise (in a phased and protracted way) the international trade regime for domestic "industrial" products, in order to progressively integrate the Indian industry into the global economy; 3) To soften previous and exaggerated restrictions concerning FDI; and 4) to selectively get rid of the budgetary load of public firms, many of them under heavy losses. All these principles led government to take serious initiatives in relation to industrial licensing, accessibility of FDI, reduction of former tariff barriers and privatisation of public industrial firms (euphemistically called "disinvestments" in India).

4.3.4.1. Licensing, Public Firms and FDI

In the field of industrial licensing, the previous system of authorisation was abolished for all industrial activities with the exception of a "short list" of industries related to security and strategic concerns, social arguments, and environmental reasons.[216] A new list of activities and products to be produced exclusively by the SSI sector was also officially published.

When in new industrial projects, relevant imported capital goods were involved (more than 25 per cent), an authorisation was

214. The basic advantage of this broad-banding conception was that, after initial authorisation, firms could devote their activity to similar products, although without exceeding licensed capacity.

215. In the spring of 2004, after renouncing, Sonia Gandhi—Indian-Italian widow of Rajiv Gandhi—to Prime Ministership, subsequent to the electoral victory of the Congress Party led by her, Manmohan Singh was appointed Prime Minister of the Government of India.

216. Among the more surprising (for Westerners) exceptions, required of explicit authorisation to start business, one could find the following activities: distillation and brewing of alcoholic drinks, sugar, animal fat and oils, cigars and cigarettes, decorative veneers, raw hides and skins, tamed or dressed fur skins, paper, newsprint, entertaining electronics, and white goods for homes.

required; likewise, when the location of the new factory was a city of more than one million inhabitants, a license was also necessary.

In the field of FDI, it was decided to provide approval of limited stakes (depending on the priority of different industries), while the payment of dividends would be monitored by the Reserve Bank of India.[217] These approvals, when granted, would mainly be in relation with export activities.

Consequently, after a protracted period (1947-91) in which the goodness of establishing public firms across almost all activities was almost taken for granted in India,[218] the pendulum (officially) started moving in the opposite direction, although with a considerable delay with respect to the big Chinese neighbour that had initiated the liberalisation movement in 1978.

In relation to the long term feasibility of public firms, the Union government redefined in 1991 the priority areas in which it would continue supporting the development of public units (defence equipment, essential infrastructure and services, exploration and exploitation of mineral resources and development of technology). In these fields of activity, the government would strengthen the financial basis of public firms devoted to the above mentioned reserved areas. The government also declared that it would support those public firms that generate high profits, in order to help the attainment of public financing balance. These profit-making public firms would be provided with greater management authority. In these cases, competition would also be induced by means of private sector participation in financing and in the board.

The liberalisation was also extended to other matters, as for instance by generalising the exception of previous authorisation for so-called MRPT companies[219] (up to then these companies had to be monitored before initiating activity).

---

217. This was done to ensure that the outflows on account of dividends would be balanced with export earnings along a pre-determined period of time.

218. Notwithstanding that, we have already mentioned that in the 80s, the private corporate sector had much more opportunities for development than before.

219. These companies, before initiating activity, had to apply for clearance in relation to the Monopolistic, Restrictive and Fair Trade practices (MRTP) Act. Under this Act, allegedly one to protect consumers, the volume of assets of the companies to be established was limited.

Note that along 90s and first years of 2000, the government also removed some limitations (established in 1991) to private undertakings in the fields of motor cars, white goods, raw hides and skins, patent leather, etc. In some cases this liberalisation was a consequence of the increase of the middle class people demanding these goods (cars, white-goods, etc.); in others it simply occurred because the SSI sector was not capable of gaining world exports share, as it happened in the shoes and leather industry.

4.3.4.2. Assessment of the Current Industrial Policy

As a general comment, we have to say that the end of the era of the *"license-permit raj"* was most welcome in 1991. Nonetheless, many aspects of the new industrial policy were sharply criticised, although in two opposite directions according to the different views of the critics: 1) the staunch supporters of the old and exaggerated version of the "*swadeshi*" policy, who claimed for a more consistent reform to further defend the Indian economic sovereignty; and 2) most of foreign representations of Western countries in Delhi and liberal Indians, who were mainly interested in finding new commercial and financial opportunities in India.

Specifically, concerning FDI, some members of parliament of the BJP have for long considered that even the mild and cautious opening policies of 1991, were against the Nehruvian project of nationalisation-indianisation of the Indian economy at long run. On the opposite side, liberal Westerners use to opine that the velocity of opening of the Indian economy was exaggeratedly slow and too much full of misgivings.

As the truth may be somewhere in the middle of the way, both mentioned extreme interpretations seems to be biased. Balancing and phasing the opening was necessary to not jeopardise the convenient evolution of the Indian economy, which with a 5.8 per cent annual average GDP growth rate in the last 24 years, have actually behaved rather satisfactory.

Nevertheless, one should not forget, that although India is in general in the good economic direction, this country has to deal in the mid-term with two main economic problems related to its Industry: 1) the slow progression of the so-called disinvestments process,[220] in particular in relation to sick public firms; and 2) the lack of a significant and formal Social Security system for the protection of workers that temporary or definitely will lose their current jobs. Note that these two problems are intertwined. India (as China) is not a rich country, and a Social Security system for mitigation of the casting out problems, is not easy to be financed and implemented.

4.3.5. The So-Called "Second Generation" Reforms in India

When Narasimha Rao initiated the reform process in 1991, the term "first generation reforms" was not used. Nevertheless, it is commonly admitted today in India that there is an urgent need for implementation of a "second generation reforms." Note that the so-called first generation reforms were implemented in a context of external economic crisis,[221] which had to be overcome. Now that the mentioned economic crisis and most of the annexed problems have been solved, and the economy has become much more balanced, the intention with the second generation reforms has to be the strengthening of the market forces and to reach or consolidate additional economic equilibriums.

First generation reforms were undertaken under the premises that removal of industrial licensing, opening certain areas from the public sector to the private one, opening the economy to freer flows of investment carried out by MNC, and liberalising of trade while reducing import and export duties, would result in the achievement of higher rates of economic growth.

---

220. The disinvestment process under BJP (till 2004) gained criticism concerning two aspects: this process mainly started by the privatisation of profitable public firms and not by the sick; and instead of privatising them in open market, it was decided to realise strategic sales to pre-existent private groups, which could accentuate the monopoly degree in some activities. Of course, the Supreme Court has recently intervened in favour of the option of stocks-sales in the Indian open market.

221. The annual average growth rate of the Indian GDP has moved along the 90s—as well as in 80s—near 6 per cent, thus by far surpassing the famous "Indian growth rate" (3.5 per cent). The foreign exchange reserves have steadily grown in the last 14 years up to a figure of around 135 US bn dollars. India has solved its former problem of external outstanding debt, being its current short-term commitments practically negligible. The ratio of Exports to Import has also improved significantly and the previous inflation rate has been tamed. As an exception, only the fiscal problem of India (public deficit) has not been solved in the last 13 years.

4.3.5.1. Agriculture and Pending Reforms in the SSI Sector

Note that, as it occurred in the first years of accelerated industrialisation of India (in the 50s), the agriculture sector was again bypassed by the 1991 reforms. Simultaneously, the industrial growth rate has not generated enough jobs for further stepping-up the absorption of redundant labourers in the primary sector, as suggested in the Lewis model commented in Chapter 2.

In a parallel way, while the agricultural inputs coming from industry have meaningfully grown, the share of agro-based industries in total industry output has dwindled. This means that the Indian agricultural policy, although succeeding in achieving reasonable food security, has failed in the exploitation of its comparative advantages (not setting up a relevant food processing industry), thus not providing rural population with enough purchase power as to foster the internal demand of manufactured goods coming from peasants and farmers.

Consequently, one could deduce that the post-reform process has been incomplete and mainly directed to the corporate industrial sector of the Indian economy, while it has not duly encouraged the SSI sector[222] which, as it happens in many other (even industrialised) countries, should have generated the bulk of new jobs.

To the extent that the first generation reforms did not succeed in relation to sufficient poverty alleviation[223] and job creation, some policies to enhance employment opportunities should be implemented. For this purpose any further reform process should encourage the creation of micro-enterprises and medium sized firms. In this regard, policy initiatives to provide these firms with significant and cheaper financing—introducing *ad hoc* subsidies—and

---

222. This policy of reservation of certain activities to the SSI sector is partly a Gandhian legacy for protecting and promoting traditional handicrafts and cottage or households production. It was also motivated by the official desire of promoting employment through labour-intensive manufactures. Paradoxically, this policy for long resulted in an ironical situation in which successful small firms had no incentive to grow (and generate more employment) beyond the officially defined size to be entitled to receive special treatment from the government. Consequently, this was a policy that indirectly averted within the SSI sector the reaching of favourable economies of scale and the promotion of employment.

223. Dr. Datt, of the World Bank, has highlighted the fact that while the urban sector appears to have continued its trajectory of growth and poverty reduction through the 90s, rural poverty reduction has been derailed by lack of enough rural growth.

export facilities, could help to increase employment in the SSI sector. Encouragement for grouping these firms by means of promotion or consolidation of more efficient clusters of small and medium firms could also be a good measure to be implemented.[224] Of course, public investment in education and health would in due time enable Indian SSI to profit from more qualified employment. In order to improve health, safer water supply and sanitation should also be enhanced, as well as housing for shelter the modest strata of the Indian urban and rural families.

4.3.5.2. The Problem of the Public Sector Deficit

Letting poverty alleviation aside, we have to say that a major conditioning factor for the implementation of the new desired reforms is the control of fiscal deficits at both levels of Union and states. Regrettably, the first generation reforms, although achieving some reduction of the public deficit in Union and states in the first years, after a while, did not deliver. The result was that the total public deficit rose again, being currently situated around 9-10 per cent[225] of the Indian GDP. This is in normal conditions a non-sustainable result, conducive in mid-long term to monetisation and to stoke inflation. Consequently this is a problem that should be fixed at mid-term at the latest.

The underlying causes of the growing public deficit, mainly since the second half of 90s, are very well known: the relatively high increases of wages and salaries of civil servants in comparison to the capabilities of the Indian public sector, the heavy and growing load of interests that both Union[226] and state governments have to pay, the relevant load of losses of public firms covered by the budget, and the inflexible paid subsidies, are the main items on the side of the expenditures.

On the other hand, the reduction in personal and corporate tax rates enacted under the first generation of reforms, far from being

---

224. To this respect, Vide Assaf, G.B. (2004:88). *Too Many With Too Litle*. Kornark. Publishers. New Delhi.

225. The deficit of the public sector in India has been in 2003-04 of the tune of 9.5 per cent in GDP terms. Note however that a bad monsoon could rise again this figure over 10 per cent if fiscal reforms were not undertaken.

226. In the last budgets, the Union government has reckoned that it needs around 1/4th of its revenues to pay for interests.

profitable in the sense of the Laffer curve assumptions, induced a significant relative reduction of revenues. The same happened with the reduction of customs and central excise duties (as a consequence of the undertaken process of liberalisation), the substitutes of which have not sufficiently offset the revenue losses generated by mentioned reductions. One should not forget either the tax rebates implemented by different states to encourage investment in their territories—in last years by setting up SEZ—in competence with other Indian states.

Accordingly, we believe that there are several potential aims that could form the public finance sub-set of the second generation reforms: 1) reduction of total fiscal deficit (Union plus states) from its current position of 9-10 per cent of the GDP to a level of 5 per cent in the next 4-5 years. 2) Rising capital expenditure, in particular in rural infrastructure, in order to step-up the growth rate of agriculture and to alleviate rural poverty. 3) Continuation with the disinvestment programme, in particular by means of getting rid of sick public firms. 4) Progressive reduction of non-necessary subsidies, to some extent collected by the most affluent layers of society. 5) Introduction of a system for "recovering", via fees, part of the cost of some economic services provided by Union and states.[227] 6) Last but not least, the administration of the Union should be reorganised, to avoid current waste of money as a consequence of redundancy and overlapping of public functions, due to the recent creation of new ministries mainly founded on building up political coalitions to rule the Union.

4.4. Indian Demography and Employment

As it is well known, the Indian population is not only large, but also overcrowded[228] and rapidly growing. According to the last Census, the number of Indians in 2001 was 1027 million (1080

227. Some state governments have provided free electricity and water to rural areas. This absurd populism conducive to squandering of resources, has to end. Cost recovery of higher education and health supplied have also been minimal or nil.

228. In 2001 the population density in India was of 324 Indians per sq. km. This figure in not far away to those of the most overcrowded countries of the world such as The Netherlands or Japan. The case of Bangladesh with a human density of more the 900 people per sq. km. is completely out of the norm.

million today). Note that this figure reflects a clear unbalance in sex[229]—the same occurs in China although in a less dramatic way—while it way, undergo significant growth in next years. Population projections obtained as a by-product of the recently elaborated census, place India as the most populated country of the world around 2050, even over China.[230]

Although the current annual population growth rate is very high (1.9 per cent), the recent trend shows a mild propensity to slowdown.[231] Nevertheless every two years around 40 million new Indians embody the population (a figure around that of South-Korea) and in 2015 there probably will be 200-225 million more Indians than in 2001 (more than a new Russia).[232]

The subject of the Indian demography is a very important one for the Indian authorities, mainly due to the negative consequences at short-mid term of the rapid population growth on the development process, as we have mentioned in Chapter 2. As a result, a new population policy for India was formulated in 2000. This policy, which tries to move in a more human direction than that practised in China since a quarter of century ago, seeks to encourage men to take a greater role in limiting the reproduction. The problem is that a voluntary policy may take decades to achieve its targets.

In particular, we will mention that the new population policy of India, established the aim of bringing down the total fertility rate per woman in 2010, to the replacement level of 2.1 children from the one

229. The figures in 2001 were 531 million males and 495 females. Note that although the gender unbalance at birth is a natural constant all over the world, the data obtained in India in past years shows that the shortfall in female registered births in India is larger than usual. On the other hand this unbalance significantly grows for the slab of 0-6 years old children. According to international experts, the causes of these two phenomena may be on the one hand the selective abortion and the female infanticide, and on the other the neglect of the girl-child, which is the cause of their higher mortality.

230. This opinion is shared by many institutions, such as WB, UN Population Fund, Indian Census 2001, etc.

231. Note that although during the first 20 years of the 20th century the Indian population hardly grew, the next 30 years witnessed a significant population growth (40 per cent). What is actually shocking is the population explosion suffered by this country between 1950 and 1980. If we take into account the population of 1950 and that of 2002, we may easily deduce that it multiplied by three in 52 years, reaching 1045 million in 2002 from a figure of 361 in 1950.

232. As recently suggested by the WB, between 2002 and 2015 the average annual growth rate of the Indian population will reach the figure of 1.2 per cent. Vide WB (2004) *World Development Indicators*.

of 3.1 in the 90s. Obviously this will not be an easy task to be fulfilled in time. On the other hand, even if the target of the government was reached, the "demographic momentum"[233] will still provide for the continuation of a meaningful Indian population growth during a significant period.

4.4.1. Encouraging Low Fertility: Relevance of Literacy Rates

There is a very powerful factor that contributes to the reduction of the fertility rate: the state of literacy, in particular that of females. Indeed, one may expect that rising female education, may help to reduce the desired family size for several reasons. Firstly because women will have more control over household resources and personal behaviour, and greater involvement in family planning decision-making. Secondly, because educated women will be less dependent on their sons as a source of old-age security.[234] Finally, because educated women will face a higher opportunity cost if they devote a lot of time to a time-intensive activity as that of child bearing and child rearing.[235]

Considering all these circumstances and others,[236] educated mothers will need to plan fewer births in order to achieve the desired family size. Knowledge of modern contraceptive methods, better child care as well as better heath environment (all these variables associated to higher incomes and economic development) will lead to a decline in birth rates. Taken for granted the declining evolution of the death rate with development, the mentioned reduction of the fertility rate will finally induce a population levelling off (of course after a transition period explained by the "demographic momentum").

Therefore, if rising education, specially that of women, induces (after a while) a reduction of the population growth rate, a significant increase of public expenditure for improving the general

---

233. Although the fertility rate reaches in a moment the rate of replacement (2.1 children per woman), it is probable that in countries like India, with a rapid population growth rate, total population continues substantially increasing (perhaps for two or three decades) before the achievement of levelling off.

234. Doubtless, the development of a conventional Social Security system would reduce the incentive to have more children (sons) for old-age security reasons.

235. Vide Todaro, M. (2003). *Economic Development*, 7th Ed., Pearson Education.

236. A rise in the opportunities of female accession to non-agricultural jobs, would also reduce the fertility rate of the Indian women.

and female literacy levels of India, would be a very profitable operation for the country.

4.4.2. Indian Population and Future of Employment

Once considered all the mentioned circumstances, and before making any comment on the future evolution of labour force in India, we will now refer to the age composition of the Indian population.

Doubtless any country with a high growth rate of its population, similar to the Indian one[237] has to have a very young population.[238] Although the economic progress of India has been conducive since Independence to a longer expectancy of life (at birth),[239] the current and recent high rates of population growth—although with symptoms of dwindling—have made possible that the group of people under 15 remains around 33 per cent.

The importance of this group, which peaked in 1971 (41.4 per cent), will induce that the volume of people ranged between 15 and 60 years continues growing during a certain period. This means that the amount of people in working age has grown and will continue growing for a while at rates over those of the population. This makes expectable annual increases of the labour force of the tune of 1.8-2.0 per cent, which translated to absolute figures means that, just to keep the position of the current rate of unemployment (open, and disguised in agriculture), the volume of new jobs should rise to a rhythm of 8 million. If, on the other hand, the government tries to reduce the joblessness at an adequate rate, it would be necessary to annually create from now onwards around 10 million jobs, mainly in the non-agricultural sectors. This is a big figure as compared to what has been achieved in the recent past[240] (creation of around 4 million jobs a year).

---

237. This rate of growth has been 1.9 per cent in last decade, and for 2001-15, as calculated by World Bank, it will be 1.2 per cent,

238. In India, the young population in the slab from nil up to 15 years is around 33 per cent of the total. This is not the case in China, whose population has already clear symptoms of ageing. Currently (2002), its population under 15 does not surpass the figure of 25 per cent.

239. Thus increasing the number of people over 60, that nowadays maybe around 7 per cent. Note that the number of people over 60 years in the 50s of last century was only around 2 per cent of total population.

240. According to NSSO, only 23 million jobs were created in the seven years 1993-2000, which means an average of 3.2 million jobs a year.

In this context, given the fact that in India no more than 8 per cent of labour population works in the Organised Sector, and that the employment in this sector has grown in last decade at an average of 0.6-0.7 per cent, the economic policy will need a significant change to absorb the difference between this figure and that of the growth rate of the labour force (1.8-2.0 per cent). Doubtless, the Non-Organised sector will have to absorb the bulk of the mentioned labour force. Therefore, although India may achieve in future spectacular growth in its domestic investment ratio (over 30 per cent) and its GDP, it will be a priority to encourage production in the SSI sector to solve the unemployment problem and to accelerate the development process. In particular, taking into account the huge figure of peasants with assumed nil marginal productivity trapped in countryside.

4.5. Financial Capacity of India

As deduced in Chapter 2, a *sine qua non* condition for unrestricted economic catching up is to have a high domestic investment rate. Although the current one in India is not negligible, of the tune of 23-24 per cent in GDP terms, we have to underline that to reach official targets of steady growth, currently figured out by government for the period 2002-07 at 8 per cent, it will be necessary to increase the mentioned domestic investment rate.

In this regard India should look to China, which in last years has reached figures of domestic investment ratios of around 38-40 per cent, and GDP growth rates of around 10 per cent. Indeed, it is not a mere coincidence that China and India, respectively with average investment rates around 36 per cent and 24 per cent in the 90s, have reached average GDP growth rates in the same period of around 10 per cent and 6 per cent. Rates that to some extent are proportional to their respective rates of domestic investments.

4.5.1. The Case of the Indian Internal Savings

To increase domestic investment, India has to generate a larger internal excess of incomes over consumption, be this private or public, which in professional jargon is called "internal or domestic savings". This domestic savings complemented by received "foreign savings" has to accurately finance the internal domestic investments to avert macroeconomic disequilibria.

Although Indian history has reflected a significant increase of domestic savings in last decades, moving to 22 per cent along 90s from 14 per cent in the 60s, neither the current internal saving nor the received foreign financing are adequate to accelerate, as officially desired, the investment growth.

Private saving in India, as in any country, has two components, that of the families and that of private firms (non-distributed benefits). Although a low percentage of families have significant saving capacity,[241] the household sector generates around 90 per cent of the total domestic savings, recently almost equally distributed in financial savings[242] and in physical assets.[243] The private corporations contributed with 3.7 per cent points,[244] while the public sector in last years has behaved in a very negative way (that is to say, dis-saving).

In effect, in the Indian public sector, as it normally happens in many developing countries including China, expenses are higher than revenues, thus inducing deficit and some times negative public savings. Tax revenues being clearly insufficient in India to meet the current expenditure, leave a negative margin for financing the necessary public investments required by the development process (infrastructures, energy, health and education). This deficit has to be financed with borrowing, the interests of which represented recently a significant portion of total revenues.[245]

Accordingly, an increase in public savings is not an easy task but definitely essential. In order to reach the target of a significant

---

241. The World Bank has recently estimated that, in 2001, 34.7 per cent of the Indian population lived on less than 1 dollar a day, and 79.9 per cent on less than 2 dollars. Vide World Development Indicators (2004).

242. In the 90s, bank deposits turned to be the most popular way of households savings. Contractual savings like those materialised in Life Insurance Funds and Provident and Pension Funds have also recently emerged as important financial assets in the households portfolios.

243. In 2000, of total domestic savings, which reached the figure of 22.3 per cent of the GDP, 19.8 per cent was saved by households (10.5 per cent materialised in financial assets and 9.2 per cent in physical assets), 3.7 per cent by firms, and –1.2 per cent, a negative figure, by the public sector.

244. To understand the relevance of the household sector savings, we have to clarify that it includes savings of unincorporated enterprises. In particular a large number of small business, which are not registered, may contribute decisively to the formation of the Indian saving rate.

245. In the case of the Union Government, the expenditure on interests in 2001, represented a figure around 28 per cent of the Total Expenditure of the Union. Vide WB (2004). *World Bank Indicators.*

increase in public savings, the public sector will have to be reorganised. And not only by means of privatisation of many public firms, particularly the sick ones, but also by reforming the public services.

The fiscal system also requires a systematic modernisation to gain sufficiency. The latter is likely the most important pending issue that has to be confronted by the Union government as well as by states, given the fact that there are indirect taxes constitutionally allotted to the states, that have to be reformed and homogenised to create a unique market[246] across India. And this will require consensus for a clearer "functional" delimitation of the respective tax competencies of Union and states. Additionally, the establishment of an objective Grants-in-Aid system to produce automatic solidarity among the different states of the Union would also be relevant to eliminate past misgivings among states and Union government.

Besides a reorganisation of taxes, directed towards the attainment of sufficiency in a context of a larger delivery of services, the development of a conventional social security system (including the creation of a health system) is another pending issue in India, as it occurs in China. Consequently, Indian authorities will have no remedy but to significantly widen the sources of public revenues,[247] taxing more and more services.[248] They should also fight against fiscal evasion, which is very high in India,[249] as a result of the magnum component of its informal economy.

On the other hand, note that to reduce public expenditure in a country like India, where so many public services and infrastructures need to be provided, is simply unthinkable. Therefore, far from

246. A totally implemented value added tax will be a good way either to increase indirect taxation or to avoid tax evasion.

247. Although growing in the 90s, the volume of direct taxes in the Union Budget of 2000-01 amounted 36 per cent of total tax revenues, while indirect taxes were 64 per cent (being Sales and Excise Taxes 36 per cent, Custom Taxes 28 per cent).

248. Since in India the contribution of services to the formation of the GDP is 51 per cent, it seems astonishing the reluctance of the involved potential service-tax payers to contribute to the common good. Recently (2004), the Manmohan Singh government has risen the Services tax rate up to 10 per cent, while it has added new services to the list of the taxable ones.

249. As a curious example, a survey made in 1981 reflected amazing data: it was found that taxes were avoided on at least 40 per cent, and possibly 60 per cent of potential taxable income. Vide Perkins, *et al.*, (2991:451) *Economics of Development*. 5th Ed., Norton.

reducing the size of the public sector—as some fiscal fundamentalists use to defend even in India—it should be rather restructured and upgraded, although simultaneously getting rid of significant dead-locks such as unfounded subsidies and transfers to sick public units.

4.5.2. The Indian Financial System

The funds that form part of the households savings mainly flow to other families, to companies, or to public sector through the financial system. As any other financial system, the Indian one consists of a multiplicity of interconnected financial institutions. The formal financial institutions of India[250] are supervised and monitored by the central bank, called in India the Reserve Bank of India.

In developing countries, as India and China are, the commercial banking system is the most powerful group of intermediaries. In India the number of commercial banks, being the most relevant in public hands since 1969,[251] has increased from 148 in 1980 to 297 in 2000, and the number of bank offices has also risen from 30,400 in 1980 to 67,300 in 2000.[252] Bank deposits and granted credits, as one could have expected, have significantly multiplied in last 20-30 years at a higher speed than the nominal GDP.[253]

Besides these classical intermediaries, there are in India others more modest and less relevant, such as saving banks, cooperative banks, insurance companies, pension funds and mutual funds.

In relation to stock exchanges (mainly Bombay), institutions in which are interchanged financial assets previously issued by companies or public sector, we have to mention that the importance

250. Remember what has been previously explained in relation to the informal financing of Agriculture.

251. In July of 1969, under Indira, a momentous event occurred in the economic history of India since its independence. Fourteen major commercial banks were nationalised on the alleged ground that commercial banking did not play an appropriate role for the country's development financing. As then alleged, SSI as well as the agriculture activities, that were clearly under-funded, were continuously ignored by commercial banks. In 1980 another six commercial banks were nationalised.

252. The massive bank branching implementation of the last 20 years cannot hide the fact that today many of the 600,000 existent villages continues without banking services.

253. As it is well known, the enlarged money supply, the so-called M3, which contains all kinds of deposits plus circulating currency, has significantly grown in India in GDP terms. This ratio M3/GDP had moved from 29.5 per cent in 1975 to 46 per cent in 1995. This is a clear indicator of a significant improvement in the financial mediation of the commercial banks and rest of banking institutions.

of the assets (potentially) interchangeable in the stock markets (level of capitalisation) relative to those mediated through the banking system has emerged notably in India in the last 20 years.[254] This confirms that the development of the Indian financial system, as it has occurred in the developed world, has entered into a process of relative banking dis-intermediation.

Summing up, we find that the Indian financial system, although containing some dysfunction—as that of the sectorial segmentation of the provided funds, the existence of high ratios for privileged financing systematically exceeded by banks,[255] and the significant volume of non-performing credits accumulated by the public banks[256]—is relatively more developed than the Indian economy itself. The opposite is the case in China. The Indian Financial system also seems more advanced than the financial systems of other significant developing countries as for instance that of Argentina or Brazil.

4.5.3. *External and Internal Financing in India*

If India wants to reach GDP growth rates of catching up (8-10 per cent) with China, it should experience accumulation processes compatible with investment rates of 30-38 per cent, as it has recently been the case in China. In order to finance this higher and desired domestic investment rates, India not only should increase its public saving rates, currently negative, but also to count with higher figures of foreign savings (mainly FDI, Portfolio investments, private creditors, etc.), to complement the current insufficient domestic private savings.

Broadly speaking, we can say that in the 90s the general trend in foreign savings received by developing countries has changed

254. The assets mediated by commercial banks in GDP terms moved from 40 per cent in 1980 to 59 per cent in 2000, while the stock exchange capitalisation (also in GDP terms) moved from 9 per cent in 1980 to a figure of 47 per cent in 2000. Note that in the 80s the degree of stock exchange capitalisation grew at higher speed than in the 90s, as a consequence of the waking up of the private corporate sector induced by Indira and Rajiv Gandhi governments in the 80s.

255. Rakesh Mohan, current Deputy Governor of the Reserve Bank of India, has termed this behaviour as "lazy banking". Typically, the bonds held by banks account for between 35-40 per cent of total assets, this being a figure well over the "statutory minimum of 25 per cent"—the compulsory coefficient for financial investments—and roughly similar to their total lending. Vide *The Economist*. Sept. 11th. 2004. Page 76.

256. Although with figures of around 10 per cent, much less relevant than those of China.

drastically, with relative decrease of ODA and heavy increase in private funding, particularly in the form of private creditors[257] and FDI.

In relation to the ODA received by India, one has to underline the recent decision (2003) made by Indian authorities to relinquish any bilateral aid, because allegedly it was too small, too fragmented, too conditioned and thus too time consuming, just for peanuts[258]. To once more prove the ludicrous geographical distribution of ODA, nothing is better than to quote the cases of China and India we are now analysing. Being China a country with practically double per capita income than India, the former received in 1999[259] a higher per-capita ODA than the latter. As a curiosity, stemming from the current ODA non-system, we could mention that India, which along 90s accumulated more than one third of the poor of the world, it only received 1-1.5 dollars per person per year, a shameful low figure that does not require additional comments.

Focusing now on FDI received by India in the 90s, we have to say that although this source of external funding has been significant in absolute terms, its low relative amount—which since 1995 never has surpassed the figure of 0.7 per cent in GDP terms—is a clear proof of the failure of the Indian government[260] to gain external confidence[261] of foreign investors. Nevertheless, note that this relative failure may also be a consequence of a "financial diversion effect" generated by the "irresistible attraction" of more fashionable China, which receives massive flows of FDI, equivalent to 4-5 per cent of its GDP, while the profitability of these investments is currently far from being guaranteed.

---

257. In India this figure of the private creditors has meaningfully grown, basically due to the funds received from officially called "Non-Resident Indians".

258. Consequently the Union government decided to count only with the multilateral aid, although its relative figures were also meagre.

259. Vide *World Development Indicators* of the World Bank, July 2001.

260. Note that all FDI is constitutionally monitored by Union Government, although part of that FDI is materialised in projects undertaken by state governments. Note also that the methodology of reckoning the FDI gathered by India has recently changed to the extent that the re-investments are now included in it. All the above mentioned figures should be increased, although the sense of the comments would not meaningfully change.

261. The instability of economic and fiscal rules in India, the so-called rollbacks in legislation projects, and the alleged slow progress of its economic reforms, use to be a constant source of criticism coming from the MNC and some Western Embassies in India.

Given the fact that Portfolio Investments are much more instable[262] than FDI, India should encourage reception of FDI, to complement its insufficient internal savings. As we have mentioned before, in 1991 a timid and shaking reform pro-FDI encouragement started, to seemly gain momentum in the first years of 2000. Notwithstanding that, given the past registered figures (very low in GDP terms), it will not be easy to approach those of China.

4.5.3.1. Evaluation of Indian External Debt

Mainly as a consequence of the rapid rate at which external assistance was obtained and utilised in former decades, the Indian external debt meaningfully increased. Nevertheless, its weight, although at times growing in terms of total public debt, never has been relevant in GDP terms, even in the worst moments of crisis in 1991.[263]

In any case we have to underline that during the 90s, there has been a consolidation of the external debt in India, the sustainability of which is clearly guaranteed. Although absolute long-term debt has increased in the 90s (while short-term debt has reduced its amount in absolute terms), total figures of external debt has decreased in GDP terms, moving from 28.7 per cent at the beginning of 90s to around 20 per cent at the time being. If we add to this "moderate indebtedness" of India—as it has been recently classified by multilateral financial institutions—the fact of the rapid building up of its foreign reserves,[264] it is clear that the current external situation of India is actually robust.

4.5.3.2. Perils of the Growing Internal Indebtedness

While the current external position of India is solid, one cannot say the same in internal terms or as a whole. As a proportion of the

262. Note for instance that in 1998 the volume of the received Portfolio Investments by India suddenly changed into negative as a consequence of the Asian crisis.

263. The problem in 1991 was not one of a relative high volume of external outstanding debt, but another related to the dangerous-small position reached by the volume of foreign reserves.

264. According to Western patterns, the current volume of Indian foreign reserves, around 135 bn. US dollars, is clearly excessive per comparison to annual Indian imports (as it has been the case of China in last years). It is likely that both countries have built them up to avoid any future dependence from IMF. A dependence that, if existed, could enable the IMF, unwillingly or not, to break for years the brilliant trajectory of these two countries in the last two and half decades.

GDP, the outstanding liabilities of the Union government, comprising the external and the internal ones, were of the tune of 55 per cent in 1991. This figure after experiencing a decline up to 1999, in the last years has recovered its previous negative trend to reach a position of 61 per cent in 2003.[265] If we add to this figure that of the relative indebtedness of the states, of the tune of 27 per cent in GDP terms,[266] we find out a total indebtedness near 90 per cent. Although it is clear that the external position of India is robust, the arrival to an exclusively internal indebtedness of 70 per cent, should unleash a fiscal reform to increase the direct taxes revenues[267] and to restate the currently non-updated indirect taxation. Otherwise, a future resort to monetisation of the public deficit should not be excluded, which would induce a resumption of inflation.

4.6. Trade Orientation of India Since 1947

Since only countries with large domestic markets could "rationally" adopt an Import Substitution strategy (IS) to develop their industries, India decided in the 50s to follow this path. The main economic target of India was then the attainment of national self-sufficiency to meet domestic needs of food, raw materials and manufactured goods.

In the context of the developing economies which practised the IS strategy, the case of India resulted paradigmatic, although—to say the truth—many others[268] followed the same path. From the mid-70s onwards, however, with the generalised return of neoclassicism as the theoretical mainstream, an alternative Export Promotion strategy (EP) was increasingly adopted by a growing number of countries, as it happened with South Korea, Taiwan, Singapore and Hong-Kong (then a British colony). All of them, being small and with narrow domestic markets, needed external expansion to continue growing rapidly.

---

265. Vide Datt, R. (2004:938). Book already mentioned.
266. *ibid*
267. In 2002 the Finance Minister of the Government of India—Jaswant Singh—established two task forces to reform the fiscal system, directed by Prof. Kelkar. When the Kelkar Report was released in 2002, in our opinion a useful piece for fiscal reform, there was a bitter criticism regarding some of its suggestions on direct taxing, which were not finally accepted by the Government of India.
268. As for instance Chile, Argentina, Pakistan, Philippines, Bangladesh, etc...

To be accurate, we have to underline that most of LDC have deployed, normally in succession, both strategies with different degrees of emphasis. However, it is well acknowledged that India adopted a very stringent IS strategy practically since its Independence till the liberalisation reforms, initiated in 1991. Since that year the process of opening of the Indian economy started, although cautiously and at different speeds.[269]

If we measure, as usual, the degree of opening of an economy as the quotient of Export plus Imports over corresponding GDP, we have to underline that current Indian ratio is well under 50 per cent of that of China.[270] Accordingly, there is a clear consensus, even among Indian officials, that India needs to additionally open up if it wants to grow at a more rapid catching up rhythm.

Changing the argument, and looking to the evolution of the Indian share in world exports, we have to clarify that India significantly under-performed in the first 3 decades of its post-colonial life (1947-1980). Specifically India moved from a share of 2.1 per cent of total world exports in 1951, to a figure of 0.4 per cent in 1980. Nevertheless, this share has positively moved in the 90s to reach nowadays a figure of 0.7-0.8 per cent, although in our view this percentage will meaningfully increase in future.

Note that the observed catastrophic results in trade performance of India along the period 1950-80 also had its counterpart in China, whose exports share in total world trade decreased from 2.7 per cent in 1959—moment of the commencement of the "Great Leap Forward" policy—to 0.7 per cent in 1977 (end of the Maoist age). Note however that, after the reforms, China has experienced a shot

---

269. As we have mentioned in another essay, a progressive higher degree of opening of an economy is not by itself a guarantee for achieving higher GDP growth rates, as experience has proven. Logically, if it was patent that opening degree and growth rate were narrowly correlated, then all countries had selected the same strategy. Vide Andreu, J.M. and Soler, M., (2002:35). *Fundamental Issues on Indian Economic Growth*. Restricted Document for European Union Authorities. New Delhi. Vide also Rahman, R. and Andreu, J.M. (2004:132). Book already mentioned.

270. Although paradoxically not significantly lower than that of the US, which is a good proof that this indicator has its limitations (all big countries reflect a low degree of opening, as measured with the mentioned ratio). Conversely Singapore had in 2002 an opening ratio greater than one, as typically happens with small countries, or regions, that have no other remedy than to trade for amounts over their own added value (GDP).

up of its exports reaching a share of 3.9 per cent in 2000 and another of 5.9 per cent in 2003. A progression speed that has little to do with the recent painstaking Indian gain in world export share.

4.6.1. Evolution of the Indian Trade Policy

After a first period (1950-56) of good harvests and quasi-equilibria in the Balance of Payments (BoP), the heavy industry oriented Second Five Year Plan initiated in 1956, shortly brought a BoP crisis in 1957. To correct this problem the Union government imposed a regime of Quantitative Restrictions (QRs) on imports. Besides holding back the demand of foreign exchange by means of this instrument, the selectivity of the applied QRs also served the achievement of industrial priorities, as designed by the chosen IS strategy.

Years later, in 1962, export subsidies were introduced to partially offset the penalties that the QR regime imposed on exports. At the same time the use of import duties increased.[271]

4.6.1.1. A Shy Attempt for Liberalisation in the 60s

Later on, in the period 1966-68 there was a relevant nominal devaluation of the Indian rupee (by 57.5 per cent).[272] Since the devaluation was accompanied by elimination of export subsidies and some import duties, the net devaluation was less than the nominal one, and varied among different commodities.[273] Unfortunately, the derivatives of two severe droughts in succession and the appearance of political problems in times of the first Indira Gandhi Prime Minister-ship, made that the mentioned incipient steps towards liberalisation were abandoned.

Along the period 1968-75 import premia rose again, export subsidies were reintroduced and augmented, and industrial licensing reverted to its previous and severe modes. Note however that in this

---

271. Note that the combination of export subsidies with import duty hikes could be viewed, because there is an equivalence among them, as a selective devaluation of the exchange rate.

272. The value of one dollar moved from 4.76 Indian rupees to 7.5.

273. According to Bhagwati and Srinivasan, the net devaluation on trade account was 21.6 per cent for exports and 42.3 per cent for imports. Vide Bhagwati and Srinivasan (1975). *Foreign Trade Regimes and Economic Development: India*. Columbia University Press. New York.

period the good results of the "Green Revolution" eased the needs of grain imports, thus giving a relief to the Indian trade accounts. This also enabled a certain relaxation in the severity of the QR regime: most non-competitive but "essential" imports were liberalised, while main industrial protective quotas remained intact and domestic industry continued armoured against import competition.

Besides some stealthy reforms already commented, in April 1985 the government of Rajiv Gandhi introduced a new innovation—fixation of an import-export policy durable for periods of three years—just to create stability in the exchange rate market. Nevertheless, the complexity of the QR scheme did not substantially diminished.

4.6.1.2. Trade Liberalisation of the 90s

With the reforms posed to the Union Parliament by Narasimha Rao and Manmohan Singh in July 1991, the country finally embarked in a truly liberalising trade policy with a "shorter"—or less longer—negative list of non-liberalised imports and exports. Quantitative controls over imports of goods were withdrawn for all items "except for industrial consumer goods and agricultural products." A new devaluation of the rupee was also implemented.

In fact, it was acknowledged in July 1991 that exchange rates and industrial policies (remember that in this period the industrial licensing also ended, although with exceptions) must form part of an integral policy framework, if their aim is to improve the joint productivity of factors and the efficiency of the economic system. It was also recognised that the deep interventionist industrial policy followed by India since its inception, by means of establishing a cobweb of controls and red tape, had failed and that it had to be updated according to the new economic trends in the world, initiated by some developing countries in the late-70s, such as China.

Then onwards successive steps in the liberalisation process were put in operation. Finally, the QR regime ended in April 2001,[274]

274. In April 2001 the QRs previously imposed in the wake of the article XVIII of GATT were removed. A total of 1,427 commodities were affected. Notwithstanding that, some products previously restricted under article XVIII then onwards passed to be restricted under articles XX-XXI of GATT (those connected with national security, health, culture, scant natural resources, etc.)

although with some limitations. We have to add that in the recent years, the so-called "basic tariffs"[275] have been reduced by 5 per cent points every year as an average. Plans were also made to finally introduce two rates in basic duties: 10 per cent for raw materials, components and semi-finished goods, and 20 per cent for the rest of finished goods.

4.6.1.3. Composition of Indian Trade in Goods

Considering imports, the main items the country needed in the period 1950-2001 were food, raw materials and investment-goods, necessary for domestic consumption, production and exports. Entering into details we have to highlight that in the 70s the imports of edible oils registered a huge growth rate (around an annual average of 40 per cent). Gems and diamonds imports also experienced a notable growth rate in the 70s, with an annual cumulative increase of the tune of 35 per cent.[276]

Other imported raw materials that experienced notable growth in the 70s were petroleum, oil and lubricants. Note that the share of these items in total imports value rose from around 6 per cent in 1960-61 to the 40 per cent registered in 1980-81, as a consequence both of the development of the Indian industry and the two oil crisis registered in those years. Later on, this share fell to 23 per cent in 1990-91 reflecting the registered fall in oil prices. Along the late-90s and mainly in the first years of 2000 this share has experienced relevant volatility, given the recurrent instability of the dollar exchange rate and the economic uncertainty which appeared after the September 11th events.[277] We will add that the growth rate of capital-goods imports has remained steady since the 50s, although reaching a peak in 1995-96.

As regards exports, manufactured goods and agricultural products were the most important items in 2000-01. The main merchandise

275. In India besides "basic tariffs" or "basic duties", there are "additional duties" which act as countervailing duties of the taxes given back to exporters in origin-countries. Recently the so-called "special additional duties" have been removed.

276. In this last case the imported commodity was re-exported after being treated. Note that there has been a strong correlation between the growth rates of imports and exports in this item, both in the 70s and in the period 1990-95.

277. The volatility of the dollar since September 11th has not been so significant against the Indian rupee.

within manufactures was textile fabrics, with a very important annual growth rate (around 41 per cent in the last 20 years). In second place gems and jewellery reached a peak in 1999-2000. The third most important export category in manufactures was "machinery, transport and metal manufactures," which is a clear indicator of the attained degree of industrialisation of India. Note that this export category experienced in the last 20 years a remarkable annual growth rate of the tune of 22 per cent.

4.6.1.4. Evolution of Indian Protectionism

As mentioned before, along the four decades in which India embraced the IS strategy, all the existent and imaginable measures to protect the domestic industry—as a whole and selectively—were put in place: import and export quotas, high nominal tariffs for imports, export subsidies, and exchange rate adjustments were combined to purportedly fulfil the devised targets. Moreover, other controversial policies were adopted during the period, such as the reservation of certain commodities for production by the SSI sector.[278]

Entering into tariffs, we have to remember the theoretical distinction between Nominal Protective Rates (NPR) and Effective Protective Rates (EPR). The first one shows the extent, in percentage, to which the domestic price of imported goods exceeds the price which would have prevailed in the absence of protection. The EPR however shows the percentage by which the added value at a particular stage of processing in a protected domestic industry exceeds the value which would have prevailed without protection. So the Effective Rate of Protection (ERP) will increase when nominal tariffs on outputs increase and/or when nominal tariffs on inputs decrease,[279] and *vice-versa*.

To better evaluate the liberalisation and tariff disarmament of the Indian economy, we have to say that on the eve of the 1991 reforms, the import weighted average of basic tariffs was around 80 per cent,

---

278. The liberalisation process that started in 1991 de-regulated a number of commodities that before that year had been exclusively produced by the SSI sector. Note however that until now not all of them have been removed from the official SSI "reservation list".

279. To refresh the differences between these two concepts, the reader may review any handbook of International Economics. Vide for instance Krugman, P. and Obstfeld, (2002) *International Economics: Theory and Policy*.

with the average for consumer goods being around the double (164 per cent). Additionally, there was a huge typical tariff deviation across commodities, with rates on some imports exceeding 300 per cent. When the liberalisation process started in 1991, ruling licensing and QR on most imports submitted to this regime were abolished, except in consumer manufactured goods.[280] Note that the external trade in agricultural commodities was left out of this reform.[281]

Against common feelings of many westerners, we have to say that the reduction in the Indian basic tariffs along 90s was remarkable. From its average level of 57 per cent established in 1991—remember the higher levels at the eve of the process—the tariff average came down to 33 per cent in 1995 and to 30 per cent in 1998-99. The standard deviation was reduced as well. And the recently[282] liberalised consumer goods imports had in 1995 a weighted average tariff of 48 per cent, only a 50 per cent higher than the overall average. Years later, in 1998-99, the mentioned disparity was only 39 per cent.

If we add to this downward trend the already explained position of the Indian protection (2004-2005), we have to admit that the adjustment effort done by Indian administration has not been negligible. If we additionally review the variations of the nominal tariffs of different countries during the 90s,[283] we have to conclude that from a group of countries analysed by the World Bank, the relatively bigger effort in tariff reductions was done by Bangladesh, followed *ex-aequo* by China and India. And this while the EU and the US, although with low average tariffs, increased them along 90s.

Turning now into considerations on the effective protection of the Indian industry before the reforms of 1991, we have to stress that, against many a time trumpeted in the West, it was not the highest of the world at all. In this regard we have to highlight that, in the context of other developing countries, the effective protection of the

---

280. Along the 90s some consumer manufactured goods were additionally liberalised, as f.i. cars, white products, etc.

281. On many of these issues about the evolution of protectionism, Vide Srinivasan, T. (2000). *Eight Lectures on Indian Economic Reform*. Oxford University Press.

282. Vide Note 280.

283. Vide World Bank. (2001) *World Development Indicators.*

Indian industry before 1991 was not as high as in countries, as for instance Uruguay and Pakistan.[284]

After the reforms of 1991, "we have witnessed a significant decrease in both nominal and effective rates of protection of the Indian industry".[285] On a simple average, the nominal rate of protection in 1995-96 in some industrial sectors was much lower than those in 1989-90. But even their effective protection was situated under the nominal one at the same fiscal year 1995-96, which means relative under-protection. We are here referring to "other primary intermediate goods" and to "capital goods" industries. Another extreme case of under-protection of the Indian economy has been the Primary Consumer goods sector, which in 1995-96 had an average protection of 6.7 per cent against the average of the country situated in 64.6 per cent.

4.6.1.5. Why Traditional Indian IS Strategy Failed

Let us finally analyse why the Indian IS strategy failed. As it happened in other developing countries, the IS strategy followed by India, focused on the domestic industrial production of final goods, for which a sufficient market was presumed to exist. Production of final goods is in general technically less sophisticated than the intermediate primary and capital-goods production. It was expected that, in due time, rising demand and economies of scale in production of final goods would create strong "backward linkages"[286], leading to the creation of domestic intermediate primary and capital-goods industries. Nevertheless, in this regard, the performance of India as well as that of many other developing countries has been disappointing.

The main cause of this generalised failure is attributable to the fact that the tariff structures of developing countries—as it has also

---

284. Vide Greenaway and Milner (1987). Trade Theory and Less Developed Countries, Oxford University Press.

285. Vide Kapila, U. (2003) *Indian Economy since Independence*. Academic Foundation. New Delhi.

286. Remember Chapter 2, in which we have mentioned the theory of unbalanced development, original by Hirschman, A. (1956). According to this theory, the different strength of the linkages of every industry—captured through input-output coefficients and inverse matrix—are a clear indicator for the selection of industries in which the scant financial resources have to be invested.

been the case in India—were implemented in such a way that the resulting effective protection of final-goods industries was much more higher than those of the intermediate primary and capital-goods industries. The effect of this biased tariff structure has been the diversion of the scant resources away from the intermediate primary and capital-goods production, towards the often inefficient production of highly protected final consumer manufactures. Consequently, backward linkages did not worked and, consequently, the domestic capital-goods industry did not take off.

Regrettably for India, on continuing in the 80s with its policy of economic quasi-isolation, it squandered a decade or more in comparison to significant competitors (mainly China). Although, at the end of the day, India performed well in terms of GDP growth rate during the 80s, due to the cautious internal reforms of the Gandhis and the applied deficit spending policy, the Indian economy could have performed much better if it had been opened earlier, thus averting the external crisis of 1991 and part of the current growing gap with China.

5

A Joint Economic Analysis of China and India: Opportunities and Challenges

In former chapters, we have explained the theories of economic growth and development (Chapter 2), and we have outlined the economic policies implemented along the last 50 years in China (Chapter 3) and India (Chapter 4)[287] as well as their results. From now onwards, in order to understand the brilliant economic future that some authors and econometricians attribute to these two big countries, we will analyse their peculiarities and opportunities as well as their underlying problems in an Asian and world context.[288]

There is a more clear consensus in relation to the bright future of China than that of India. Indeed, as we will observe, the current economic (quantitative and qualitative) differences between these two giants are relevant. Notwithstanding that, some traits of the Indian economy could make that this economy strongly emerge from underlying own current problems. Indeed, it already seems (in 2004) that the process of the Indian catching up is brisker than before.

5.1. Evaluation of Current Economic Situation of China and India

Although China and India are nowadays fashionable countries and seem to have a very large growth capacity—annually and for a long period ahead—a fast survey on their main social and economic

---

287. As the reader may have observed, the volume and accuracy of the supplied data by governments and economic institutions of China and India is very different, of course in favour of India. As a consequence, and along all this essay, the analysis of China has been more shallow than that of India.

288. Along this chapter, we will make constant comparisons of the figures of China and India, with those of some developed countries, those of other relevant developing ones, and those of other Asian countries. To this respect, the reader may consult the Statistical Annexes of this book.

indicators, may return us to the harsh reality of these two countries at the dawn of the 21st Century. Indicators that effectively show the austere, although differentiated situation, through which they are moving at the time being.

5.1.1. *Variables Related to the "Human Development Index" (HDI)*[289]

To start with, we will here refer to the per capita GDP of China and India, which in 2002 respectively was 960 and 470 US dollars.[290] In consistency with the importance of their respective rural populations[291] we have to mention their levels of poverty, particularly that of India. With a figure of 34.7 per cent of the population of India under the 1 dollar a day "poverty line" (only 16.6 per cent in the case of China), and almost 80 per cent under the "2 dollar poverty line," India accumulates more poverty in absolute and relative terms than any other of the rest of the analysed countries,[292] be these Europeans, Americans or Asians. Nevertheless, one should not forget either that China has a higher proportion of people under the 1 dollar poverty line, than all the considered countries, except Vietnam and of course India.

While the income distribution pattern of China and India, is respectively worse or alike than that of some EU countries—but better than that of other South-East Asian ones of the selected sample (Table 1)—their public expenditure on health is rather low.

---

289. The Human Development Index (HDI) basically takes into account life expectancy and education, as well as GDP per person.

290. These are figures of the World Bank (2004), reckoned at current exchange rates. If the reckoning was done in US dollars in PPP terms, their respective per capita GDP would be 4,520 and 2,650. Certainly small figures compared with the 35,500 of the US and with the 26,000-27,000 of the analysed EU countries.

291. In 2002, the proportion of rural population in China was 62 per cent of the total, and in India 72 per cent. Note that the rural population is a rather different concept to that of the agricultural population atached to this activity. The latter is in relative terms less important in China than in India, moving the two agricultural populations rather proportionally under mentioned figures of rural population.

292. In order to put these two countries into a global perspective, we have considered them in parallel to a lot of statistical figures of some big EU countries (such as France, Germany, Italy and UK), and other relevant countries of the world as Brazil, Japan, Russian Federation and the US. In addition we have also considered those corresponding to South-East Asian countries, such as Indonesia, South Korea, Malaysia, Philippines, Singapore, Thailand and Vietnam.

In this regard we have to mention that while China overcomes the figures of many other South-East Asian countries, the case of India is shockingly disappointing, with a figure of public expenditure in health of only 0.9 per cent of its GDP.

Note however that the total health expenditure (public plus private) of China and India, is in GDP terms higher than that of the South-East Asian countries, most of them with higher per capita incomes than the two giants. Curiously this is an indicator of the importance that Chinese and Indians privately give to their health.[293] In connection with the mentioned expenditure in health, but also in connection with the per capita income, one has to agree that, although the life expectancy in India has significantly grown in last decades, it continues being the lowest of all the analysed countries (only 63 years of life expectancy at birth in India in comparison to 71 in China).

Surprisingly, barring Indonesia, the current Chinese public expenditure in education (in GDP terms) is the lowest of all considered countries of the sample (India devotes 4.1 per cent *versus* 2.2 per cent of China). Nevertheless, this small relative expenditure may be counteracted in China by the existence of a significant complementary education of a "private" character. Anyway the smaller figure of Male Adult Illiteracy rates, much lower in China than in India (7 per cent *versus* 31 per cent of the total) may reveal the public efforts in education realised in the Maoist period. Note additionally that, although the figure of India in public education expenditure is rather similar to those of the EU and US in GDP terms, the huge differences in per capita income terms between India and the Western countries establish a colossal difference in the absolute per capita expenditure devoted to education.

The former deficient traits, stemming from the comparative economic situation of China and India, make that the levels of the three selected pointers (per capita income plus indicators of education and expectancy of life) used to build the HDI, currently

293. Note however that the total expenditure in health in Europe, Japan, and particularly in the US is, in GDP terms, around double or more than that of China and India, with the US leading the list (13.9 per cent of its GDP is devoted to health expenditure).

place China and India on an unsatisfactory position—94th and 127th of the world ranking—in terms of their "human development index".[294]

5.1.2. *Energy, Infrastructure and Communication Indicators*

A parallel indicator to the per capita GDP, to asses the current level of development of the different countries is the per capita consumption of electric power. In this regard, it must be understood that despite the rapid progress of China and India concerning their economic growth rates, their per capita consumption of electricity continues to be rather small, particularly that of India. Although China had in the year 2001 a per capita consumption of 893 *kwh.*, that of India was only of 365, being the latter lower than that of all analysed Asian countries with the exception of Vietnam (325). Note that the per capita consumptions of China and India are very far away from those of the Western countries of the sample.[295]

The figure of Indian per capita consumption of electricity is particularly astonishing and in contradiction with its economic and political aspirations. Even more, in terms of its transmission and distribution losses, in 2001, India reached the maximum figure (27 per cent) of all the analysed countries. The fact that the "stealing" of power has only recently been declared a penal fault, jointly with the fact that some states use to provide practically free energy for the poor (peasants and villagers), have made that the energy in this country has become a comparatively expensive and scant item[296] for those who pay for it. And this, while its supply is lower than its

294. In the World ranking of per capita GDP (PPP), India was placed at the 117th place in the year 2002 (amongst around 200 countries referred to in the World Bank Statistics). Nevertheless, this position worsened a little taking into account the Human Developing Index (HDI), worked out by the UN (in 2002 India was placed in 127th place). Concerning China, this country was placed in 2002 in 99th position concerning per capita GDP (PPP), and in 94th position in relation to HDI.

295. Note for instance that in 2001 the per capita consumption of electricity was 11,714 kWh. in US, around 5,000-6,000 in the analysed European countries, and over 1,000 in all analysed countries except in China (893), Philippines (489), Indonesia (404), India (365) and Vietnam (325).

296. As a consequence of these facts, people or companies that pay for the power they receive, have to pay for the bill not paid by others, as well as for the technical losses of energy, which in India are abnormally high due to the lack of adequate investments in the grid.

demand. As a result of the current energy deficit production, recently figured out around 10 per cent, many firms and individuals have to invest in private generators of electricity, which is a costly and aggregated inefficient solution.

Letting aside the case of infrastructures—mainly roads, railways and ports— in general more favourable in the case of China than in India in per capita length terms or in Km-Tn. transported, we have to mention that in relation with the available main lines of telephones per 1000 inhabitants in 2002, the cases of China and India were also shocking.[297] In particular India, with 40 main lines (per 1000 people) compared with 646 of the US, was the worst positioned of all countries we have considered along this Chapter. Note however that the current boom of cellular phones has made that the "main lines" indicator has become rather obsolete. Notwithstanding that, in 2002 India also had the smallest figure of cell-phones per 1000 inhabitants of all analysed countries.

Conversely we have to mention that China is rather well placed in terms of its GDP percentage devoted to expenditures in ITC, as well as in its relative expenditure in R&D. Indeed two very favourable indicators for its future economic progress (remember the conclusions of Chapter 2).

Finally, to complete this panorama of the sociological and economic traits of China and India, we should not overlook that their expenditures in Defence, are relatively high, only overtaken in GDP terms by US, Russian Federation, Korea and Singapore. Of course this is a derivative of their assumed roles as global or regional players, a role which will become more and more relevant along coming years or decades.

5.2. Recent Economic Evolution of China and India (1980-2003) in the Asian and World Context

It is well known that in the second half of the 20th century, the world economy obtained its best ever results. For the convenience of the analysis of this half a century, historians use to divide it in two periods: 1) the so-called "golden age of capitalism" (1950-1973);

297. Vide. World Bank (2004) *World Development Indicators*.

and 2) the "neo-liberal period" (1973-98).[298] As a whole, the global GDP grew along the last 50 years at an annual rhythm of 3.9 per cent, which is the average of what the world grew in the first period (4.91 per cent) and in the second one (3.01 per cent).

5.2.1. Recent Evolution of the GDP in the World, China and India

Regarding the neo-liberal period,[299] in which the global GDP grew annually at the mentioned rate of 3.01 per cent, we should first of all note the remarkable economic failure of Eastern Europe, changing its annual growth rate into negative (-0.56 per cent) from earlier 4.84 per cent (in the golden age). Also Japan decelerated its previous spectacular rhythm of growth, converging to the average growth rate of the world. Note additionally that while Western Europe had annually grown in the "golden age" almost one per cent point above the EIC countries,[300] commanded by US, this situation overturned in the neo-liberal period, with the EIC growing almost one per cent point more than Western Europe.

Significantly above the world average, the Asian (ex-Japan) countries not only maintained in the neo-liberal period the growth rate of that of the golden age (5.18 per cent), but also surpassed it (5.46 per cent), this figure being almost twofold of the world average. No doubt, this period (1973-1998) of general decline in global growth was the period of the economic resurgence of Asia.

Note however that in the last two decades, a period almost coinciding with that of the "neo-liberalism" as devised by Maddison, both China and India grew at higher rates than those of average Asia (ex-Japan): around a figure of 10 per cent in the case of China, and around 5.8 per cent in the case of India. Making the considered periods more homogeneous one should agree that China has grown in the period 1973-98 at a figure of 8.5-9 per cent, and India at

298. Vide Maddison, A. (2001:125). Book already mentioned. The periods selected by Maddison are arbitrary and consequently arguable, but we will not enter in discussions on the frontiers of these two sub-periods.

299. The international comparisons of China and India in the "golden age of capitalism" have been done in the first Chapter, under the heading "Initial Economic Under-Performance of China and India" in the period 1950-1978 (80).

300. The so-called European Immigration Countries (EIC), quoted in Maddison (2001: 126), include US, Canada, Australia and New Zealand.

around 5.1 per cent. The latter is a little lower figure than the average of Asia,[301] but higher than what few Indians and even less Westerners could have imagined in the middle of the period, that is to say before the initiation of the reform process (1991) in India.

Note additionally that of all considered countries of South-East Asia in our sample, only Philippines (2.2 per cent) under-performed with respect to the Asian (ex-Japan) average. South-Korea and Singapore behaved exceptionally, letting aside Taiwan and former British colony Hong-Kong.

5.2.2. Current Structure of the GDP in China and India

Although China and India have grown very quickly in the last two and a half decades—let us remember that the former three decades were those of economic under-performance of these two gigantic countries—they have not had time enough for catching up. This lack of sufficient catching up of China and India has its replicate in the per capita income they have reached, well under that of Europe, Japan, US, Brazil, and even under many of the South-East-Asian countries, as observable in Table 4 of the Statistical Annexes.

This up to now unfavourable economic positioning of China and India has also its expression in the relative structure of their output composition. In particular, the Chinese agriculture production represents today a 15 per cent of the total output, a figure equivalent to that of the lesser developed Indonesia, although inferior to that of Vietnam.

Indeed, of all the analysed countries barring Vietnam, the Indian agriculture production registers the highest and most unfavourable figure (23 per cent) in relation with its GDP (Table 4), this being clear indicator of its relative degree of development.

If alternatively we look at the share of industrial production in total output, we have to certify that the Indian economy is also the worst positioned of all considered developing countries in Table 4. Only 27 per cent of total Indian output is generated by the Indian

301. Note that the average global growth rate of Asia over the period 1973-98, was pushed forward not only by the extraordinary growth rate of China but also by the high growth rhythms of the so-called Asian tigers (Hong-Kong, Singapore, South-Korea and Taiwan) plus Malaysia and Thailand.

industry, a figure identical to that of France or UK, although in these cases their low industrial share is a consequence of the development of their Services sector, as it corresponds to their so-called "tertiary societies", and not of their insufficient industrialisation. If we additionally consider the share of manufactures in total GDP, we may also deduce that India keeps the most unfavourable position of all analysed countries.

Conversely, this is not at all the case of China, whose relative industrial production moves well over all the analysed, developed or developing countries. And this in relation to Industry (51 per cent in GDP terms) as well as in Manufactures (35 per cent of GDP).

In relation to the contribution of Services to GDP, we have to certify that while the Indian economy exhibited in 2002 a figure of 51 per cent, that of China was only 34 per cent. Indeed a surprisingly coincidence of 51 per cent, being this percentage the contribution of Services in India to GDP and that of Industry in neighbouring China. A coincidence that far from being a twist of fate is just the result of the different chosen strategies of growth.

5.2.3. *Evolution of the Population in the World, China and India*

As it is well known, the annual average population growth rate of the world lost momentum in the "neo-liberal age" (1973-98) in comparison to that of the "golden age of capitalism" (1950-1973), moving from 1.92 per cent to 1.66 per cent. Most of the regions reduced their population growth rate with the dramatic exception of Africa, that reached an average figure of 2.73 per cent per annum, a figure capable of doubling the population of this continent every 26 years. Latin America also reduced its annual population growth rate to a figure of around 2 per cent, a little bit over the annual growth rate of Asia (1.86 per cent).

Nonetheless, the population behaviour of China in the "neo-liberal age" was rather different from the Asian one. Although the Chinese population had undergone a population explosion during most of the Maoist period, alike to that of India, from then onwards the new almost compulsory population policy devised by Chinese authorities induced a significant slowdown. This meant a noticeable change in the velocity of augmentation of the Chinese population, which moved from an annual growth rate of around 2 per cent in the golden age, to a figure of 1.1 per cent[302] in the neo-liberal age, thus reaching an absolute figure in 2002 of 1280 million people.

The Chinese population policy of "one child per couple" quickly fulfilled its target concerning reduction of fertility rates. Nevertheless, the "demographic momentum"—accompanied by a perceptible increase of the expected life—played its role, and the Chinese population did not suddenly stop growing, but just grew slower than before while rapidly started ageing.

This policy accompanied by some primary innovations in the financial system and other reforms, made possible a rapid growth of the private savings ratio of Chinese families. As a consequence, at the edge of the 21st Century the total domestic savings ratio reached a figure of around 40 per cent (almost 44 per cent in 2002), a surprising level for a country with a relatively low per capita income.

Note however that the induced process of ageing, currently undergone by the Chinese population as a direct consequence of the applied population policy, in combination with a perceivable gender unbalance, may create serious problems in the future, unless a sufficient Social Security System for protection of the elder is set up in due time.[303]

The case of the evolution of the Indian population has been very different from that of China, particularly in the last two decades of the 20th century. Far from experiencing a sudden turning point in the 80s,[304] India only experienced a slow reduction of its annual population growth rate. As a result, after the population bomb suffered in the period 1950-1980, with growth rates similar to that of the Asian average (2.2 per cent), it only mildly reduced the speed of its annual population growth rate in the period 1980-2000, to currently reach a figure of 1.9 per cent, and an absolute amount of 1,050 million people in 2002 (vide World Bank figures).

---

302. This figure could be around 1 per cent according to other sources.

302. Perhaps the lack of a generalised Social Security system may be the root-cause of the current galactic "saving domestic rate" of China, placed at 43.7 per cent in GDP terms.

304. Note that in the first months of the so-called Emergency Period (1975-77), the government of India also attempted to reduce the annual fertility rate by resorting to sterilisation of males. The final result of this programme was a total failure from all perspectives, included the political one, which further undermined the credibility of Mrs. Gandhi's government, that soon after would lose the power.

Note that this Indian figure of 1.9 per cent annual population growth rate not only is larger than that of China but also clearly superior to that of many South-East Asian countries with some exceptions (Table 2).[305] To put things clear we have to say that the recent Indian population policy (based on voluntary corrections) has not been successful, although international institutions (WB) expect that, as an intrinsic trait of the development process, the population growth rate will flex down to 1.2 per cent in the period 2001-2015.

Although the currently high population evolution of India continues being worry-some, it might induce in decades ahead a significant comparative advantage. The cause will mainly be the youthness of its population: currently a 33 per cent of the Indian population is under 15, a figure well over that of China, Europe,[306] US, Brazil, and many South-East Asian countries.[307] This relative figure of the young population of India will additionally protract for decades the high capacity growth of this country, although it will probably keep during the next decade a relatively lower growth rate of the per capita income.

The mentioned differences in growth population rates among China and India, and those of these two countries in comparison to those of Europe, Japan and US,[308] will additionally induce meaningful differences in the growth rates of the labour force among all considered countries. According to recent estimates, while as for instance Italy, UK, and Japan will undergo negative growth rates of their labour force in the current decade, India will increase its labour force at an annual rate of 1.8 per cent.[309] This could be a short term problem for the Indian government, but also an advantage. To the extent that, if the second generation reforms became a reality at mid-term, the economy would annually absorb a larger proportion

305. The population growth rates of Malaysia, Philippines, and Singapore are well above that of India, and always over 2.3 per cent.

306. Indeed the relative volume of young people in Europe, and mainly in France and Germany, should be a very serious concern for the authorities of these countries. Their political reactions however, do not seem supportive enough.

307. Of the different countries considered in Table 2, only Malaysia and Philippines have younger populations than that of India.

308. The case of Japan is also a paradigmatic. This is a country that, in a similar way than France and Germany, will experience a reduction of its population in the current decade.

309. Note (Table 3) that Indonesia, Malaysia and Philippines will experience growth rates of their labour force larger than those of China and India.

(than before) of the excessive labour force currently attached to agriculture, thus thrusting higher GDP growth.

5.2.4. *Evolution of the Per Capita GDP in the World, China and India.*

As we have stated before, in the "neo-liberal era" the rhythm of prosperity experienced a generalised downfall[310] except in the case of Asia (ex-Japan). This region moved from an annual per capita GDP growth rate of 2.92 per cent in the "golden age" to a 3.54 per cent in the neo-liberal period. In Eastern Europe, on the contrary, this period was a clear catastrophe, not only in terms of economic performance, which significantly reduced the standard of living of the citizens,[311] but also in its political functioning.[312]

The per capita GDP in Africa did not grow at all in the neo-liberal period (0.01 per cent), while Latin America grew only at a rhythm of 0.99 per cent. Note that the loss of steam in Western Europe was also significant, experiencing an annual growth rate of its per capita GDP (1.78 per cent) which only surpassed those of Latin America, Africa and Eastern-Europe.

In the context of the economic success of Asia (ex-Japan), whose per capita GDP grew in the neo-liberal period at a rhythm of 3.54 per cent, we have to insist that the performance of China has been outstanding. An annual growth rate of its per capita GDP of around 8-8.5 per cent in the period 1973-1998, similar to that obtained in the "golden age of capitalism" by the then seemingly unstoppable Japan, is a clear indicator of the relevant success of the Chinese economy.

In relation to India, we have to underline that this country, often under-considered by Western observers,[313] has performed significantly

310. Among other things, the sharp increase of the price of energy in the 70s, and the appearance of internal environment legislation in Western countries, forced a reduction of the former higher growth rate of productivity of labour in the West. Only in the second half of the 90s—with the IT revolution churning up—the productivity of labour recovered or surpassed past trend, in particular in the US.

311. The per capita GDP growth rate of this region fall at an annual rate of 1.10 per cent.

312. Note that in the middle of the period the communist political and economic model of the region became bankrupt, this being followed by a period of high economic instability.

313. These observers use to look almost exclusively to the current level of the Indian economic and social indicators and not so much to the Indian potentials.

well in the last two decades in per capita GDP growth rate terms (3.8 per cent), mildly above the Asian (ex-Japan) average, which was of around 3.5 per cent. This is praiseworthy for a country that, captured in its administrative cobweb, and with huge problems in economic decision making, started the 80s in a bad economic condition. Note additionally that India was then much worse positioned than many of the current 168 "shaking countries" in terminology of Maddison.[314] Nevertheless India has grown much more than most of them in the last 25 years in terms of per capita income.

5.2.5. *Current Relevance of China and India in a World Context*

It is clear that the current absolute per capita incomes of China and India—although rapidly growing—are not the real cause of the observed deep concern among Western governments, particularly with reference to China. This concern is rather motivated by the rapid evolution of its GDP and the overwhelming growth of the Chinese exports to the West.

If we start considering the GDP of China (in US-dollar terms) and compare it to those of other countries, we may deduce that China's GDP is rather similar to that of Italy, or alike to the addition of the GDP of all the South-East Asian countries analysed in Table 4. Of course this comparison would drive us to mis-consideration of China, as it would be to judge the Russian Federation as an economic power of the tune of half of that of Spain.

For different (economic and political) reasons, the "top leaderships" of the world assess the current importance of China (and to lesser extent that of India) well over its GDP relevance in US-dollar terms. This is mainly due to its current economic potentialities, and its current and future political weight. Do not forget that China nowadays count with a joint middle and high class,[315] which in Western standards is roughly equivalent to 110-125 million people, being that of India around half of this figure.

---

314. This "shaking countries" group is formed by 40 countries of Asia, 44 Latin Americans, 27 ex-Soviet Union satellites, and 57 African ones. Vide Maddison, A. (2001:129). Book already mentioned.

315. Of course in the today China it is not possible to officially talk about different economic classes but about different strata of purchase capacity. This is a mere case of semantics typical of the official communist wording.

Consequently, if we changed the former assessment criterion (that of the GDP measured in US-dollars terms), substituting it by the GDP reckoned in PPP terms, the results of our analysis would be very different.[316] To start with, we have to affirm that China and India would gain relevant positions in the global stage (Table 4). After the US, currently the most powerful country of the world in economic terms, would be China; after China would appear Japan, and immediately following it, India. Note further that the addition of the GDP (PPP) of China, India and the analysed South-East Asian countries would be (today) equivalent to that of the US. And that the GDP (PPP) of China is (today) equivalent to those of France, Germany and UK altogether.[317]

Logically, if we bear in mind the rapid growth rate of the GDP of China and India in the last two decades, as well as those of the rest of neighbouring countries, the concerns of the Western governments are understandable. In this regard it seems that time is running against the West and in favour of East and South Asia, and particularly in favour of China and India, as deducible from the extrapolations recently published by Goldman-Sachs, as mentioned in the Introduction (Chapter 1).

In this regard the politicians should not forget that the problems for the West, in particular for Europe, will not start when the mentioned Asian countries reached a significant per capita income—which could only come after decades—but just when they grow in absolute and aggregated terms more than the Western ones, being this growth—as it currently happens—partly supported by exports to the West. As forecasted, this economic phenomenon that doubtlessly would negatively effect the Western creation of employment and create political problems, will likely start in just half a decade.

---

316. Note that the indicator GDP in PPP terms may also be imperfect, in particular if we are assessing the short term international trade potentialities of the different countries. Note however that, due to the fact that a significant part of the goods and services reckoned in this way does not pass through markets—particularly in the agricultural sector—these produced goods and services exist and consequently must be evaluated. Not to evaluate them would be equivalent to ignore all the people currently in subsistence positions and their potentialities in coming years, and to ignore all transactions typical of the underground or informal economy.

317. Continuing with these comparisons we could affirm that the analysed economies of South-East Asia are jointly larger in GDP (PPP) terms than that of Germany.

5.3. China, India and the New Direction of the International Trade of Goods

Continuing with our analysis of the main economic trends of the different regions of the world, we will now consider the recent evolution of the international trade of goods. Before entering into the recent direction of trade, we will refer to the geographical structure of the international trade of goods in 2002. These data will enable us to have a better knowledge of the potentials of the involved countries at short-mid term.

5.3.1. International Economic Structure of Commerce of Goods

According to recent figures provided by World Bank,[318] the structure of the commerce of goods had the following profiles in 2002: 1) the export value of *high income countries* was 74.6 per cent of the total export of goods; and 2) the export value of *low and middle income countries*, that is to say the rest of the countries of the world, only reached 25.4 per cent of the mentioned total exports.[319] To this unbalanced profile, one could add another meaningful traits: 3) the volume of the total exports of Asia (ex-Japan) were of the tune of 53 per cent of the total exports of the developing world; and 4) the exports of mainland China plus that of Hong-Kong represented altogether 61 per cent of total exports of Asia (ex-Japan), that is to say 8.25 per cent of the total world,[320] well over the exports of Japan, the third world exporter.

---

318. Vide World Bank (2004:311) *World Development Indicators.*

319. According to figures of IMF—International Financial Statistics, Year Book, 2003—the share in 2002 of total exports of the Industrialised Countries was 62.4 per cent, and that of the Developing Countries was 37.6 per cent. Following this source the share of Asia (ex-Japan) was 20 per cent. Following another publication of the IMF—Direction of Trade and Statistics, yearbook 2003—the figures would respectively be 65.4 per cent and 34.6 per cent. If we alternatively used figures of the WTO we would arrive to lower figures for the share in world exports of the developing countries. Surprisingly, according to WTO, the export-share of Asia (ex-Japan) in 2002 would be 19.2 per cent, a figure alike to that provided by IMF.

Looking for the consistency of our analysis we have chosen those of the World Bank commented in the text. Anyway, in a long term analysis as that realised in this book, differences in departure positions are less relevant than the speed and direction of the involved variables. Notwithstanding that, one have to acknowledge that current higher positions of Asia (ex-Japan), reflected by figures provided by IMF and WTO, could change the schedule of possible political derivatives that we will comment in Chapter 6.

320. In 2003, this joint figure of mainland China plus Hong-Kong represented 8.9 per cent of total world exports. Note however that this aggregated figures of "total China" contains China-Hong-Kong intra-trade that should be excluded.

Although the 90s have been a good decade for the exports of goods of the developing countries and mainly for the Asian ones, the nuke reality is that, as a whole, its total exports share continues moving around 1/4 of the total world exports, as it was the case 30 years ago. This circumstance, stemming from past biased international trade rules, has not helped the developing countries as a whole in their catching up intentions along the last three decades.

Note additionally that of the mentioned share of 25.4. per cent of the total exports of goods realised by the low and middle income countries, 19.1 per cent points were exports directed to the high income countries, while the developing countries only mutually exported 6.3 per cent points,[321] which means only 1/3 of their total exports.

5.3.2. *General Trends in the Direction of Commerce Along the 90s (1992-2002)*

Although a magnitude may be small—we are here referring to the mutual trade of goods of the low and middle income countries, which in 2002 was 6.3 per cent of the total world exports—this does not imply that this magnitude cannot grow, nor that it cannot grow very quickly. On the contrary, we are convinced that this figure is going to experience a fast growth rate in the future, as well as that of the total exports share of the developing countries (mutual plus those directed to the industrialised world), today 25.4 per cent. In consistency with the former statement, we are also convinced that the share of high income countries in total world exports, is already decreasing fast.

To specify, the high income countries have generated along the 90s (1992-2002) growing total exports at an annual rate of 4.5 per cent, a figure well below the world average that was 5.4 per cent (Table 5). If this disparity continues up to 2015 the share of high income countries could reach the figure approximately 65 per cent instead of the current 74.6 per cent.[322]

---

321. This figure would change into another of 7.2 per cent, according to figures of WTO for 2002.

322. The mentioned total exports share, forecasted for 2015, in 65 per cent and 35 per cent for respectively developed countries and developing ones, would change into others, respectively around 55 per cent and 45 per cent, if we had used for calculation the figures provided by IMF.

Conversely, along the 90s the export of goods of low and middle income countries has moved in an opposite direction. Their total exports have grown at an annual average rate of 8.7 per cent, a figure well above the world average (5.4 per cent). If these trends and disparities are confirmed in next years, the total export share of the low and middle income countries could reach in 2015 a level of the tune of 35 per cent, from the current 25.4 per cent.

5.3.3. Evolution in the 90s (1992-2002) of Intra-Regional Trade

Dividing the "developing world" in seven geographical areas,[323] we may deduce that all these regions except one—Middle-East and North-Africa—have registered annual growth rates of their total exports (towards inside and outside the region) well above the annual growth rate average (5.4 per cent). Note additionally that in all developing regions, except in the already mentioned one—the total exports of goods have grown between a minimum annual rate of 8.3 per cent in South Asia and a maximum of 11.2 per cent in the East Asia-Pacific region.

A more relevant detail of the commercial figures of the 90s, is the "intra-regional" export growth rate registered in the different regions of the world. In this regard, only the "high income economies" have experienced intra-regional growth rates of trade below the world average (4.0 per cent *versus* 5.4 per cent).

Conversely, the "intra-regional trade" was more than extraordinary in two developing regions of the world that share borders: East Asia-Pacific and South Asia. In these two regions the disparity "intra-regional annual growth rate/total annual growth rate of exports" was 1.47 and 1.18 respectively along the 90s. Particularly outstanding was the intra-regional growth rate of the Eastern Asia-Pacific region, which grew at an annual average rate tripling the world average (16.5 per cent *versus* 5.4 per cent), while the annual intra-regional commerce growth rate in South Asia was the double of the world average (9.8 per cent *versus* 5.4 per cent). This is a clear indicator of the present and future trade performance of these two regions, of course commanded by China and India.

---

323. These regions are: Eastern-Asia and Pacific, Eastern-Europe and Central Asia, Latin America-Caribbean, Middle East-North Africa, South Asia, and Sub-Sahara Africa.

Even more, if we consider the mutual import-export relations of these neighbouring two super-dynamic regions, we find something extraordinary: 1) that East Asia-Pacific region has exported to South Asia in the period 1992-2002 at annual growing rhythms of 14.7 per cent, while 2) South Asia has exported to East Asia-Pacific at an annual growth rate of 15.5 per cent. These figures jointly with those mentioned above, have generated along the 90s an average growth rate of exports, inside the common perimeter of these two regions, of the tune of 13-14 per cent, which means tripling of the growth rate of total world exports.

If we turn now to the "high income countries" we will deduce some additional interesting traits. First of all, we have to mention the fact that the US, EU, and Japan have exhibited along the 90s growth rates of their total exports well below the world average. Actually the cases of the US and EU, although not so serious as that of Japan, are also worrying. Indeed, according to the figures provided by WB, the total exports of the US and EU grew along the 90s at an annual rate of 4.5-4.4 per cent, well under the world average (5.4 per cent). Even worst the intra-regional trade of the EU, that is to say its intra-EU trade, moved along the 90s at an annual rate of 3.5 per cent, a rhythm of around 60 per cent of the world average.[324]

In the case of the international trade of the EU (extra-EU trade) it is clear that things have not been as bad as the intra EU-trade. However, letting aside the EU exports to the US, Eastern Europe and East Asia-Pacific, the rest of the EU exports have not properly worked.

5.3.4. Underlying Automatism of Growing Chinese-Indian Trade

Although the drums of fear are already sounding in Western countries in relation to the quick gain of total (world) exports share by China[325]—note that the rapid annual growth of exports coming

324. Trying to find some explanations for the above mentioned poor behaviour of the EU intra-trade along 90s, we could mention: 1) Wearing out of the "trade creation effect" after the implementation of the single market, agreed in 1986; 2) The low GDP growth rates experienced along 90s by the EU as a whole, which may have provoked scantly growing purchases of every EU country to its commercial partners; 3) The not very competitive environment in industrial matters across the Union.

325. Some comments unofficially realised by authorities of relevant Western import countries, suggest that their registered imports from China are larger than corresponding exports declared by China to the WTO. Accordingly, if these undertones were right, the world exports share of China (ex-Hong-Kong) in 2003 could be significantly higher (perhaps 7-8 per cent) than that (5.9 per cent) stemming from official figures of WTO.

from China is enlarging the imports in the West, thus reducing Western aggregate demand against internal production and internal job opportunities for its nationals—the worst for them perhaps has not started.

Observing the commercial process of the last decade (1992-2002), one has to agree that a substantial part of the growth in Chinese exports has had as protagonists Western MNC (Multinational Corporations), which have selected this country for dislocation and further (partial) exporting of their outputs, thus taking advantage from the lower wages paid to the Chinese industrial workers. This strategy, materialised in huge FDI directed to China, is consistent with the more strict logic of globalisation and open capitalists economies. Consequently, Western countries could not significantly misbehave against China in trade matters if they want to protect the interests of their own MNC*.

Letting aside former considerations, we do believe that Asia (ex-Japan) has entered in a clear virtuous circle for their exports. The causes of the export share gains of Asia are double and differently rooted. Firstly, the main Asian regions (East-Asia and Pacific and South Asia) are gaining quota in the internal markets of "all high income countries," due to their higher competitiveness based on their comparative low industrial wages. And this despite the low GDP growth rates of Western countries in comparative terms—particularly in Europe and Japan—which has forced smaller than potential growth rates for their total imports along the 90s.[326]

Note also that while the EU has shown total annual import growth rates of 3.9 per cent along 90s, the export growth rates to the EU coming from East Asia-Pacific and South Asia have respectively been of 12.1 per cent and 6.1 per cent. These growth rates of the exports of the Asian countries to the EU, well above those of the average EU-GDP or EU-export growth rates, explain by themselves the difficulties for the creation, or simply for the maintenance, of the industrial employment in the EU.

---

326. The annual growth rates of the total imports of the EU and Japan along the 90s have been low and equal, 3.9 per cent. Total imports of the US grew however in the 90s at an annual average rate of 7.7 per cent.

* In the first days of June 2005, the Chinese Government implicitly referred to this issue when it announced the elimination of export taxes on some textiles and garments.

Almost the same, although in a minor tone could be said with respect to the US, which only has registered along the 90s (1992-2002) annual growth rates of 4.5 per cent in total exports, while its imports from East-Asia-Pacific and South Asia have respectively been 14.4 per cent and 10.9 per cent (Table 5).

Although the former figures and arguments spread by themselves serious doubts about the long term stability of the current geographical distribution of international trade and support our predictions, there is second line of reasoning even more detrimental for the economic future of the Western countries. Note in this regard that the current GDP growth capacity has clearly shifted towards Asia, as proven by figures of Maddison (OECD) and World Bank. At the same time, Asia (ex-Japan) counts as a whole with an enormous potential for additional growth during decades, given the low level of its development and the huge absolute and relative figures of people attached to agriculture. Particularly in China and India, the two colossal countries of the continent.

This current and future higher growth rates of the two involved regions, led by China and India, will *ceteris paribus* induce significantly higher growth rates of their total imports. Notwithstanding that, given the superior current trend of the intra-regional trade growth of the two mentioned regions of Asia, plus the progressive lower competitiveness of the EU and the US in these two sub-regions, the Western countries will have serious difficulties in future to keep their current Asian export shares. Note in this regard that the share of the exports of the EU and US to East Asia-Pacific and South Asia have already dwindled in last decade. And this despite the fact that the EU and US exports have grown in these regions more rapidly than their total world exports.

Consequently, under the *ceteris paribus* clause, we do believe that the "die are cast" and that in the future the gains in total exports share will continue for Asia, and for long. As a result, it is almost sure that in the short-mid term, the net creation of industrial employment will take place mainly in Asia, commanded by China and India.

To face this difficult situation, the sole (acceptable) economic strategy at disposal of high income countries—in the context of the ongoing biased interpretation of the neo-classical model—will be the continuation or even the acceleration of the economic penetration in these Asian regions, by means of increasing FDI. Note however that this strategy will enhance the acceleration of job creation in the Asian regions while it will undermine job creation in the EU and the US. And this while Western GNP will grow quicker than its GDP.

To the extent that China seems nowadays to be relatively overloaded with FDI, we should not rule out the possibility that the better economic times of India are near to arrive. Positive modifications in the economic and political *modus operandi* of this country—second generation reforms plus certain top legal framework changes—could generate the "miracle" which the Indians have for long been waiting at.

5.3.5. Degree of Opening and Limits of the Trade Structure of China and India

After "explaining the future" of the international trade of China and India, we will now make some comments on the current degree of opening and on the current structure of exports and imports of these two big Asian countries.

In relation with the volume of exports over corresponding GDP, we have to mention that in 2002 the ratio of India was the lowest of all the considered countries (Table 6) with the exception of those of Japan and US.[327] If we compare China with India we find that the value of the corresponding Chinese parameter is almost the double of that of India (29 per cent *versus* 15 per cent), being the Chinese one placed well under that of some analysed EU countries such as Germany and UK. As expectable and stemming from their smaller size, all the analysed South-Asian countries (in Table 6) have higher quotients Exports/GDP than China and India. Note that Malaysia and Singapore have quotients over 100 per cent, which is a clear pointer of their very open economies (in a framework of small sized economies).

Letting aside additional comments on the ratio imports/GDP, which in general moves in parallel to that of the exports/GDP,[328] we

327. As we have mentioned before, this paradoxical result is a derivative of the limitations of this indicator, which tends to have a low value in big countries.

328. One should take note of some few cases in which there are relevant differences between these two ratios. An outstanding example is the case of the Russian Federation, a country very tilted to the exports of oil in its goods trade.

will additionally consider the value of the indicator "annual growth rate of the real trade, less growth rate of real GDP". As easily deducible this is an indicator of the current effort of a country to an additional opening to external trade, irrespective of its current commercial scale, and the size of its internal market.

Concerning the last indicator, and with the exception of South Korea with a figure of 6.9 per cent, India and China, and by this order, have been in the 90s (1992-2002) two of the countries more involved in continued and serious efforts pro-opening to international trade, respectively with figures of 5.6 per cent and 4.5 per cent.[329] Consequently, it would be incorrect to say that India has only mildly reacted pro-opening to globalisation after the reforms undertaken in 1991.

Going now to the current structure of exports of China and India, we note that the exports of India are relatively tilted to food—only surpassed by Brazil among the considered countries in Table 6. This peculiarity of the Indian exports makes this country prone to Western pressure concerning fulfilment of international WTO agreements.

Looking to the current imports of China and India as well as to the rest of the considered South-East Asian countries, one may observe (in Table 6) the great dependence of India from the imports of fuels, well above that of other also deeply oil-dependent countries, such as South-Korea and Japan. Note furthermore that, given the recent registered high growth rates of China, this country is becoming a much more oil-dependent one than it was some years ago. This change is already forcing a rise, or at least limiting a downwards trend of oil (and other raw material) prices.

Significant growth of oil prices could initially be a problem for both China and India, although also for the rest of players, thus likely inducing in the mid-term a general resumption of the inflation rate, and in long term a change of the relative prices of energy and other raw materials. Unquestionably, the necessary global adjustment to the new relative prices of energy, could establish an additional obstacle to the global growth of the planet, thus probably

329. The figure of Brazil (4.8 per cent) was a little higher than that of China.

redistributing, again in favour of China and India—due to their great competitiveness—the current geography of trade and development.

5.3.6. Position of China and India in the Interchange of Services

While the trade of goods in Asia has experienced a very significant rise in the last 40 years and in particular in the last decade, the gains of China have proven to be almost un-stoppable in the last two decades, moving from a world share in total exports of 1.2 per cent in 1983 to a figure of 5.9 per cent in 2003. This represents a shift much more relevant than that experienced by India,[330] which in the last 20 years has only moved from 0.5 per cent to 0.7-0.8 per cent of total world exports.

Nevertheless the evolution of the internationally traded services has been rather different; and not only in relation to Asia but also concerning the comparative positions of China and India.

First of all we have to underline that the evolution of the share in total exports and imports of services in Asia as a whole, has positively evolved in the 90s, although with a trend to a stagnation in the second half of the mentioned decade. Note additionally that while in the last 20 years the global international movements of goods of Asia were positively balanced, the international flows of services have shown in the 90s a non-negligible deficit in the region.

In relation to China, one has to note that its share in the total exported services has significantly moved upwards along the 90s, reaching in 2002 a figure similar to that of India (2 per cent); and this while China began the 90s with a lower share than India in the total world exports of services (0.7 per cent *versus* 1.2 per cent). However, while India has in any moment along the 90s kept a positive balance of services, the case of China has been rather different turning in the second half of the 90s into a deficit position.

It is noteworthy that while the current share of India in the total world export of services is 2 per cent, its quota in total world exports of goods is only of 0.7-0.8 per cent. This means that in the

330. Note that recently the case of the Chinese exports is one of simple and constant acceleration. In the year 2003, the Chinese share in total world exports has moved to 5.9 per cent from 5.2 per cent in the year 2002. Observe that the gained share by China "only in 2003" is practically equivalent to the current one of India.

international arena India has shown a significant comparative advantage in its export of services (particularly in IT services), an advantage that according to mainstream economists could *sine die* continue,[331] unless defensive and protective manoeuvres of the West force its stagnation.

To conclude, we have to underline that the future exports of tradeable services of China and India seems to be optimistic, as it currently happens with their trade of goods. Although of course, mentioned future exports will depend on the global development of these markets at world scale, and on possible hurdles that the West may establish to avoid outsourcing of own firms and public sectors to China and India.

5.4. The Financing Process in China and India

As we have mentioned in Chapter 2, the size of the rates of saving and investment (in GDP terms) plays a relevant role in formation of the annual growth rate of the countries.

Notwithstanding that, favourable changes for improving the deficient political and economic organisation and/or eliminating sociological and psychological habits or conceptions contrary to development, use to generate fast steps forward, thus nearing the current level of economic activity to the "frontier of production possibilities".[332] We have to say, however, that these specific and transitory accelerations of the measured GDP growth rates are exclusively a consequence of the reorganisation of the production machinery—from an inconvenient position to a more pro-market and efficient one—than a derivative of the internal forces of growth, as currently explained by the Theory of Growth (Chapter 2).

As a result, once the country is conveniently reorganised, the GDP growth rate will mainly depend on the domestic investment

331. Note that the export of services of India, is not only growing at high rates in relation to IT activities. Additional services as f.i. laboratory and other medical analysis, as well as medical treatments, which are more costly in the West, are also expanding at high speed.

332. This comment is particularly appropriate to India. In our view, a mere change in the top legal framework, favourable to the redistribution of power of Union and states for reaching a less time consuming decision making process, to the improvement of the judiciary system for shortening the litigation process, to the rescheduling of the state-elections making them simultaneous, etc., could by themselves step up the growth rate of the country up to two points throughout half a decade.

rate (be this materialised in additional physical or human capabilities), according to some patterns devised by professional economists (neo-classical model and endogenous growth theory). Note additionally that this domestic investment will have to be totally financed by internal or external savings in order to keep macroeconomic equilibria and to avoid inflation acceleration.

5.4.1. The Investment and Saving Process of China and India

To begin with, we will make some comments on the current (2002) Gross Capital Formation of the different analysed countries of our sample. As it occurs with other parameters, China is the leader of the group, having an almost stratospheric domestic rate of 40 per cent in GDP terms.[333] Note however that although Vietnam (32 per cent), Korea (26 per cent), Japan (26 per cent) and Malaysia (24 per cent) have higher domestic investment rates than that of India, the domestic investment of the latter (23 per cent) is far from negligible (Table 7).

5.4.1.1. The Case of India

The Union Government of India, conscious of the relevance of the rise of the domestic rate of investment for the acceleration of the annual growth rate up to 8 per cent, as it was programmed for the Tenth Five Year Plan (2002-07), established a target for the domestic gross investment rate of around 32 per cent, a figure very far away from that of the year 2002 (23 per cent) as already mentioned.

Given the fact that the Indian economy is far from an optimum organisation in conventional terms, the Union government intention of significantly increasing the investment rate of India for stepping-up the growth process, seems an acceptation of the intrinsic difficulties that it has to significantly reschedule the Indian economy at mid-term to reach the intended economic result (8 per cent of growth rate). Observe that this result could temporary be attained just by means of a more rational economic reorganisation of the country.

---

333. We should not forget that, historically, the economies with central planning have in general exhibited higher figures for the registered increase in "inventories", than those of the economies of market. Even more, in the latter, after the ITC revolution, the contribution of stocks piling to the investment is significantly lower than before.

Now then, to achieve the mentioned rate of domestic investment in a balanced way, it is indispensable at the same time to rise the internal savings rate and/or the external one (mainly made up by FDI, Portfolio investments, credits from abroad, etc.). Consequently, to achieve a GDP growth rate of 8 per cent in India without a meaningful economic reorganisation, it will be necessary to raise the Gross Domestic Saving (in 2002 around 22 per cent), with no less than 5 per cent points in GDP terms. Only with this boost in domestic savings and with an additional enlargement of the received foreign capital up to 5 per cent points in GDP terms from the recent level of around 2.5 points, it could be possible to reach the programmed figure of 32 per cent.

However, we think that these figures will be difficult to be accomplished in the programmed period. Indeed, without a greater and *sustained*[334] growth rate and without a significant reduction of the population growth rate, the private savings of Indian families cannot meaningfully grow. On the other hand, the fiscal and expenditure situation of the country is rather difficult, with a sustained deficit of around 9-10 per cent in GDP terms,[335] reason why to expect significant increases in public savings—recently (2002-03) in negative position—is not expectable either[336] unless the Union government initiates a drastic fiscal reform to noteworthy increase fiscal sufficiency.

Note additionally that the total expenditure of the Union government in 2001 was only of the tune of 13 per cent of the GDP,[337] too low a figure for the setting up of a modern public service

334. Note that the evolution of the growth rate in India uses to be highly fluctuating, due to the large contribution of its agriculture—of very variable results according to variations of the monsoon rains—to the formation of GDP.

335. The total Indian public deficit in 2003-04 may have reached a figure of around 9-10 per cent. However, we believe that last fiscal year has been exceptional. This means that in future the Indian deficit could come back to old figures (10-11 per cent) if second generation reforms are not undertaken or they do not perform.

336. The constant discussion in Indian newspapers and official meetings on the capacity of the so-called disinvestment process (privatisation) to reduce the public deficit use to be a typical case of economic mis-focussing. Many a time, these discussions centre on the obtained revenues to partially cover the current public deficit by means of selling profitable public firms, and not on the more favourable aim of getting rid of the sick firms in order to annually save in the future subsidies transferred from government to these sick public units.

337. This is a figure taken from WB. (2004) *World Development Indicators.*

capable of a sufficient provision of indispensable public and merit goods. In particular, if the Union has to face interests payments which are equivalent to 28 per cent of the expenditure and 37 per cent of the current revenue,[338] and has to promote a conventional Social Security which currently is in an embryonic situation.

Finally, although the long term prospect of India is optimistic from several points of view, this does not mean that the current problems of "business environment," with which foreign investors have to deal, have been overcome. This is the reason why much more affluent inflows of FDI and Portfolio Investment are not expectable.

Certainly the relevant differences among the current figures of internal and external savings of India and the expected ones by the Indian Planning Commission for the period 2002-07, seem to us not easy to be bridged. Indeed the saving figures projected by the Planning Commission appear to be very optimistic and rather inconsistent with the backlog of pending reforms. Note also that the over-success of the Indian economy in the fiscal year 2003-04—growing at an average of 8-9 per cent—has had more to do with the favourable past monsoon[339] than with the necessary corrections to be introduced, or with the significant increase of the investment ratio, to reasonably follow the more successful and steady economic growth of China.

5.4.1.1.1. Bad Performance of India in Relation to FDI

Since India is in great disadvantage to China concerning its internal growth capacity, due to its significantly lower domestic savings rate (22 per cent *versus* 43.7 per cent), India should encourage the external contribution of foreign savings in order to additionally finance a greater domestic investment rate and to accelerate its catching-up process.

Unfortunately, the traditional misgivings towards foreign financing—rooted in the nationalistic Nehruvian principles which

338. No other country among those considered in Table 7 had such a big burden of interests than India.

339. In a country in which the agriculture contributes 23 per cent to the GDP, a shift from a situation of two or three successive droughts to another of good rains, may have resulted in an agricultural growth rate around 9-10 per cent in last fiscal exercise.

shaped economic policies up to 1991— followed by a over-cautious approach of India in this issue after 1991, placed the country in a second tier position in relation to the geographical priorities of FDI, which decidedly continued leaning to China.

If we add to these traits the many a time hesitant applications of FDI rules in the 90s, the legal formulation of some backtracks concerning stimulation of FDI, and successive Union budget discussions[340] in which so-called "roll backs" have been more rules than exception,[341] the confidence of foreign investors on the future "profitability" of their business in India had to fade.

Following the example of China although with a huge delay, India has finally recognised the "convenience" of the creation of economic enclaves—the so-called Special Economic Zones—in which FDI "might" enjoy relevant economic advantages. This has been a significant step forward in encouraging FDI, given the traditional and converse propensity of the Indian administration to negatively discriminate foreign investors (charging them higher corporate tax rates, power prices, etc.), as a consequence of frustrations over negative practises carried out by foreign capitalists in colonial times.

It is noteworthy that, again as a consequence of the distribution of power in India, many states have initiated a competition among each other for offering the best conditions to FDI, while at times forgetting the need for urgent improvement of local "business environmental conditions."

Anyway, we do believe that in the current decade, due to the exaggeration of the emphasis put by FDI in China—where many MNC are already facing insufficient internal demands and decreasing profits—and following the correction of the adverse Indian treatment of FDI, the FDI directed to India will necessarily grow in terms of the GDP, thus overcoming the meagre figure of less than 1 per cent of

---

340. In last years, formulation of Budget Drafts by the Union Government containing interesting fiscal reforms and many other rules concerning external opening, has frequently occurred. Nevertheless, many a time relevant proposals have finally been dismissed before being enacted. This has been a consequence of political pressure of members of the ruling coalition in government, trade unions, industrial lobbies, etc.

341. Since 2000, the problem of the insufficiency of the states budgets has made it difficult to reach a consensus on the creation of a general VAT.

the Indian GDP[342] registered during the 90s. This will additionally help India to increase its GDP growth rate, provided that India continues with its second generation reforms.

5.4.1.2. The Case of China

Although we have paid attention to the financial case of China in Chapter 3, we will now enter into additional considerations. Indeed, besides its frightening (for competitors) Gross Domestic Savings rate, situated in 2002 at a level of 43.7 per cent, almost the double of India, thus supporting by itself a greater long run growth capacity, China receives substantial additional inflows from abroad (in particular FDI). All this generates a total financing capacity which by far surpasses the current domestic investment needs, thus forcing China to be an international net lender.[343]

Notwithstanding the great propensity of families[344] and private firms in China (many of them familiar) to save, it is clear that the Chinese Central government, after the process of dismantling a significant part of its public firms sector, has paradoxically become a tiny "full socialist" government that counts with a small capacity for public saving, while it generates a significant public deficit (3-4 per cent in GDP terms). And this whereas its expenditures (10.9 per cent) are even lower (in GDP terms) than that of the Indian Union government (13 per cent).[345]

Although we do not forget that the Chinese GDP is almost 2.5 times that of India, which enables the government of China to spend and fund much more public services in absolute and per capita terms than India, actually the mentioned figure of 10.9 per cent is the

342. In 2001, FDI in India reached the figure of 3.2 per cent only in terms of total domestic investment (10.1 per cent in China). In 2002, Indian FDI reached 0.6 per cent only in GDP terms (3.9 per cent in China). All these figures of India have recently registered "statistical" increase, due to the inclusion of the reinvestments in the total figure of FDI.

343. The mentioned financial unbalance of China, with total (internal plus external) available savings overcoming the needs of its high domestic investment (40 per cent in 2002), generates a significant accumulation of reserves, today reaching a figure of around US $ 650 bn., that has partially to be lent to the US for the financing of its public deficit. Note, consequently, that in this regard China is partially substituting the traditional US external financial function of Japan.

344. In absence of a conventional Social Security system, families have necessarily to save for their retirement.

345. These are figures of World Bank (2004). *World Development Indicators.*

lowest of all the countries considered in the list of Table 7. Note however that although China lacks a conventional Social Security, as India does, the former has the advantage (in comparison to India) of counting with protection granted to citizens by the economic and political system as a whole.

5.4.2. *The Role of Domestic Credit and Stock Exchanges in Private Financing*

An indicator of the role played by domestic credit in the support of private production, is the ratio of the volume of credit granted to private firms, over the corresponding GDP.

In relation to this indicator it is noticeable that, although China continues being the largest socialist economic system on Earth, the support of its "deficient" public banking system to private firms is one of the most relevant of the listed countries (Table 7)[346]. Only Japan, Malaysia, UK and the US clearly surpasses it, while the Chinese domestic credit is significantly more supportive to private firms than the domestic banking systems of Korea and Singapore.

In comparison to the high value of this ratio in China, currently placed at a figure of 136.5 per cent, the position of India with a figure of 32.6 per cent is, with the exception of Indonesia, the most deficient of all considered countries (Table 7). This is a figure that clearly points out that the privatisation process in India has a long way ahead, and that the continuous resort of the Indian public industrial sector and public administration to the banking system for seeking domestic financing, makes up an additional hurdle for the development of the private one.

Although it is clear that in India, as it has occurred in many countries of the world, the progression of banking de-intermediation has become an indisputable fact, we find that in India the current ratio (2002) of market capitalisation of the stock exchanges in GDP terms (25.7 per cent), is with that of Indonesia and Malaysia, the lowest of all listed countries (Table 7). The low Indian value of this

346. This comment and allied, are based on the figures provided by World Bank (2004), *World Development Indicators*. Although it is always difficult, the evaluation of the accuracy of the available information concerning the Chinese economy, we have paid more attention to this figure than to others also published, because we have found it more consistent with the rest of the picture.

indicator may be another sign of the difficulties undergone by Indian listed private firms for gathering sufficient private financing to conveniently thrust their activities.

In this regard, the case of China, which reflects a figure of 36.6 per cent of capitalisation in GDP terms, though less dramatic than that of India, is also another indicator of a long term under-funding of private projects for launching "big business initiatives" in China.

5.5. External Net Position of China and India and Implications for the Future

Although we have mentioned in Chapters 3 and 4 the current solid positions of China and India in relation to their foreign creditors, we will here refer to certain lateral derivatives of their policies related with the issue.

First of all we have here to underline the huge relative volume of the international reserves accumulated by China and also by India (let us remember that at mid-2005 they were of the tune of 650 and 135 billion of US dollars respectively). Note that this is a shift that follows the policy of reserves over-accumulation, for long practised by Japan.[347]

Certainly, if we compare the available international reserves (in 2002) with the annual imports of the analysed countries (Table 8), we have to conclude that the relative volume of kept reserves was maximum in Japan (1.14), followed by those of China (0.90) and India (0.87). Although these high foreign reserve positions of the mentioned countries have gathered criticism from a financial point of view,[348] we consider that in the case of China and India their cautious positions are entirely supported by an economic and political rationale based on a long run prospect.

In this matter we should not forget that China and India are embarked in a speedy process for catching up. As far as possible and

347. As the reader may observe (Table 8) the Gross International Reserves of Japan reached the figure of US 469 billions in 2002, equivalent to 1.14 times annual imports. These figures are taken from WB (2004). *World Development Indicators.*

348. Note for instance that this ratio has levels in the Western countries of around 0.1-0.2, with a minimum in the UK of 0.09.

for their own convenience, this process should be independent of the international business cycle. In this regard, if conversely, these two countries had scant positions of available international reserves, when the Western economy entered in a slowdown situation or in recession—let us remember that, for the moment, the Western countries (US and EU) are the main customers of China and India—their trade revenues would dwindle, and thus their capabilities for increasing imports at the velocity required by own internal markets would be choked by lack of external demand.

As a result, the practised policy of reserves "over-accumulation" by China and India, far from being a waste of resources, as many commentators use to say, could alternatively be considered as a wise strategy, framed in a long term prospect from the point of view of the business cycle. And also from the perspective of keeping these two countries away from disturbances stemming from policies eventually forced by IMF (remember the case of Russia in the 90s) in case of appearance of external unbalances.[349]

There are, however additional reasons whereby China and India cannot run the risk of maintaining relatively short volumes of foreign reserves. We are here referring to the weakness of the financial system of China,[350] and to the problems that suddenly could appear in India if Deposits and Portfolio Investments realised by Non-Resident Indians, would flow out as a consequence of a lost of confidence in the short term capabilities of the country to instantly meet demands of foreign exchange.

Connected with all this are the problems of the exchange rate controls practised by China and India. The first country has for years remained pegged to the dollar (at 8.28 Yuan one US dollar), and the second has administered the value of the Indian Rupee, in consistency with the desired foreign reserves accumulation. In recent months, the EU-US authorities have tried to force the Chinese

349. Observe that to some extent, South Korea, and Taiwan also follow this policy of reserves over-accumulation.

350. We have here to mention the huge indebtedness of the sick public Chinese firms with the domestic banking system, the viability of which has many a time unduly put under suspicion. Although in India, something alike could have happened in recent years, we think that the seriousness of the so-called "non-performing credits" held by Indian public banks, is much lesser than that of China (probably under 10 per cent of their assets).

financial authorities to re-value the Yuan against the dollar and the Euro, but with scant success.

The lack of interest of the Chinese authorities in a Yuan revaluation has to do not only with their desire of accumulation of reserves—as we have already mentioned—but also with the need of preservation of the rapid growth rate of China by means of a fast growth of its exports for encouraging the creation of internal employment.[351]

Finally, we should not forget a new situation that probably will appear in next decades in relation to the dollar-pattern currently applicable to most international economic transactions. In this regard we do believe that the dollar pattern, and the "seigniorage rights" stemming from it, favourable today to the US,[352] will progressively degrade in future to the extent that two huge countries as China and India—will jointly accumulate bigger GDP and international transactions than individually most of the rest, including US.

In this faraway framework, the process of over-accumulation of foreign reserves (mainly in US dollars) recently undertaken by these two big countries, although currently useful for softening cyclical problems coming from abroad, will become progressively worthless, specially for China. This is because in next decades the Yuan, will necessary become a substantial part of the then international monetary system. Let us not forget that, at present, the dollar is at the centre of the international monetary system, due to the comparative and indisputable strength of its economy, and not because of its accumulated volume of foreign exchange, which is comparatively low (Table 8).

351. Note that a revaluation of the Yuan would force a reduction of the Chinese exports and an increase of the Chinese imports, and consequently a reduction of the Aggregate Demand of Chinese goods and services, thus inducing a lesser creation of employment, being this opposite to the interest of the government.

352. As calculated, the nominal value of US-dollar notes circulating outside the US, which are credit titles that never are presented to the debtor (US), generates for the US a seigniority right of around 0.1 per cent of the US GDP. Incidentally we will mention that this is a figure equivalent to the current "called" ODA provided by US to some developing countries, that the US mainly uses to achieve its geopolitical targets.

5.6. Current Internal Obstacles and Economic Perspectives of China and India

Once we have reflected on the current situation of the Chinese and Indian parameters related to human development (not very exciting, particularly those of India), and on recent comparative evolution of the main macroeconomic variables of China and India (some of them threatening Western competitors), we will now review some internal political and economic hindrances that the two Asian upcoming giants will have to deal with.

5.6.1. Political Problems of China and India

5.6.1.1. The Case of China

Many a time one hears in the West that the alleged brilliant economic future of China—as some econometricians have recently forecasted—could be arrested by coming internal political problems.

In this regard it is frequently said that, from one moment onwards, the growing political demands of a society progressively richer, will generate a pro-democratic movement in China that will change its current style of doing politics. Such a movement, after the creation of democratic institutions—parliament open to all parties, independent trade unions, etc.—would politically and economically homologate China to the West, depriving China from its current "comparative advantage" of rapid decision making and management of the core economic variables for development (as the domestic saving rate, labour wages, etc.). As a derivative, according to suggestions of some authors, the new political process would by itself curb the fast speed of the economic progress of China.

Nevertheless, there are other authors, perhaps more piercing in their insight, who think that along the last decades of economic progress the freedom of Chinese citizens has already significantly changed for the better[353] and that a stratum of "middle and high class" with substantial purchase power has emerged. Although members of this stratum have undertaken shy political initiatives, many a time smoothly channelled through the CCP, most of them have remained

353. Note that in comparison to the Maoist period, the Chinese citizens, particularly in the urban areas, may travel inside and outside the country, may choose their own studies, may move from one job to another (in the urban private sector), may access to a variety of cultural expressions, etc.

extremely cautious in the political arena. This may have happened because the new middle and high class Chinese citizens are well aware of two traits of the current economy that, if inconveniently managed, could adversely affect them: 1) the recent propensity of the personal income distribution to worsen, a phenomenon which has precisely profited these urban middle and high income strata; and 2) the restriction of the external sector, since this sector, as one of the main determinants of the future economic progress of China,[354] could experience derailing from its current trajectory causing generalised welfare losses, if a sudden and disorganised democratisation movement would start. These are reasons why some observers, remarking that political opposition is practically non-existent, do not expect any alternative to the CCP in the short-mid term.

However it is clear that it will become more and more difficult to maintain a progressive capitalistic economy in a stiff socialist political framework. Consequently, it is doubtless that China will have to advance towards a more democratic political system. Steady and significant economic growth, progressive international integration and, above all, *freer information* will be variables which will bring democracy to China. A democratic transition which, according to some observers, will be managed in due time by the CCP.[355]

To finalise reflections on the main "internal" political problems of China, we have to consider the issue of Taiwan, in the mainland referred to as the "renegade province." In our view and comparing sizes of mainland China and Taiwan, be this in inhabitants, or in GDP (PPP) terms, or in international clout, the reunification—with perhaps a long transition period as implemented in 1997 in Hong-Kong—is a simple matter of time. In particular, given the overwhelming expectations for the future of the Chinese economy.[356]

---

354. Had not existed this "foreign sector" limitation, the political repression after the Tiananmen Square revolt, would have been much harder than it was.

355. Indeed we have the reference of Taiwan—another Chinese society—in which the transition to democracy was done in the beginning of the 90s by the KMT (the party created at the beginning of the 20th Century in the mainland, after the fall of the Empire), which won the first general elections and also the recent one. It is plausible that in the People' Republic of China a similar process takes place in due time. On the other hand, the necessary strong bet that China should do in its own interest to internationally encourage a UN democratisation, could additionally force this country to initiate its own democratisation process.

356. Note however that the Taiwan issue could be used by the hegemonic power as a pretext to politically or economically arrest the rapid progression of China.

5.6.1.2. The Case of India

In relation to India, which from its inception has always been a democracy—although to say the truth, not a fully informed democracy due to the existing number of illiterates[357]—we also find some non-negligible problems. The main one is that of Kashmir. From time to time this conflict looks as if it is near to be solved and one may hope that the current ongoing negotiations between India and Pakistan will finally finish with a durable peace for all.[358]

Although India has not to undergo a transition to democracy, which in principle is an advantage in comparison to China, even the Indians acknowledge that the top legal framework that today rules the country generates some dysfunction. Note however that legal changes related to relevant issues could also bring political adjustments which could introduce some difficulties into the Indian economy.

The Indian Constitution establishes the financial relations between the Union and the states, while it distributes the different competencies among them.[359] It is understandable that at the time of the approval of the Indian Constitution, a significant autonomy was given to the states in relation to indirect taxation. At that stage, given the economic underdevelopment of the different states and the overwhelming relevance of agriculture in the GDP formation, combined with a petty inter-states commerce, the significant autonomy of the states had little influence on the allocation of resources.

Today the case is totally different. Significant improvements of infrastructure, transports and communications have made possible that the internal market of India is now growing at quick pace. Therefore, if the Indian government wants to accelerate economic

---

357. Reaching a figure in 2002 of 31 per cent of the male adult population.

358. Unfortunately, in all confictive proccess of long duration, the longer the duration the larger the number of people proffesionally "involved" in them, and the wider and abundant their political stances. This creates a complex structure of politicians, to some extent reluctant to agreements, because if they eventually solve the problem, most of them will massively go to the dole. This induces maximalist behaviour and planning, conducive to deadlocks in negotiations which use to feed back the problem. This may be the case in Kashmir as well as in Palestine.

359. In particular, there are some concurrent competencies among Union and states that are in need of a redefinition for improving efficiency.

progress, it is time to modify the financial autonomy of the states. Important in this regard is that states should be authorised to overrate[360] part of the direct taxation (income tax), while all of them should homogenise the general indirect taxes, in order to promote a unique market throughout India. Since no one of poorest states should however lose financial resources, due to relative poverty and current problems of sufficiency, we consider as urgent to reach a consensus on the rates of general indirect taxes currently controlled by the states and, simultaneously, to enact an objective "grant-in-aid system" for the whole Union.[361]

According to complaints coming from some states, the use of grants and loans in the last decades has resulted in a complete domination of the Union government[362] which sometimes has generated biased behaviour in funding when political parties in charge at state level were not coinciding with the one (or those) in charge in the Union government. Conversely, Union government is regularly complaining about financial irresponsible behaviour of

360. Under this scheme the fiscal revenues stemming from the income tax would have two segments. The main one, roughly coinciding with the current rates (personal income tax) would be administered by Union government. On the same fiscal basis the states should be authorised at will to establish surcharges, this being the second segment of the income taxation.

361. In our opinion the complaints of States when the Union government is trying to modernise the indirect taxation are not tenable. Keeping different rates on sales taxes, or even the *octroi*—a tax which is in files many decades ago in developed countries—is simply nonsense. Logically, as the indirect taxes and their rates can not be homogenised without guaranteeing the sufficiency of the poorest states and the solidarity among all of them, a superior norm for making an objective and stable "grant-in-aid" system, should be simultaneously introduced.

362. Note that the Indian Constitution attributed to the Union Government competencies on banking system, railways and ports, national planning, exploitation of mineral resources, regulation of foreign trade, etc. besides of course defence. The states had to deal with maintenance of law and order, irrigation, road transport, energy, etc. as well as education and health facilities, promotion of agriculture etc.

In order to carry out the mentioned responsibilities, the constitution provided different types of financial resources. The Union would mainly administer income tax on people and corporations, plus excise duties and customs duties (all of them being flexible when development occur, except customs taxes which tend to reduce its revenues when tariffs go down). And for the states, the land would constitute the most important base of taxation, which being fix and inflexible would produce in time insufficiency, thus forcing the states either to increase other attributed indirect taxes (as tax State excise duties, duties on electricity rates, motor vehicles tax, etc.), thus breaking the unity of the Indian market, or to demand grants and loans to the Union government for balancing their budgets. This last way of financing—without lasting and stable revenue sharing rules—gave the Centre the opportunity for dominating the states.

states, which in last years have contributed, legally or in a veiled way, to the increase of the total public sector deficit. And this while the Union—as suggested by others—has invaded or complemented, in particular in issues of law and order, constitutional competencies of the states.[363] Obviously, this dissatisfaction on both sides indicates that India should consider the administrative and fiscal reorganisation of the Federation.

Another issue which seems to be in need of urgent reform in India is the working of the justice system, and its derivative of the current long litigation process, one of the longest in the world.[364] Unfortunately, and for different reasons, the Indian system of justice is infuriatingly slow,[365] reason why in the business world the habit of gathering a complete set of guarantees for avoiding possible juridical disputes has emerged, consequently, as the current performance of the justice system also prejudices the expansion of commercial credit (and also the institutional one), so vital for the stepping up of the development process, the justice system should urgently be reorganised.

Last but not least we share the opinion that the current status of private property is another issue to be modified in India as well as in China. Taking into consideration the different historical backgrounds of these countries, as well as their differences in political organisation, we do believed that in China private property recognition has to advance, while private property in India should be less revered than currently is. Private property has to be enjoyed by individuals, as an stimuli for the wealth accumulation (in China), but also more submitted to the common interest (in India).

---

363. Since Independence, the Centre has been gradually extending its functions. Some opine that it has been done to keep the states relatively depending on it; others claim that the Union has taken some constitutional responsibilities from the states because their performance in some activities has been deficient. In other cases, the Union has to recognise that, just for political convenience (building up coalitions), it has duplicated the number of departments, that have no real functions to perform, as for instance in the fields of education and health, which Constitutionally are competencies of the states.

364. Periods of up to more than 10 years to recover the money in bankrupt cases is simply a mockery of the creditors rights. In this field India is regrettably the leader of the world, accompanied by Brazil and Chad. Vide World Bank (2004:262). *World Development Indicators.*

365. The Indians inherited from the British a very slow justice system, which by itself favours the richer or the more powerful of litigating parties.

Finally we expect that the mentioned top legal modifications in India, plus the rescheduling of state elections performing them simultaneously in all states, would radically change the mood of Indian private entrepreneurs and FDI directed to this country, which would help India to position itself on a different and higher path for growth in benefit of its large poor population.

5.6.2. Additional Economic Problems of China and India and Opportunities

Although different in their political organisation but sharing similar social concerns since their inception as countries, China and India also have to deal in the short-mid term with additional and alike problems: 1) the underdevelopment of their public sector, particularly in relation to a practically non-existent or very incipient Social Security; 2) Their reliance on foreign supply of certain raw materials, in particular on oil, a dependence which is much more visible in India; 3) The current trend in both countries towards a worsening of personal income distribution as a consequence of the recent rapid growth rates, tilted to the development of the private sector; and 4) their deficient banking systems.

In front of these common economic problems, these two big countries have an opportunity never enjoyed by any other country in the world history: their large and long lasting growth capacity in the future, based on their huge populations which are mostly stuck to elemental agricultural activities. As expectable, in due time these economically "vacant" factors will be transferred to the non-agricultural sectors, a transfer which only will require adequate financing. Note that this financial operation has an almost absolute guarantee of success, given the lower and long-lasting relative wages in these two countries.

5.6.2.1. On the Necessary Correction of the Fiscal Systems

In relation to the alleged underdevelopment of their public sectors, we have first of all to underline the scant tax-revenues of these two countries in GDP terms in comparison to the rest of the analysed countries. Indeed the case of China is different from that of India, although not so much.

Both countries decided in the very moment of their inception that the industrial public sector would be the core sector for economic progress, and that it should be promoted by the state. This meant that practically almost all profits of the main industrial activities of these two countries would at the end be driven as non-tax revenues to the public sector budgets.

If we add to this initial and sustained approach, the low per capita levels of an overwhelming majority of these two nations, the huge number of people working in subsistence conditions (outside the market), the limited taxation to services—a reminiscence of the socialist approach to economics—and later on the initiated process of privatisation, earlier in China than in India, their current low comparative levels of "fiscal load" in GDP terms is not difficult to understand.

These tax revenues were in 2001-2002 (only for central governments) of the tune of 7-8 per cent in China[366] and of 10 per cent in India, figures very faraway even from those of the rest of the analysed Asian countries (Table 8). This trait reveals the "different nature" of the Indian and Chinese economies in comparison to the rest.[367]

Both countries are now embarked in significant public deficits, even though they have not developed a formal Social Security.[368] These deficits, that could be of the tune of 3-4 per cent in China and 9-10 per cent in India, both in GDP terms, are rather structural (not cyclical). As a consequence, if both countries want to develop their public sectors—in particular a Social Security system—and avert in the mid-long term the subsequent reactivation of the inflation, they will have to reform the tax structure progressively, and the level of

366. Vide WB (2004:274) World Economic Indicators. If we take into account the entire public sector the figure for China would be around 17-18 per cent. Vide National Bureau of Statistics (2003) China Statistical Yearbook.

367. Note for instance that the available figures of UK and Italy—of the tune of 35 per cent of their GDP—have to do with the relevance of their Central Administrations in raising taxes in these two countries, and with the higher degree of their development.

368. We have already mentioned in Chapters 3 and 4 the partial systems of Social Security that a very limited number of Chinese and Indian workers enjoy. They are mainly workers of the public firms in China or Chinese civil servants; or just functionaries or labourers working in the organised sector in India, which only employs 8 per cent of total working population.

the tax rates in order to achieve financial sufficiency in consistency with economic efficiency in microeconomic markets.

One should not forget that the rapid growth of these two countries will facilitate the achievement of the necessary reforms. Reforms that will be easier to implement in China, since its political organisation is more prone to rapid and efficient action than that of India.

5.6.2.2. Energy and Income Distribution Problems

A second relevant problem that China and India will have to confront and solve in the near future, is the one referring to their growing needs of oil.[369] We have already made some remarks on the issue, but the most important one is that India and China, should politically ensure the provision of oil for the next decades. This will be vital for their economic progress since growing oil deficits of these two giants could provide outsiders with the means of cooling down their rapid catching up process.

The third significant problem that China and India will have to address is that of the recent worsening of their income distribution. The case of China is actually paradoxical because this is a country, for more than half a century commanded by a communist party, the CCP, that undertook the revolution under chairman Mao precisely to improve the income distribution and to rescue the country from the feudalist rulers of those days. Surprisingly this CCP, after the two failed *magnum* experiments towards real socialism—Great Leap Forward and Cultural Revolution—decided to partially change its economic model, entering into a process of cautious and progressive privatisation while starting its opening to international trade and financing.

All of us know the spectacular aggregate economic results achieved by China, with annual growth rates of near 10 per cent during more than two decades. However this rate is just an average that does not explain the distribution evolution. Although we only know the evolution of the Gini indicator in the last years, and not

369. Note that the case of India is much more serious than that of China. India starts today from a very low level in electricity production and per capita consumption, and it has to import most of the used fuel for different purposes, thus being very dependent on oil imports for the continuation of its development process.

that of the last two decades,[370] there is a general consensus shared by Chinese authorities and multinational institutions, on the direction of the internal income distribution: this has significantly worsen (although, of course, in consistency with a significant reduction of the relative volume of poverty).

Indeed this negative evolution of the personal distribution of income does not come as a surprise for professional economists, because this is an expectable derivative from the first phase of a capitalistic economy, when it starts its development process with an almost non-limited supply of industrial labour, as explained in Chapter 2, following the Lewis model.[371]

Specifically, we have to say that in China around 800 million people who live in the countryside have been relatively left behind the recent boom. A boom that has basically taken place in the coastal regions, and mainly in the SEZ (Special Economic Zones) and other special areas for the promotion of business, as we have explained in Chapter 3. These areas not only have attracted relevant FDI but also have siphoned financial resources from other areas through the financial and fiscal systems.

To the extent that China will annually need around 10 million new jobs just to keep pace with the labour force growth—and it would need much more jobs to step up the necessary transfer of human resources to the urban non-agricultural sectors, something rather difficult to achieve according to the recent history of Chinese employment creation—we do believe that, a durable trend to the worsening of the personal income distribution in China is, *ceteris paribus*, expectable.

Due to the fact that this trend towards adverse movement along the Kuznets-curve of income distribution is manifest, it should be a priority that the Chinese government additionally redistribute part of

370. We have already made some comments on it in Chapter 3. The last known value of the Gini coefficient for China is of 44.7, well over (and worse) that of the US (40.8).

371. Note that in the current debate on the evolution of the international convergence of per capita incomes, it has recently been said that, there is a case of non-convergence in the period of globalisation if we exclude the case of China (and vice-versa if we include China). Vide *The Economist* of 16th April 2004. However this seems to us non-rigorous because one cannot use the evolution of the weighted per capita GDP average of the different countries to deduce a case of unconditional convergence, if the evolution of the personal distribution of income within the different countries is not considered.

the fruits of the economic development in order to keep the "social tenability" of the chosen mix model. Otherwise social peace would not be completely guaranteed, which could be detrimental for the continuation of the boom till now registered. Indeed, it would be better to grow 2-3 per cent points less and to improve distribution than to maximise growth with more and more people left behind for a longer period.

The case of India seems to be rather similar to that of China with reference to the evolution of the personal income distribution and the fight against poverty. Although the National Accounts Statistics of India do not generate any data on the evolution of income distribution among household or persons,[372] there are some indicators that prove a regression in the personal distribution of income (although in consistency with an effective reduction of poverty, certified by official and international sources).

First of all an urban and rural break up in India is observable.[373] Available data reveal that the urban-rural disparity of per capita incomes grew at least in the 80s[374]. On the other hand, if we consider the disparity ratio between the maximum per capita income of the state of Punjab and the minimum per capita income of Bihar, we find that this disparity grew enormously in the 90s, moving from 2.74 to 4.6.[375] Consequently also in India a better redistribution of the fruits of development is a priority; although at a considerably lesser speed than China (given the lower Gini value of the former) in order not to reduce the progression capacities of the Indian economy. Logically this is an additional argument for stepping up the second generation reforms in India, as well as to reform some aspects of the top legal Indian framework.

5.6.2.3. The Banking Systems of China and India

One additional problem of these two countries is their banking systems. While the Chinese banking system is clearly an

372. Vide, Datt, R. *et al.*, (2004:39). Book already mentioned.

373. The continuation of this urban-rural break-up, against the expectations initially created by the BJP in rural India, may have been the main cause of its electoral defeat in 2004.

374. Vide again, Datt, *et al.*, (2004: 38) Book already mentioned.

375. Vide again Datt, *et al.*, (2004:467). Book already mentioned.

underdeveloped one, the Indian banking system is predominantly in need of updating the instruments used to fulfil the formulated targets. Specifically, as a derivative of the continuation of the "Five Year Plans" implementation in India, and in order to fulfil these Plans, a system of sectorial loans and privileged credit lines or ratios[376] is periodically defined and enforced.

Although we perfectly know the situation of the Indian Banking System—let's remember that the Reserve Bank of India publishes practically all the necessary details to accurately understand the situation and working of the banking institutions and that of the economy of India—the same does not happen in China. Regarding the latter, the available information is fragmented and contradictory and this makes it difficult to formulate a consistent judgement on its working. In any case the degree of the development of the Chinese banking system is in significant delay with respect to that of India, and even in larger delay with respect to the rest of liberalising policies undertaken in China along the last 25 years. Perhaps the existence of a "two speeds" China explains the mentioned dysfunction of the banking system.

On the eve of the reform, which started in 1978, China only had three public banks and a bad fledged net of elemental rural credit cooperatives. The most important of these banks, the People's Bank of China, changed its status in 1984, becoming a real emission bank and consequently the regulator of the banking system. The remaining two (Bank of China and China Construction Bank), plus the Industrial and Commercial Bank of China and the Agricultural Bank of China, both of new creation,[377] became the core of the current Chinese banking system (the so-called "big four"). In the late-80s and 90s new commercial banks (national or regional) were created, of which some were of private nature (f.i. the Minsheng

376. As theorists of banking proclaim, these lines or ratios do not work properly, because the money is fungible, thus every segment finally financing other issues different to those politically pursued. And this whereas the imposed segmentation generates additional costs.

377. In 1984, taking over the commercial banking functions of the People's Bank of China—which then became the Central Bank— the Industrial and Commercial Bank of China, the most important of the state owned banks, was formed. This bank with the upgraded Bank of China, the China Construction Bank, and the Agricultural Bank of China, created in the late-70s, form the so-called "big four", owned by the state.

Bank). Beside these developments, several "policy banks" and a large number of rural and urban credit co-operatives were created in 1994.

Note that the mentioned "big four" public banks—the core of the banking system—currently dominate the banking activity, managing around 60 per cent of total banking assets. Needless to say that these banks are not in good shape, since a significant part of their assets is "non-performing".[378] On the other hand, the administrated interest rates charged to different operations, do not match with the different involved risks of the latter. In essence these anomalies are rather parallel to those experienced by public Indian banks, although more overdone in the Chinese case.

Although the Chinese "big four"—as well as Indian public banks—count with the guarantee of the public powers for sustainability, the allocation of financial resources carried out by them should significantly improve in both countries. Recently the Chinese government, by means of intermediate institutions,[379] has injected fresh funds into the "big four" up to an amount equivalent to 200 bn. US-dollars (in local currency), a figure equivalent to the total revenues of the Central Government in 2000. In a further attempt to improve the quality of the assets of the public banks, a complementary figure of around 30 per cent of the former one, served as a base for an interchange of bad loans for shares of the debtor public firms.[380]

Although foreign banks have recently entered in the Chinese financial market, they are restricted in action to certain geographical areas, and to certain activities, as for instance foreign currency operations realised by foreign firms in China.[381] These limitations—also partially occurring in India[382]—will progressively be relaxed,

378. In the banking business, "non-performing credits" are all over the world defined as those credits or loans which remain non-reimbursed for more than six months after maturity. Vide Andreu, J.M. (2000) *Teoría del Dinero y de la Banca*. Dickynson. Madrid.

379. In 1999 "assets management companies"—one for every one of the "big four"—were established to buy "non-performing assets" to the banks in order to write them off in their books.

380. This is an operation similar to that undertaken in Japan in several occasions, with a limited result.

381. A certain restriction on allowed activities is also currently practised in India for most of the new foreign banks, which entered in the 90s.

382. Note that in India there are several traditional foreign banks, which, established before Independence (1947), have continued doing all typical domestic banking operations, as done by Indian banks.

making it possible that in 2007, as a Chinese concession in exchange of its accession to WTO, the authorised foreign banks could start operations in Yuan with domestic borrowers.[383]

In a frame of great misgivings—as it also happens in India—the foreign banks have been discriminated by the Chinese monetary authorities, concerning expensive licensing and branching permits. Of course these discriminations reduce the profitability of the foreign banks, which however at mid-term will start gaining market share from the bad administered and inflexible local public banks. Note in this regard that many foreign banks have recently obtained significant profits in India, well over those achieved at home or in other markets abroad.

As we have briefly reviewed, there are clear parallels between the Chinese and Indian banking problems, although we do believed that the Indian system is much more familiarised with Western operations and with the mainstream theory of banking than the Chinese one, thus economically behaving better.

5.7. China, India and their Economic Future

In this Chapter, we have reviewed more in detail the current traits of the Chinese and Indian economies. In order not to lose the real perspective of these two countries we have started with a brief analysis of their main socio-economic indicators which has generated an illustrative picture of their current socio-economic situation. Note that China, and to a less extent India, after rapidly progressing in the last 25 years, have not sufficiently overcome the initial backward conditions of most of their citizens.

However, what is really frightening to Western observers is the velocity of their progression, particularly in the case of China. The

383. In May 2004, for the first time in the history of the Chinese Banking, an American institution (Newbridge Capital) has taken a stake in a Chinese bank (Shenzen Development Bank). Although the legal limit of the individual stakes is 20 per cent of total own resources, a participation as this or below—as recently signed at 18 per cent—may be more than enough as to control the institution if the rest of capital is very distributed among small shareholders, as it happens with the mentioned SDB. Note that this is not the case with other relevant private institutions as Minsheng, Shanghai Pudong Development or China Merchants, in which ownership is very concentrated. Vide *The Economist*, June 5th, 2004.

speed of China in the growth of the GDP and total exports in the last two decades, combined with the economic resurgence of India and the rest of the region, seems to be conducive to an unquestionable shift in growth and trade capacities in favour of East and South Asia. Observe that this shift will affect the West, which has scant possibilities for a "convenient" economic reaction at mid-long term. Clearly, targeting on industrial dislocation towards Asia will not be a satisfactory solution.

Indeed, the extraordinary performance in economic growth and in total international and intra-regional trade of goods of the East Asia-Pacific and South Asia regions along the 90s (1992-2002), in relation to those of the high income countries, seems to be the prelude of a relevant shift concerning the role played by these regions as engines of the world economy. And this despite the comparative much higher per capita incomes that the West will enjoy along next decades, and its even for long relevant clout in international politics.

China and India seem to be the natural leaders of this economic shift. Although the case of China is already noticeable and actually scares Western governments which do not seem to have an economic idea as to how to deal with the issue—probably because there is no favourable "neo-classical" solution—Western governments should not forget the case of India either.

In some years, if India recovers from "its lost decade", overcome the remains of its population explosion problem, and implement the rest of the pending reforms, it may share with China a leading role in economic growth and in the international trade of goods and services.[384] In this regard one should not overlook the Indian advantage over China stemming from its younger population and its quicker labour force growth rate, which could support an even faster GDP growth rate than that of China from 2013-15 onwards.[385]

384. In the last months, the qualitative and quantitative spreading of the export of services by India is also unleashing deep concern in the West. Outsourcing to India is not anymore a matter of just "call centres", "back office" and all that, but much more.

385. As proclaimed by the commented study on the economic prospects for the next 50 years, realised by Goldman-Sachs.

As a derivative of the commercial success of China and (in future) India, Western countries should not overlook the current foreign exchange reserves accumulation practised by China (and India). If the trend continues, this policy, being in principle a policy to de-link internal growth from the western business cycle, could change in two decades, or before, into a Yuan pattern for the Asian trade or even for the international trade, in demerit of the US dollar.

All this does not mean that the future economic path of China and India is going to be easy. These countries have significant internal problems, be these strictly economic, or political with economic repercussions. And these letting aside the economic or political problems that could come from abroad, which will be commented in next chapter.

From a strict political viewpoint, China has to move in the future on a delicate equilibrium between rapid growth, redistribution of incomes, and unavoidable democratisation. Although the initiation of the democratisation process at this moment does not seem to be very pressing, a more decided policy of redistribution that favours those left behind (at countryside) appears to be convenient. If this policy was not undertaken at mid-term, China could enter either into a situation of economic involution—let us remember that the negative situation of the personal income distribution could force the CCP to more decidedly act in favour of the poor by means of changing its current pro-market economic criteria—or perhaps it could "automatically" move in an accelerated way towards democracy. Two options that could be judged as inconvenient.

The case of India is rather similar, although with advantages for the Indian government because in this country democracy is well rooted. However a case for further redistribution of the fruits of development also exists in India.

Although a political reform is always by itself less traumatic than a change of the political system, something that sooner or later will occur in China, the Indians should start seriously reflecting on some legal reforms, if they actually want to step up their velocity of economic progress. Financial relations among Union and states and their respective competencies, the organisation of justice, the role of private property, and the reform of the electoral process[386] are main issues that should be reviewed.

Continuing with "internal politics," we do understand that, since the problem of Hong-Kong has been solved, the case of Taiwan is the most convoluted that China will have to confront in future. Although we believe that this case will finally be resolved with similar criteria as those applied in the case of the former British colony, we do understand that complications in international politics could appear, if other powers try to avoid the consolidation of China as the leader of Asian countries.

Letting aside former "internal" politics, and referring now to additional economic matters, we cannot forget the ones related to indispensable fiscal reforms, the setting up of conventional Social Security systems, and the corrections of the financial systems of China and India.

If these two countries want to count with enough public financing for the sufficient provision of public and merit goods, including a Social Security system, they will have to restate their fiscal systems, putting the stress on direct taxing (corporate and personal), ruling out the old taxation, and rationalising and homogenising (particularly in the case of India) the indirect taxation. And this while the established rates and broaden bases for taxation (mainly on services) will rise the fiscal contribution of taxpayers.

These reforms are urgent and indispensable for the correction of the current negative trend of income distribution, for the alleviation of fiscal deficits, and for the development of integral Social Security Systems to protect the unemployed and retirees. Of course the absence of these reforms would provoke uneasiness and so it would be counterproductive. And this when the political costs of rising taxes would be bearable in these two countries, since they would be introduced in a phased way and in a context of rapid growth.

To finalise, we will mention the need of significant corrections to be introduced in the financial systems of China and India in order to

386. The electoral process in India, with ongoing successive elections in the different states, generates a sort of constant situation of electoral campaign which, introducing additional uncertainty, averts rationality in the political decision making process.

make economic prosperity easier. In both cases, the significant involvement of banks (mainly public) in the financing of sick public units may have introduced some difficulties in the access of private firms to banking credit. The same could be said in relation to the financing of the public deficit.

Note that in China and India fiscal problems of insufficiency, with its sequels of public deficit and insufficient provision of public services, are intertwined with the non-healthy financial investments of public banks. As a result, to correct the dysfunction of their banking systems, China and India will have to implement their fiscal reforms with priority.

In conclusion, China and India are two large and highly populated countries that, although comparatively poor, are very dynamic, thus having great economic expectations for the future. Nonetheless, to gain the brilliant future that many economist forecast for them, they will have to overcome a set of internal (political and economic) problems as those mentioned above, as well as to deal with possible external hurdles that other powers could put in front of them in the coming years, to cool down their aspirations.

6

China, India and Possible Hindrances from Abroad

6.1. The International Political Context

As we have already mentioned in the Introduction, one thing is to count the extraordinary potentials that China and India possess to reach economic leadership positions at the end of the first half of the 21st century; and another is to effectively attain these privileged ranks, which would change them into political powers and top global players, as currently the US is.

6.1.1. The International Political Profile of the World

Before reflecting on the possible course of facts along next decades, it is necessary to briefly outline the current political international profile of the world.

First of all we have to underline the prominent position of the US, as the alleged hegemonic power in the world. Strongly connected to it in international political matters, we find the UK, an unenthusiastic EU-member that apparently does not want to share higher political risks with its partners, while trying to exploit all the commercial and financial advantages of the EU-market.[387] Effectively while the UK has firmly supported enlargements, it has refused some "inconveniences" which could come from the third and following stages of integration.

For long politically connected with the US, we find a relevant part of Latin America—pejoratively called "the backyard of the US"—formed by

387. Note that within the EU, UK is currently the leading-country among all those which do not want to transfer any sovereignty in matters of direct taxation, foreign representation or defence. Even in issues connected with the access to the fourth stage of European integration—the Monetary Union—the British have remained insensitive.

countries that usually adjust themselves to the US in international political matters, particularly in the UN and the Security Council.

Less important than the US in influence, we find a group of EU countries, mainly France and Germany, that although interested in the political integration of the EU, have wasted time promoting a watered down EU Constitution, while the creation of a political European power in the form of a voluntary federation among sincerely interested countries would have been a more profitable strategy. Observe that this voluntary federation could be built up in consistency with all economic treaties historically signed with the rest of partners, including the new comers of the fifth enlargement.[388]

As we have mentioned in another essay,[389] although for long rich in future, the former EU-15 area is nowadays a region in relative economic and demographic decline, with low GDP growth capacity and perceivable inability to gain relative commercial penetration in the most dynamic region of the planet, as Asia (ex-Japan) is. And this whereas the EU internal transnational trade grows less than its total world exports (the latter also growing below the world average), and while many of its most significant industrial firms have entered into a process of location abroad (European dislocation). Besides this, as a result of the political underdevelopment of common political institutions, the EU organisation as such is not but a political appendix of member states, thus less influential than some of its members (particularly UK, France and Germany).

In the other extreme of the planet we find also a comparative economic declining Japan, a country that although rich as the European countries are, seems unable to further relative progress in trade and GDP terms, as a consequence of the current and growing competition of China and South-East Asian countries. Japan has also entered into a negative demographic dynamic—with its population rapidly ageing as equally occurs in most EU countries—while many of its firms are also dislocating mainly in benefit of China. Politically Japan uses to behave as independent, although often adjusts to the US in UN affairs.

---

388. We have already explained in another essay how this consistency could be achieved. Vide Rahman. R. and Andreu, J.M. (2002:75) *A Federation with Enlargement for European Prosperity*. Rashtriya Printers. New Delhi.

389. Vide Rahman, R. and Andreu, J.M. (2002:54). Book already mentioned.

At a different layer, we find the cases of Brazil and the Russian Federation. Brazil is a country of relevant economic expectations, currently richer than China and India in per capita income terms, that nevertheless has not had a brilliant economic behaviour along last two decades (only 2.7 per cent annual GDP growth rate and 1.1 per cent in per capita terms). In international politics it nowadays plays a very independent role, as the most important country of Latin America. On the other side we find the Russian Federation, which as successor of the Soviet Union in international institutions, formally enjoys a relevant role in the UN—backed by its nuclear inheritance—while economically it has only a second tier significance, well under that of some EU-partners.

Letting aside the cases of some rich but not very populated countries (such as Canada, Australia or New Zealand), with little influence in international political affairs, we have next to refer to Africa, the "forgotten continent." In the North of Africa we find a more developed area than the Sub-Saharan one, the latter being the most underdeveloped region of the world despite its huge deposits of raw materials and rapidly growing populations.

Let us remember that most of these Sub-Saharan countries have for long been stagnant: as an average, their real per capita incomes have not grown at all in the last two decades. This has been a consequence of their fast population growth[390] combined with scant rates of investments, which by itself has created a vicious circle of underdevelopment and poverty. This bleak situation has become worse as a result of the neglect of the West, which has taken many of these countries away from its agenda, except for raw materials. This dreadful combination of circumstances has made it possible that these countries have become the main nursery of the world in ongoing unsolved civil wars. Logically, these countries have scant influence in international matters, if they do not adjust to the rich or to the non-aligned countries league. Indeed, some of them, those placed in the South-East, seem to be called to the establishment of closer political ties with rising Asia.

Note additionally that some of the North African and Middle-East (Muslim) countries, have become—since their over-abundance

390. Today significantly affected by the HIV-AIDS problem.

in oil and gas production and due to the internationally unsolved Palestine-Israel conflict—a sort of time bomb that could condition the future economic and political role of the different regions of the world. One should not overlook either the fact that many of these Muslim-Arab countries are failing in relative socio-economic progress, thus adding motives for the discontent of the poorest layers of their population. No wonder that the US and allies are worried with the matter, although managing it in a counter-productive way and without results.[391]

Finally, we have to mention the Asia (ex-Japan) case, nowadays the most dynamic region of the world in economic terms, whose more populated nations (China and India), involved in a fast catching up process, seem to be called to play a much more relevant role in international politics in the future.

6.1.2. Growing Economic Gap and Its Causes

Although according to the neoclassical economic model, flexibility in prices of goods and services and free mobility of *all* factors, will in the long run automatically tend to equalise the per capita GDP of the different countries and regions—remember the case of "unconditional convergence" as defined in Chapter 2—the reality is that there are some natural[392] and artificial barriers[393] that have averted the per capita GDP convergence.

Even though there are some non-sufficiently justified and "optimistic" conclusions on recent convergence,[394] according to the figures of Maddison the process of convergence has not worked in the world since 1870 with the exception of the "golden-age period"

391. Note that the US, while constantly neglecting the Palestinians in their recognised rights and almost unconditionally supporting Israel against the former, try nowadays to establish democracies in some Arab countries, while it supports oligarchies in others. Actually a ludicrous strategy in a world of perfect information, that has deeply undermined the prestige of the US all over the world.

392. Among natural barriers, we may quote the so-called transactional costs, and the transports and communications costs. Note that the costs of transport have dramatically fallen in the 19th and 20th centuries, and that those of communications have even more dramatically decreased in the second half of the 90s with the ICT revolution.

393. Among artificial barriers we could quote those of tariff and non-tariff protection to trade, and prohibitions to the freer mobility of the human and capital factors.

394. In particular that realised by Sala-i-Martin, already quoted lines above.

of capitalism (1950-73). Therefore, the non-convergence has also become a fact in the neo-liberal era (1973-98), also called the "age of globalisation," in which the disparity of the per capita GDP of the different regions of the world has ascended to a ratio of 19:1 in 1998, from another of 13:1 in 1973.

As a consequence, the naked reality observed in the "age of globalisation" is that despite fabricated expectations on convergence of the per capita GDP of the different regions of the world by means of progressive (but selective and asymmetric) liberalisation, convergence has not become a reality,[395] although the absolute number of poor has dropped.[396]

Of course this adverse result does not mean that the international community should get rid of the current economic model to guide international economic transactions. Conversely, what it should do is to get rid of its dysfunction and inefficiencies while introducing a more rational approach to it with a political priority for catching up and social sustainability of the poorest countries in a reasonable time-span.

In this regard, inaccurate thinking and biased behaviour of international economic institutions (International Monetary Fund, World Bank and World Trade Organisation) and persistent bilateralism, as recently explained by us,[397] have partially induced a long run trend to growing gap. Typical treatments of balance of payments crises by IMF, as that practised in South-East Asia in 1997, which forced the developing countries of the region to practise a

---

395. The most truthful we could say, playing with average per capita incomes of the different countries, is that, if we exclude China from the analysis, the convergence has not become a reality in times of globalisation. If we included China, we could find a certain soft convergence, but if we decomposed China in rural and urban regions, the divergence would again become a reality. Indeed, the degree of economic convergence or divergence generated by globalisation can only be reasonably measured by a Gini index on the evolution of income disparities of all the 1300 million families living on Earth.

396. The non-ambitious target of halving the absolute number of people located under poverty line (one dollar a day) consecrated in the Millennium Objectives of the UN, accompanied by others alike (primary education for all and improving health by 2015), may be useful for sedating Western governments and citizens, but not to actually solve current international problems, which are becoming more and more complicated. Vide Rahman, R. and Andreu, J.M. (2004:62). Book already mentioned.

397. Vide Rahman, R. and Andreu, J.M. (2004:74) book already mentioned.

"beggar-thyself policy",[398] are clearly counterproductive strategies for convergence. Likewise, "adjustment programmes" devised by the World Bank have also been accused of not contributing to bridge the gap but, on the contrary, to increase inequality.

We have also to underline that the current trends in international trade, commented above, have been conducive—to large extent due to the defective access of agricultural and service products coming from the developing countries to the markets of the industrialised ones—to an overwhelming rise of regional trade in developing regions, thus not sufficiently promoting trade globalisation, the paramount target of the WTO.

Finally, we should also note that with the so-called new issues of the WTO (the Singapore issues and the sustainability ones), recently parked in the WTO meeting at Geneva, 2004, the rich countries have for years put pressure on developing countries on certain matters, such as competition, labour-social developments, environment matters, etc., forgetting their own development history[399] and practising an asymmetric international policy based on myopic own interest.

6.1.3. Asia as a Possible Future Champion in Commercial Matters

Although the majority of the international trade of goods is currently carried out by the so-called "high income" countries (they export around 75 per cent[400] of total world exports), the different growth rates of the diverse regions of the world along the last 10 years (1992-2002), seem to point out that around 2015, the distribution of the total world exports will be very different.

---

398. This policy consisted of the reduction of the GDP of the involved countries in order to cut their imports and rebalance their current accounts, thus inducing cuts in the exports of neighbouring countries. With this policy, instead of solving the crisis, the IMF induced a deepening of the crisis, thus provoking a regional one.

399. Note that while the Western countries have for years taken the WTO as a playground for disputes and conversations on movements-restrictions of capital as practised by developing countries, the rich countries have sent developing countries to the International Labour Organisation (ILO), when the latter have tried to introduce in the WTO agenda a progression in the liberalisation of labour markets, the other main factor of production. And this while the human "factor" is the last reference of Economics as a social science.

400. This figure could be around 10 per cent points less if, instead of using WB figures, we would have used IMF figures.

Extrapolations of the current trends show us that around 2015 the "high income" countries will export around 65 per cent[401] of the total world exports from current 75 per cent, while the developing countries as a whole will export the rest (around 35 per cent[402]). Note additionally that, in 2015, the developing countries of the regions of East Asia-Pacific and South Asia (China plus India plus neighbouring countries), would possibly reach a figure of around 23-24 per cent[403] of the total world exports instead of the current figure of around 13-14 per cent.

If extrapolations were taken up to 2020, it would not be weird that in that year the high income countries would "only" export 60 per cent of total world exports, while the low and middle income countries would then be exporting 40 per cent, of which 2/3rd-3/4th would be the total export figure of the developing countries of East Asia-Pacific and South Asia.

We have to say that these estimated figures of Asia will be mainly encouraged and/or conditioned by: 1) the continuation of the current relative divergent trends in GDP growth rates of these regions in comparison to those of Western countries; and 2) the continuation or not of the same behaviour of the West in the treatment of imports of goods coming from developing countries.

Note additionally that the continuation of the current high growth rates of GDP of China, India and the rest of neighbouring countries could be threatened by a *ceteris paribus* significant long term rise in the real price of raw materials and oil.

In this regard we should not forget, that—if they do not count with additional and significant new reserves of oil and gas—China and India, will need massive imports of crude to move forward their expectable industrialisation process, which would jointly employ in 2020 not less than 125 million people more than they currently do. Note that this increase is superior to the current industrial

401. This figure could be around 55 per cent if the departure base has been the figure of the IMF.

402. This figure could be around 45 per cent if the departure base has been the figure of the IMF.

403. This figure could also be 30 per cent if the extrapolation has been realised on the figures of IMF. Vide. *International Financial Statistics*. 2003 yearbook.

employment of the US and the Euro-zone altogether. Connected to this, we should also consider the possible oil supply problems that could appear if the Middle-East continues with a process of unending conflict.

Finally one should not take for granted the continuation in the future of the current commercial behaviour of the West which, although asymmetric, has enabled a rapid increase of the export shares of Asia (ex-Japan) and its leading countries. Conversely, if in future things continue rolling in an unpleasant way for the West in the field of international trade, thus compressing Western internal employment, one should not rule out the possibility of a limitation (relative or absolute) of their imports from the South. And this despite the negative experience in the 30s of the 20th century.

6.1.4. International Political Impasse, New Role for Asia and the Danger of UN Bifurcation

The persistence of unsolved conflicts due to political neglect and exclusion, and the recently observed growing economic gap due to imposition of Washington Consensus policies (as those sometimes practised by IMF and World Bank) and asymmetric rules within WTO, complemented by negative feelings over international policies on core issues (such as that of Israel-Palestine) deployed by Western leadership, seems to have generated a new kind of instability and insecurity in the world.

Unfortunately, steady implementation of a working multilateral policy to increase global stability and security in the context of the current UN seems unlikely, given the power structure stemming from the Charter of the UN.[404] As a consequence, a background of political instability and unilaterallism will probably be the international political framework in which the economic consolidation of China and India will have progress all along next decades.

---

404. Note that the Charter of the UN is extremely inflexible and non-democratic in terms of decision making for Charter reforms. In art° 108 of the Charter is written that "Amendments to the present Charter shall come into force...when they have been adopted by a vote of two-thirds of the members of the General Assembly and ratified in accordance with their respective Constitutional processes by two-thirds...including all the permanent members of the Security Council." The last nine words are, in our view an entire defy to the logic of international democracy. Opting for maintaining the decision making structure as devised in 1945 will avert rational updating.

Indeed, as a result of the recent polarisation of power, and in absence of significant reforms of the power structure of the UN[405] and affiliated agencies, it seems that these organisations will not be able to significantly work for common interest, thus not contributing to the achievement of the wanted international public goods, as general peace, security and prosperity for all.

As we have said in another essay,[406] the only way to unlock the current deadlock for reaching mentioned international public goods is to create constructive countervailing powers, capable of promoting a new balance in a more democratic Security Council, of course in need of abolition of veto rights.

To the extent that a EU-Federation does not appear soon, After recent rejection of France and Netherlands of the treaty for European Constitution, as a countervailing power—certainly a negative perspective for the European citizens at the dawn of a new economic world of large nations—one should not be surprised if China and India take over this role of countervailing power creation.

Even worse, if the current international framework worsens, thus progressively damaging the economies of the developing countries, a process of UN bifurcation could occur. This UN-bifurcation could arise at mid-long term from a generalised feeling of lack of representation of the interests of the developing countries in f.i. IMF and World Bank. It could also occur due to insufficiency of results in future WTO negotiations,[407] or due to a widely perceived miss-use of the UN by the hegemonic power and its allies in international policy matters, in detriment of global stability and/or economic development of the many.

Note that this hypothetical bifurcation of the UN is much more probable now than 30 years ago when the North-South conflict emerged in the UN without significant disruption. The probability is now higher, not only because the economic gap has grown, or the IT

405. On the possibility of implementing a significant reform of the Security Council, Vide Rahman, R. and Andreu, J.M. (2004: 127). Book already mentioned.

406. Vide Rahman, R. and Andreu, J.M. (2004: 131). Book already mentioned.

407. Although last agreement of WTO in Geneva (August 2004) on export subsidies on agricultural goods has been considered by some commentators as a success after the failure of Cancun in 2003, we do believe that the the belated and long term concessions of the Western countries will practically force in next 10 years a further regionalisation of the international trade.

revolution has generalised the access to full information of the poor of the world, but also because the economic world structure is experiencing a dramatic change, as we have mentioned in Chapter 5. A dramatic economic change that, progressively shifting the gravity centre of the world economy towards emerging Asia, will likely tend to induce a parallel political movement towards this continent.

In this framework of potential political upgrading of Asia, the West should not forget that emerging countries, such as China and India, are geographically a huge part of the planet with respectively a maximum and high economic growth rates; that jointly have a relevant part of the global population (more than 1/3rd of the total), and that are entering into a progressive mutual economic co-operation, while they also belong to the nuclear power club.

If, in this context, they seriously perceive that they have a common political obstacle for their economic prosperity, the "political" co-operation among them would be likely. Note in this regard that attempts to "divide and rule" seem to us no longer a workable solution for the West in a world of perfect information. In particular in the case of these two big countries that not so long ago, underwent humiliations from colonial powers.

6.2. Battles for Keeping Current Privileged Positions and its Limitations

As we have mentioned in the Introduction, no hegemonic nation in the history of the world has shared power with others without presenting significant economic or "non-economic" battles. In the world today, the presumed hegemonic power has a high-tech army, but its citizens are not prepared to massively risk their lives in armed confrontations. Even more, enthralled in their affluent life style, they are not prepared to significantly and for long spend in wars abroad.

Consequently, based on superiority feelings, and trying to politically and economically control the planet with its population, which is only 4.5 per cent of the total, the US has necessarily to look for allies prepared to help it in the implementation of its international undertakings, in particular in violent confrontation. Or to look for alike economic partners for the defence of common interests of the West. In this regard, nobody should forget that the current Western way of life could automatically be threatened in next decades, just by leaving the markets to work, as they currently do.

In the political context of collaboration with the US, we find relevant the recent admission of new partners in NATO.[408] Note however that this organisation, after the crumbling of the Soviet Union and the disappearance of the Warsaw Pact has lost its initial aims. As a result NATO has started undergoing mutations in its targets[409] and composition,[410] and just before the initiation of the Iraq war, it became somewhat chaotic, although the US continues, and will likely continue being in-charge.

From the second point of view, that of its economic global dominance, the US also tries to look for the support of the EU and other rich countries. Its relative supremacy in the UN and main economic agencies (IMF and WB), as well as in the working of the WTO (based on consensus and consequently on vetoes) give the US and others the opportunity of legitimising actions implemented in own interest.

In relation to future conflictive economic matters, which would negatively affect Asia and in particular China and India, we find two outstanding and intertwined issues: 1) that of oil, necessary to move the industry of the US, EU and other rich allies, as well as those of the main Asian developing countries (China and India); and 2) that of the possible and relative commercial castling of rich countries, trying to economically defend themselves, by means of limiting additional access to their markets.

Note that in relation to the first issue, the strategic supply of oil, whose main producers are currently located in the most conflictive region of the world, the Middle-East, international economic and

---

408. Remember that the NATO was born in 1949 from the Western Union. The Treaty, commanded by the US, was signed for mutual assistance and solidarity in case of external attacks to the "NATO territory."

409. Including the fight against international terrorism. And this, as if attacks of formal Western armies (under NATO structure) to certain states, could solve the problem of this so slippery and reproductive enemy, while over killing of the locals (euphemistically called, in NATO jargon, "lateral damage") is actually guaranteed.

410. Recently, candidate members for the EU enlargement have successfully applied for NATO-membership as well as some other former Soviet Union satellites and new countries which appeared as a result of the Soviet Union de-segregation.

political matters are strongly entangled. In this field, political provocations—real or imagined—of certain Arab-Muslim fractions, or pure pretexts, as for instance to allegedly preserve the international economic stability, could unleash new military interventions with or without support of the Security Council.

In this fragile environment, a continuation of the international behaviour of the US, which in last decade has acted on a case by case basis,[411] seems likely. As a result and based on their experience, it would not come as a surprise if China and India take *ad hoc* measures, for avoiding in future oil problems.

In connection with the second economic issue, that of possible relative commercial castling of the West, we have to say that its implementation would not be easy, mainly due to the dependence of the West on certain raw materials. In any case, slow negotiations in the context of the WTO, mainly resulting in delayed commitments with long phasing periods, are expectable in order to protect the way of living of Western populations. It is likely that on this second issue, the behaviour of the EU—doing common cause—will be one of followers, adjusting to the proposals of the US.

Although the future relative degrading of the living standards of the Western middle classes is simply an automatic derivative of globalisation[412] as designed by the West, we are not sure whether they will be able to accept the outcomes of the ruling system.

6.3. Probable Strategies of China and India in the Current Commercial Framework

If circumstances of trade and international politics *sine die* continue as they currently are (biased but bearable for these two dynamic big sized countries), China and India could follow some

411. Thus applying to similar subjects different *ad hoc* arguments, far from a linear and equal long term treatment on alike issues, as one could have expected from a leader with moral authority.

412. Observe that a relative degrading of the general Western standards of life, in exchange of a relative upgrading in the standards of certain successful Asian countries, would be consistent with a continuation of the current trend towards "non-generalised convergence," stemming from biased globalisation. The final result of it could be one of a limited convergence among different countries (developed and some developing), while most of the developing countries could be left behind.

strategic actions, in the context of the current WTO rules, to improve their current commercial positions.

6.3.1. Encouraging International Economic Relations with Neighbouring Countries

First of all, the signs are there that further commercial agreements will be implemented between China and India, or among them and other countries of the two adjacent Asian regions with high growth rates of GDP and exports. The more facilities for mutual commercial interchange the countries of these two regions give, the higher will be their intra-regional exports growth rate, the higher will be their GDP growth rates, and consequently the more will the citizen profit from the mutual additionally awarded facilities.

In this regard, preparations for a wider Free Trade Zone (FTZ) creation are underway.[413] If actually implemented, and in line with other experiences, this could encourage a move towards a Customs Union between China, India, and some neighbouring countries—already involved in a FTZ (ASEAN)—interested in participation into a future Asian Customs Union.

The countries of the region—in particular China and India—could also give one another additional facilities for the movements of capital and mutual FDI. In this regard, it is almost sure that a greater and progressive freedom of capital movements across the borders of the two giants would induce clear gains in their joint welfare, without significantly endangering the external value of the Yuan and the Indian Rupee, both of them nowadays very stable against the US dollar. Time after, it is expectable that other neighbouring countries join the area of mutually installed freer movements of capital.

6.3.2. Facing Future Scarcity of Oil

Given the enormous amount of accumulated foreign reserves of these two countries (respectively around 650 and 135 billion US dollars) in relation to their imports, and in presumption of future shortages of oil at world scale—generated by international political turbulence or by own comparative rapid growth—China and India

413. Note that China has recently embodied the ASEAN (Association of South-East Asian Nations) free trade zone. India is in a similar process.

could commit with oil producers, firms or countries, renewed "futures" contracts at longer term with floating "premiums." This would guarantee the oil supply of the two Asian giants.

Note that the comparative higher prices that China and India would thus have to pay in future, would not be seriously detrimental for their unitary industrial costs, given their huge and long-lasting comparative advantage induced by their much lower industrial wages. Note that in terms of costs, this action would have a similar effect as that of the so-called opportunity cost of the "over-accumulation" of foreign currency reserves, that China and India currently practise.

6.3.3. UN Reform Attempts by China and India and Secondary Way Out

Jumping from international economic matters to international political ones, it is observable that in order to politically support their current accelerated economic progression, China and India, have recently started firm moves for the democratisation of the UN.[414] Firstly because this democratising process would profit them, since they are the most populated countries on Earth. And secondly, because the maintenance of the current power structure of the UN, potentially conducive to political abuse, is in clear divergence with the declining economic power of some UN-leading countries.

6.3.3.1. Obsoleteness of the UN

As it is well known, at the moment of the UN inception, the permanent members of its Security Council were mainly the "winners" of the Second World War: 1) "China" ("represented" by the then minority and non-democratic government of Taiwan, today out of all international institutions and substituted by that of the People's Republic); 2) the "Soviet Union," which disappeared more

414. Indeed, it could be considered as strange that a non-democratic country as China promotes a more democratic UN. Note however that this apparent "non-consistent" Chinese positioning would be just a reversed one in comparison to the current status of the remaining four veto-owners which, being internally democratic, sometimes behave as non-democratic in the Security Council. China by promoting democracy in the UN would be renouncing to its own non-democratic veto right, thus at least internationally democratising itself. Observe however that an internal pro-democratic positioning of China would make a UN democratisation more acceptable for the rest of veto-owners. Additionally, one could not discard a UN democratisation in parallel with the existence of some non-democratic relevant partners. This position, could be a better one than the opposite, most of them internally democratic but at times behaving non-democratically and abusively at UN level.

than a decade ago and was substituted by the Russian Federation, which is economically and politically a very different country than the former one; 3) the two former colonial and influent European countries, Britain and France, which although continue being rich are unevenly but rapidly losing political clout at global scale, because they lack a critical economic and human mass; and 4) the US as the apparent citadel owner.

If we accept that France and UK jointly have a smaller GDP than that of Japan, while the two altogether have a similar amount of population as the latter, and also that France and UK individually have smaller GDP than Germany, we may deduce that, while others (Japan and Germany) are under-represented[415], France and UK are clearly over-represented in the UN; and also over-punching in defence and on other international political matters, thus economically prejudicing their own citizens in long term[416].

Consequently, the economic and political foundations of the current Security Council are already falsified by the economic facts reflected above. In addition in the past 50 years—a period in which almost all the remaining colonies disappeared and the GDP of the world grew more than ever—new nuclear and/or very populated countries (as India and Brazil) have entered into scene, making their influence and UN-representation in comparison to their current and (future) economic weight, unbalanced.

If we add to all these distortions, the issue of the undemocratic "veto rights" that the four "democratic" permanent members of the Security Council (plus China) have, the political foundations of the UN are even weaker. No wonder that this institution is significantly fading, because in addition to being "non-representative" in crucial political issues, it lacks enforcing capacities while its most prominent veto-owners have always refused to pool in a real UN military structure.

415. Note that Japan and Germany, without having a significant influence in the current UN decision making, contribute economically more to the financing of the UN than the UK and France. Vide Rahman, R. and Andreu, J.M. (2004:130). Book already mentioned.

416. Consequently, to avoid long term unfavourable economic disturbances, countries of this size should merge with other alike powers. In this context, letting aside the case of UK, if France and Germany want to keep a certain international clout in the future without economically exhausting their citizens, they should promote a voluntary EU Federation. We are convinced that the idea of a EU Federation will finally become a reality.

Paradoxically, aggressive veto-owners, who logically defend this anachronism, often exhibit negative positions concerning UN capabilities, stemming "of course" from the veto rights of the others. Consequently, at times they publicly declare as "unwillingly" forced to individually act irrespective of the resolutions of the UN when the latter, democratically formulated, does not adjust to their own interests.

6.3.3.2. Unilateralism and Political Re-positioning of China and India

The above mentioned biased behaviour has induced a rapid wearing out of the UN in the last decade. Note that recent unilateralism[417] in international policy actions, has further stressed the case.

Against this background there are speculations which predict different negative scenarios in order to halt the economic and political progress of China and India. One such prediction is the possible encouragement by third parties of economic or political quarrels between the two countries. Other speculations refer to the stirring up of internal political problems in every one of these two countries, or even to the creation of indirect difficulties in the oil supply to China or India. Note that in all these hypothetical scenarios, the traditional "divide and rule" policies, practised by dominant nations along centuries, is underlying.

Against the backdrop of these possible scenarios, the contemporary attempts undertaken by India and China to promote multilateralism and the reform of the UN could be seen as a healthy way out.

Besides making a case for the democratisation of the UN, China and India have also increased their involvement in development co-operation and funding, thus revitalising the case of the developing countries, but this time making it capable of more independent actions. In particular the economic support to Sub- Saharan African countries by China is a proof of the new Chinese international policy.

---

417. Unilateralism may be practised not only under formal actions, but also with resort to intelligence.

As a consequence of all former considerations, one should not rule out that in case the democratisation of the UN reaches an impasse situation, while the average economic position of the developing countries degrades as a result of the policies implemented by the Bretton Woods institutions, some Asian, African and Latin American countries could take an initiative, lead by China and India, for the creation of a UDN (United Developing Nations).

Against this possible development, and remembering the antecedent of the G-20[418] in the WTO meeting in Cancun, we hope that, in front of this increased political and economic[419] reaction capacity of relevant developing countries against assumed unfair proposals, Western leadership would react admitting a UN democratisation. This would be good news because it would avoid the risk of a de-link at large scale between the West and the emerging countries, which doubtless would be detrimental to western exports, growth and employment.[420]

6.3.3.3. Financing Development of LDC by China and India

Not only based on solidarity considerations but also to protect their long term economic interests and to gather international political support, China and India are already increasingly involved in development co-operation. Nevertheless, it is possible that in the near future, and in a context of political self promotion, they create significant funds for cooperation. These funds, given the current policy of China and India of over-accumulation of foreign reserves, could enable these two countries to jointly surpass in absolute terms the annual foreign assistance of the US.[421]

---

418. Little attention was paid by the US and Europe in the run-up to the Cancun meeting of the WTO in September 2003, when 20 developing countries established a platform, the so-called G-20, to defend vital trade interests of the developing world. Much to the surprise of the West, the group managed to make a strong fist.

419. Observe that this bifurcation of the UN would also imply a bifurcation of the IMF, World Bank, and the rest of the UN agencies.

420. Note that the growth rate of exports from the EU and US to East Asia-Pacific developing countries has been roughly double than that of their total world exports in the last decade (1992-2002).

421. Indeed, this manoeuvre, if implemented, could be unpleasant for the West, to the extent that China and India, using the exchange rates of the Yuan and the Indian Rupee as they currently do, could gather reserves from the West to further redistribute part of them as their own development co-operation.

6.4. Economic Impasse in the West as a Consequence of Own Wrong International Policies

Given the current geographical trends of international trade, now favourable to emerging Asia, it is not a surprise that concerns are growing in Western countries. Indeed, the rapid share-gaining of Asia in the total world trade of goods is already considered as a threat for jobs creation in the Western hemisphere, in particular in its industrial sector, which paradoxically is the only sector almost completely open to international trade.[422]

The new trade and financial conditions generated by the recent globalisation, although defective in its approach as we have stressed in another essay,[423] is already generating unpleasant economic and trade effects in the West. In trying to offset this trend, Western countries looking for new opportunities in the field of FDI, have put pressure on leading Asian developing countries, for further abating their FDI admission conditions. To the extent that these pressures have resulted successful, own automatisms of the market economy have induced something perhaps not considered or, at least, not sufficiently analysed by Western strategists: the problem of progressive "dislocation" of the Western industry.

Observe that "domestic" dislocation of industries has frequently played a relevant role in the internal development of many (Western) countries. In fact, and for decades, this dislocation of productive-assets from overcrowded and expensive cities towards "poles or hubs" of development—in search of lower wages and economies of de-congestion, followed by internal migration towards these poles—was encouraged by public powers in the West. This strategy created new opportunities of employment in mentioned poles or hubs, thus inducing a migration flow of the unemployed from traditional industrial cities and surrounding territories of the poles, to the mentioned poles. As a result, this policy facilitated the increase of the "average" per capita income of the country, while generating domestic employment at national scale.

---

422. Note in this regard that in the West, the access of agricultural products, services and some manufactured goods coming from the developing countries are still rather limited.

423. Vide Rahman, R. and Andreu, J.M. (2004:38) Book already mentioned.

The current situation at international scale, stemming from FDI-dislocation, is a very different one: the governments of Western countries are in splits, having to grudgingly support at short term the increase of their GNP (not GDP) by encouraging FDI to developing countries, thus creating industrial employment in those countries in detriment of the internal creation of (more expensive) jobs in the West. After a decade of exercising this policy, the derivative has suddenly appeared in front of their eyes: the industrial dislocation towards developing countries (mainly to China) cannot be followed by migration of jobless Westerners to these countries, as it happened internally in the Western countries after the Second World War.

Consequently, if things continue as they are, the options for preserving jobs in the West are either an "ultra-rapid" increase of labour productivity[424]—which is technically impossible—a huge relative reduction of Western wages to defend competitiveness,[425] something politically unthinkable, or an almost arrest or reversal of the current process towards freer trade. But if the facilitation of the commercial process quickly arrested or reversed, large parts of Western overseas investments would change into losses for the MNC which, in addition to the contractive effects of a relative depression of trade, could provoke an economic down-turn at a world scale.

However, it is likely that, in trying to meddle in the process, and paying for time, the Western governments will embark on an intermediate strategy: step by step putting new hindrances to the industrial exports of the developing countries,[426] with additional

---

424. The evolution of the labour productivity has to do with two main arguments: 1) a technical one, which clarifies the impossibility in industrialised countries to annually increase the labour productivity per hour over 4-5 per cent; and 2) an institutional one, consisting of increasing the number of annualy worked hours per worker, manoeuvre that has a ceiling not surpassable. Both of them make it impossible to rapidly bridge the current competitivity gap among the western countries and China and India.

425. Observe that if globalisation had been well implemented, with parallel freer and progressive movements of all factors, capital and labour—as we have explained in another essay—the absurd situation of today would not have become real. In parallel to greater migrations to the West—as we have suggested—Western salaries had not grown so much, and the current need for industrial dislocation would have not been so urgent. Let us remember once again that in Economics to keep segmented markets, and to asymmetrically liberalise them at different speeds may produce negative results, as described by the theory of "second best."

426. A test on the possible negative behaviour of Western countries will be their reaction after January 2005, as a result of a regime change in the international trade of textiles and garments due to the expiring of the Multifibre Agreement on 31st December 2004.

emphasis on quality and technical standards, spare-parts guarantees, sufficient branching for post-sale services, etc.

Concerning agriculture and services,[427] and reading recent history of biased interpretation of the neoclassical model at an international scale, we do believe that the West will likely arrest or delay[428] the process of the dismantling of barriers to access their markets. Further co-operation favouring political "friendly-countries," by means of bilateral preferential agreements, etc., is also an expectable derivative. Of course, in such a harsh context, one should not rule out the possibility of a collapse of the WTO.

Summarising one may say that nowadays the Western world seems to be captured in the subtle trap that the "invisible hand" has reserved as punishment for market economy twisters. To the extent that the goods, services and factor markets are tightly connected, to device a partial international liberalisation, as engineered by the rich countries, particularly in the last decade, had to be conducive to the creation of a mechanical monster which is today threatening them.

Instead of liberalising more or less at the same speed the markets of goods, services and factors, Western governments and multilateral institutions mainly promoted trade liberalisation of industrial goods (to also increase industrial exports to Developing Countries) and the movements of capital (to rise FDI opportunities). As a result of this selective liberalising approach, they stimulated rapid growth of (industrial and general) wages in the rich world, while they kept almost banned the immigration process towards the West. This policy significantly limited the creation of jobs at a world scale, while it forced the maintenance of lower wages in the developing world. After years of practising this policy, the reached disparity of industrial (and general) wages across the world (China-India-West) is

427. Note that the West has always "nominally" defended the market economy, while it has devised an approach to international co-operation really biased in own interest "at short term." After the Second World War the West has always put difficulties in the accessibility to their markets of the Agricultural and Services products coming from the developing countries, while a freer international labour market has practically remained forgotten.

428. The recent agreement achieved in Geneva (August 2004), on elimination of export subsidies to agricultural products in the West, will compulsory start in 2007 and will be phased-out in 2017. Really a new mismanage of the West in relation with the poorest farmers of the South.

really scaring because it seems non-bridgeable by means of gradual manoeuvres for increasing productivity or for wage moderation.

Regrettably, this technical difficulty could induce temptations in the West to wrongly fight—by means of introduction of new barriers to trade—against the jobs-destruction process induced by their own mistaken policy applied in the past, instead of analysing the deep causes and looking for durable solutions.

6.5. A Win-Win Solution: Positive Reaction of The West

We have to insist once again that the mentioned possibility of a UN bifurcation, chosen by the developing world as a last resort, should not become a fact. Indeed, this non-desirable initiative should be substituted by a profound re-organisation of the UN, feasible if the leading countries accept a reform of the current UN (and its economic agencies), according to the principles of international democracy and representation. This would in parallel mean that the West should accept the economic consequences of the current "special market economy" as devised in the last decades: relative decline of own exports, dislocation of industrial activity mainly redirected to developing countries in particular to Asia (China and India), and decline of relative figures of jobs in some Western countries (mainly in the EU) in correspondence with its ageing population.

The acceptance of the mentioned re-organisation of the UN would imply the disappearance of veto rights, the establishment of a system in the Security Council of qualified majorities for decision making, and the setting up of an early warning system as well as an international army for rapid intervention based on formal decisions made by a new democratic and less time consuming Security Council. The expulsion from UN of anyone who unleashes without UN-support armed confrontations with other countries, and the ex-novo more rational assessment on contribution of the different countries to the UN, would also be issues to include in the new Charter.

6.5.1. On the Reshuffling of Multilateral Economic Institutions

A re-organisation of the multilateral economic institutions depending on the new UN should also be accepted. The IMF should work more visibly in the interest of the international community, under a consistent and stable framework of rules applicable to any country in a similar situation of external financial unbalance. These objective rules for application in certain contexts (ways of granting loans, etc.) should rule during a protracted period and restated thereafter according to the variation of circumstances. These objective rules should be agreed in the UN by the international community.

The ways of financing the IMF should change significantly. The new financing should be based on the principles of transparency and ability to pay. In relation to juncture financial support to the members, past history of moral hazard and non-accomplishments of commitments should be taken into account. Steady cases of petition and granting of loans by recurrent problematic countries should be avoided, by means of establishing objective rules. In case of fundamental economic disequilibria, incumbent government should step down and convene new general elections. In case of social catastrophe stemming from a protracted period of non-performance of a certain economy, the UN, supported by the UN army, would take measures to significantly alleviate population suffering, directly implementing the programmes by itself, thus punishing the incumbent failed government.

In relation to the World Bank we do believe that at the present moment of history its way of promoting development, although well intentioned and rigorous in relation of aims and means, is clearly insufficient and somewhat obsolete. We have discussed at another place[429] how a new system for development financing should be implemented, if the international community wants to reach in a "reasonable period" of time the most desired international public goods, such as peace and human security for all.

In current times of full information at a global scale, coexistence of lasting social injustice and social stability—as it occurred in isolated national agrarian societies of past centuries—can no longer exist. Consequently, the international community, under the aegis of a new UN, will have to devise a new system for development

429. Vide Rahman, R. and Andreu, J.M. (2004:143). Book already mentioned.

financing, a system based on grants and not on loans,[430] in which the contribution of higher income countries should be boosted, pooled and reshuffled.[431]

As we believe, according to the figures of Maddison,[432] that economic convergence has not been achieved in last decades, while we assume that the future social and political stability of the world will depend more on per capita income convergence than on the reduction of the number of poor under the so-called poverty line, we understand that a more ambitious target should be set by the UN, to de-activate underlying economic problems related to international peace and security.

In order to implement this new multilateral policy for development financing, a new UN agency for co-operation should be created (UNICO), to which current World Bank system would have to be embodied. On the relative volume of funds to be transferred by higher income countries to UNICO to forward them to developing countries, on the possible regional organisation of UNICO, and on the methodology for individual or regional transfers reckoning, we have made some specific proposals in another essay.[433]

Finally we have to underline that current methodologies and approaches of the rich countries in WTO negotiations should be re-driven on the principles of acknowledgement of past biased behaviour, of historical debt to developing countries stemming from colonial times, and of a more flexible acceptation of current economic conduct of some developing countries in matters of trade

---

430. Note that our proposal for changing loans into grants made in March 2002—vide Rahman, R. and Andreu, J.M. (2002). *Financing Economic Development and Human Security*, Rashtriya Printers, New Delhi—has recently been considered as positive by Gordon Brown in his Plan directed to the IMF (vide Griffiths, B. in *The Economic Times* India. 14.2.2003).

431. This does not exclude the possibility that any donor-country continues with its bilateral grant, loans, etc.

432. We have previously mentioned the current debate on convergence. Although there are some contenders (mainly Sala-i-Martin), who opine that a convergence process is underway, we sincerely believe that convergence may not be realistic if one takes into account the evolution of internal distribution of big countries as f.i. China. Anyway, note that in case of acceptance of methodologies of those who "certify" current convergence, we have to underline that the velocity of the process "detected" by them is too slow to guarantee peace and human security in the first half of the 21st Century.

433. Our proposals are explained in the Chapter 6 of our book *Responsible Global Governance* (2004). Academic Foundation. New Delhi.

(which are not faraway from the behaviour exhibited by many today's rich countries in the first two decades of their post-Second World War industrialisation).

6.5.2. *Urgency for Reassessing the Current Economic and Political Order*

Step by step the economic gravity centre of the world is shifting to the East. In this altering context, Western politicians, mainly worried with the next domestic elections, hardly rise their sight and look with rigour into the future, meddling only with short-term internal and external problems. Despite that, they should know that some changes in the trend, although hardly perceivable from one year into another, could significantly vary the current correlation of economic and political power in the coming 10-15 years.

If we seriously analyse the world today, we have to deduce that some old colonies or countries, such as China and India, that just half a century ago barely counted in the political or economic global game, have today become relevant players. In addition to the dimension of their economies (respectively the second and fourth in the ranking of GDP-PPP of nations), and their rapid rates of growth, they have become nuclear powers, maintain huge conventional armies and have progressively more educated supporting populations. No wonder that in these circumstances their elite's in power have become conscious of the enormous importance of their countries in the current and future international power play.

Ignoring this landscape and focussing exclusively on the huge per capita income gap favourable to the rich, Western countries continue enjoying their high per capita consumption levels, while their growth expectations are comparatively low against a backdrop of small, stagnant and ageing populations. Furthermore, forgetting these two crucial unfavourable traits of their economies, they seem to believe that they can continue controlling the international institutions (UN, IMF, WB), while their high-tech armies will for ever support their dominance.

However the naked truth is that these considerations are already partially falsified by reality. In particular, their individual armies are in lack of enough human factor as to police the world. Consequently any attempt of indefinitely maintaining the current asymmetric economic and political order is a chimera. As history has proven, stubbornly trying to keep unfair positions in the context of high informed and economically uneven societies, has no other future than escalation in the form of trade wars, vetoes in multilateral negotiations, formation of regional economic and political blocs, and last but not least continuation of intermittent violent actions against the above described unfair framework.

6.6. China, India and the Future: From Dependency to Parity

In past times in which the value of individual and collective liberties were not so much rooted as they now are, and the differences in domination capacity were extreme and based on overwhelming weaponry advantage, comparative small countries were able of taking over huge and largely populated nations. In particular if infighting in these countries gave the colonisers the opportunity of practising a "divide and rule" policy.

Nevertheless, independence of colonies from former colonial powers in the second half of the 20th century, rapid economic growth of leading developing countries in last two decades, development of their elite's supported by updated knowledge, and access to full information (at the end of the 20th century) have significantly changed the picture in detriment of former colonisers.

China and India, although significantly underdeveloped in per capita income terms but quickly growing, not only count in their favour with substantial equilibrating factors, but also with the most relevant variable in the long run for achieving political and economic clout in democratic societies: huge and growing population (and a younger one in the case of India) which altogether overcome 1/3rd of the total world inhabitants.

Looking into the future one should also note that while the rich West, although with exceptions, has practically entered into a situation of relative economic decadence due to its slow growth of GDP and exports, and many developing countries of the world remain in low growth or almost in stagnant positions, the Chinese and Indian economies are enjoying high velocities of growth. And probably for long, given their huge reserves of people in situation of nil marginal productivity, transferable along next decades to non-agricultural sectors.

If we add to these traits of China and India, the economic evolution of neighbouring countries and their progressively more interconnected economic relationships in the East and South Asian regions, we have to conclude that the main countries of this macro-region not only are nowadays "formally" independent from a political perspective, but also near of reaching parity positions (with a delay of a decade and half as maximum) in economic and political negotiations with the West.

Since fighting against the law of gravity (understandable in this case as a matter of large numbers) is a rather difficult and costly policy, a more intelligent position of the West should be to gradually adjust to the new economic environment, instead of entering into a situation of economic and/or political confrontation with Asia.

We understand that it is arduous to adjust to unfavourable positions from buoyant ones, but real sailing skills only become patent when it is necessary to lean against the wind. In this regard, we think that the future 10 years hide strong tests to Western politicians, who will have to remain cold blooded in order not to unleash counterproductive international economic or political actions.

7

Conclusions and Insight into the Future

Looking through conjectures about China and India, one finds two forms of reductionism concerning their future economic behaviour. Firstly, there are observers that, exclusively focusing on their current and unpleasant parameters (small per capita income, deficient infrastructure, low per capita consumption and accumulated poverty) and/or on their "assumed" non-surmountable political dysfunction, negatively assess the relevance of their economic future "because it could arrive very faraway in time," or because their current fast development process "will rapidly arrest or enter in a diminishing returns stage."

Secondly, other authors, focusing only on the recent dynamic aspects of these countries, imagine a *sine die* rapid growth of their economies which, without significant problems, will catch up with the richest ones in some few decades. And this irrespective of whether internal economic difficulties—macroeconomic disequilibria and sectorial bottlenecks—or political ones, may appear along the process of development, or may disturb it.

The defectiveness of this second form of reductionism becomes more patent because it ignores almost certain reactions of the West in the international economic and political fields. These reactions have always occurred in history and should not be forgotten.

In our view, far from these two extreme guesswork's, the future course of the economic and political development of China and India will be an intermediate one, perhaps nearer to the second approach if Chinese and Indians strongly bet on the international game, and wisely act to remedy their socio-economic and political problems. It is true that these two countries count with enormous possibilities for keeping their relative current high cruise speeds for catching up.

Nevertheless, one cannot overlook either the internal snags they nowadays have, or the problems that other powers will put in front of them to cool their aspirations.

After reviewing the essentials of the theory of economic growth and development (Chapter 2), we have briefly analysed the economic history of these two countries (Chapters 3 and 4) as well as the political and economic traits and profiles of China and India in comparison to their Asian neighbours and to the main nations of the world (Chapter 5). Finally (Chapter 6) we have tried to imagine the possible economic developments in these two countries at long term; but done beyond conventional econometric extrapolations, which in nature ignore the future international political developments that will necessarily alter the economic framework, readjusting it.

After extracting some conclusions applicable to China and India stemming from pure theoretical corollaries, we have reached significant findings in relation with the Chinese and Indian current economic success, as well as with their economic and political deficiencies. We have also found in these two countries some meaningful comparative advantages, which could enable them to become relevant economic and political powers at long term.

Additionally, we have mulled on the diverse international scenarios that could become real (in the political and economic spheres), as a consequence of possible applied policies by the West in the future. In this regard we have furthermore analysed some economic policies that Asia, and particularly China and India, could deploy if things nearly continue as they are; and also possible political answers that China and India could give if confronted with attempts to significantly harm their current economic trajectories.

7.1. Conclusions Stemming from the Theory of Economic Growth Applicable to China and India

Although the following conclusions are mainly rooted in the conventional wisdom accumulated by professional economists along the 20th century, we will here quote them to make explicit the Chinese and Indian intrinsic comparative advantages in relation to the West and to some neighbouring developing countries.

7.1.1. Aggregate Conclusions

To the extent that—according to the neo-classical model of growth and the endogenous growth theory—the domestic investments ratio (in physical or human assets) in GDP terms is the main variable that explains the growth rate of nations, and since these investments have to be financed by corresponding domestic or external savings to reach macroeconomic equilibrium, the volume of the ratio of total (internal plus external) available savings (s) in terms of GDP will be the main conditioning variable for rapid growth. Consequently, in general terms, any economic policy that makes an increase in "s" easier (updating internal fiscal systems, reorganising public administrations, improving banking systems, facilitating FDI accessibility, etc.) will be crucial to rise the total value of "s".

In this regard it is clear that the level of the current value (2002) of total "s" is simply astonishing in the case of China. And not only because its internal and overwhelming saving ratio (43.7 per cent) overcomes by itself its very high domestic rate of investment (around 40 per cent), but also because the relevant reception of FDI (annually around 4-5 per cent in GDP terms) and other foreign capitals, adding available funds, have unexpectedly transformed China into a relevant international net lender.

Concerning the value of this parameter, total "s", India is in significant disadvantage (23 per cent) in comparison to China. Nevertheless, in general comparative terms (Table 7) the Indian figure is not negligible at all. Notwithstanding that, India should increase its ratio total "s" (at least up to 30 per cent) if it wants to step up its speed of economic progress, as desired by Indian authorities in order to quickly correct current poverty problems.

Conversely, it is today becoming a matter of discussion in China whether it should reduce its overwhelming savings ratio in order to re-orientate its aggregate demand more towards internal consumption, in order to partially substitute its currently awe-inspiring and super-growing industrial exports.

In this regard, we are convinced that to the extent that China has to solve some problems related with its income distribution, and to upgrade its incipient Social Security system, and given the fact that the West could in future put more problems to the industrial exports of China, the mentioned shift towards higher consumption should already start its implementation. A fall of the Chinese domestic saving rate to 32-34 per cent would be enough to alleviate all these problems without a significant reduction of the economic growth rate of China (perhaps two-two and half per cent points or less, yearly).

7.1.2. Bi-Sectorial and Multi-Sectorial Considerations

If we shift from the former uni-sectorial economic perspective and deep into dis-aggregation, additionally considering agricultural and non-agricultural sectors, we may deduce an overwhelming advantage of China and India over the rest of countries of the world. Following the Lewis-model of "growth with unlimited labour supply", and considering the huge volume of population with nil marginal productivity currently attached to agriculture in these two countries, which during decades will be transferred at low wages to non-agricultural sectors, one has to infer that the significant higher comparative rhythms of growth experienced by China and India in the last two decades may continue at least during three-four decades more.

A derivative of the functioning of the two-sectors model of Lewis is the almost automatic trend to a negative distribution of the per capita income in the first stages of development. This trend, that seems to have become effective in the two Asian giants in the last two decades, will have to be corrected if authorities of these countries also pursue the "social sustainability" of their undertaken approaches to growth.

From a multi-sectorial perspective, we have to underline that the growth of these two countries should be more balanced. In the Indian case the progression of the industry and agro-industrial activities should be quicker and much more tilted towards exports to enhance the external sector of India, relatively underdeveloped for the time being. In the case of China over-investments in some industrial activities (steel, textile, automobile) should be curved in favour of agriculture, and particularly in favour of services.

7.1.3. Relevance of Negative Non-Economic Factors

Although China and India are well positioned in terms of strict growth capacity—high growth speed and enormous and cheap reserve of future non-agricultural workers—one cannot overlook the fact that, beside some sectorial disequilibria, China and India will have to deal with some unfavourable non-economic factors that could relatively drag their future development.

At a national level, everybody agrees that the political transition in China towards democracy, in a context of growing private sector and property rights, is just a matter of time. We understand that a "traumatic process" towards democracy is not expectable if the recent aggravation of the income distribution changes its current trend, and a new income distribution orientation starts at short-mid term. Anyway democracy has its costs in terms of decision-making speed and changing aims (as a consequence of the principle of alternation of parties in power) and this, from a moment onwards, will reduce the Chinese economic growth velocity.

Although India is a democracy, we have few doubts that some of its top legal rules should be modified. Distribution of power among Union and states, restatement of the judiciary system to significantly reduce the duration of the litigation process, unification of the electoral calendar of the states to eliminate uncertainty and facilitate consensus, reorganisation of the public administration at all levels to avoid overlapping and long procedures as well as to improve Union and states co-ordination, and a greater flexibility in the interpretation of the limits of private property, are matters to be reconsidered.

From an international perspective, China and India have also some pending issues that could hinder its current rapid economic progress. The cases of Taiwan and Pakistan-Kashmir should be agreed respectively by China and India with their counterparts. Although rather different, both of them seem susceptible of agreed solutions by means of granting ample autonomy to the territories in dispute, while continue belonging to their respective mainland.

At least equally significant than the formerly listed non-economic problems, are the future international hurdles that almost surely will be put in front of these two big Asian countries to limit their velocity of growth and influence.

7.2. Currently Observed Deficiencies in China

Despite its amazing economic performance since 1978, which has crystallised along 25 years in maximum annual GDP growth rates, accelerated industrial progress, overwhelming average growth rate of exports, sustained growth of its per capita GDP, etc., China continues to be a country with great expectations, but also with economic obstacles for progress.

The first and perhaps the most important problem of the Chinese economy is the definition of property rights. Although this property rights definition is in progress, it is in significant delay with the evolution of the private economy. Property rights and private economy have to go hand in hand. Otherwise the economic stimuli may fade. In this regard it is noticeable that Chinese private "big entrepreneurial initiatives" in the industrial field have not sufficiently flourished—in opposition to small sized private undertakings and MNC installed in China—while in India precisely the opposite has occurred. This is because in India the property rights are (perhaps excessively) consecrated, while FDI has not played a significant role in its industrialisation.

A second significant trouble of the current Chinese economy is the partial segmentation of its labour markets, as a consequence of the remains of the old economic policy designed in the Maoist period. Restrictions on rural migration, and limitations on movement of labour working in the even today important public industrial-urban sector, are rules that avert the optimum allocation of resources. These restrains—until now in place to impede hazardous accumulation of unemployment in cities—could hinder in future the necessary absorption of the agricultural-labour excesses by non-agricultural sectors.

Despite having been an almost full socialist country, the small level of public funds managed by the Chinese Central administration comes as a surprise, being its amount even smaller in relative terms than that of India. China also lacks a sufficient Social Security system.

Liberalisation and de-nationalisation processes—depriving the state from revenues formerly coming from profitable public undertakings—have induced a reduction of crucial public expenditures and a growth of fiscal deficits, recently reaching figures of the tune of 3-4 per cent in GDP terms. Consequently, significant increases in taxation and reduction of subsidies to public firms in red, as well as higher fiscal-expenditure proposals to offset recent negative distribution of per capita income, are expectable initiatives to be taken by Chinese authorities in next years, if they want to keep the "social sustainability" of the current economic approach.

The existence of an underdeveloped banking system in China, overwhelmingly controlled by the public sector and overcharged with "non-performing credits", is also a weak point of the Chinese economy that has to change to improve the allocation of resources. In this regard there is a consensus among observers that the Chinese Banking system is considerably in delay in comparison to that of India. Note that in Chinese banking, administrative criteria predominate in the allocation of resources, thus interest rates do not significantly play that role.

Additionally, there are in China a set of variables and policies that have induced an over-accumulation of foreign reserves and have generated a very unbalanced growth from a geographical perspective. We are here referring to low industrial wages—as a result of the huge volume of people attached to agriculture—to an alleged, although disputable, undervalued Yuan, and to the extraordinary success of the SEZs (Special Economic Zones) that has attracted FDI and encouraged Chinese exports.

Notwithstanding some allegations, the Chinese level of international reserves over its imports, although high in terms of Western standards, was (in 2002) similar to that of India and well under that of Japan (Table 8). Note that this relative over-accumulation of reserves may have been caused by the government's intention to partially de-link the Chinese economic activity from the Western business cycle and to become really independent from the IMF.

Besides this, the Yuan is not so undervalued from several points of view: the trade balance of goods in China is not in high surplus (in GDP terms) while it is in decline, and the financial system is not ready to confront a liberalisation process of the Yuan. At the same time, a significant revaluation of the Yuan could provoke a reduction of exports and hazardous accumulation of unemployment in coastal cities and regions.

On the wake of its success, the setting up of SEZs and other geographical stimulated areas for FDI, has generated diverse and not entirely positive outcomes in China: 1) a temporary over-stimulation of Industrial production tilted to exports and construction; 2) a proliferation of relevant foreign firms in these privileged areas, which with the subsistent old public firms make up the bulk of the relevant industrial tissue; and 3) a geographically unbalanced distribution of the personal income, with a dynamic and more developed East and South inconsistency with a stagnant West, and with more developed and growing per capita incomes in cities and towns than in countryside.

Indeed the Chinese policy of stimulation of industrial activities, by means of encouraging FDI in SEZ and over-growing industrial credit, has generated a "two speeds" economy and a significant distribution problem. Although this trait could be considered as negative, we share the view that the Chinese authorities, when they started the reforms in 1978, had little room for manoeuvre to implement a fast growth process. The industrial exports—in the context of the then GATT rules, and following the recommendations of the then mainstream economists—were the sole group of exports that could grew massively, as to significantly thrust the aggregate demand of China.

Although in next years this country will have to modulate and rebalance the weight of the components of its aggregate demand, thus further encouraging internal consumption, its comparative higher speed of economic progress seems to be guaranteed. Nevertheless, to guarantee the achievement of these higher growth rhythms, China will have to solve its internal political problems (democratisation and personal income distribution), the main external one (that of Taiwan), and all the others which the outside world could put in front of "The People's Republic of China" to cool down its economic and political aspirations.

7.3. Currently Observed Deficiencies in India

Notwithstanding the brilliant economic behaviour of India along the last two decades (1980-2003), there are a lot of activities that will have to be improved in this country, while the current low levels of its main economic parameters (per capita income, etc.) will have to progress rapidly.

India, is mainly a rural-agricultural country, whose relevant agriculture productions (rice, wheat, etc.) are less productive per cultivated ha. than those of China. Current low productivity of Indian agriculture, although much higher than that registered before the

Indian "green revolution," continues being affected by long lasting problems that have averted the necessary productivity growth of cultivated land.

Technical, social and institutional factors, have impeded an adequate progression of agricultural and agro-industrial activities in India. An illiterate and superstitious agro-population involved at times in communal wrangling, a pattern of the tenure of land not prone to innovation, a generalised small size of cultivated plots not significantly affected by an always pending "Reform of Land," a scant institutional financing to poor farmers, infrastructure deficits that have hindered the agro-production marketing, and a relative neglect of the agriculture which has mostly been bypassed by the main undertaken policies, have maintained the Indian agriculture in a second tier position.

Concerning the Indian industry, we have to state that the delayed start of its essential reforms, in 1991, which conveniently eliminated the licensing system, and significantly and progressively began a sustained reduction of the tariff and non-tariff protection of the sector, while opening a process to degrade the excessive and bad oriented protection of the SSI (Small Scale Industries) sector, has not created a meaningful number of new jobs. This disappointing result has to be overcome in next years as to match the current need of new jobs in non-agricultural sectors, estimated at 10 million a year. Actually, this is a figure very far away from the new jobs effectively created in India in the last years, of around 4 million a year.

As it has happened in other parts of the world, the bulk of new jobs to be created in the non-agricultural sectors to absorb at a faster rhythm the excess of workers attached to agricultural activities, will have to occur in small and medium industrial firms. This means that it will be necessary to restate the policy related to the SSI (Small Scale Industries) sector. In our opinion it is not a matter of reservation of activities to small firms—as the traditional Gandhian policy purported—but just one of special fiscal treatment, better accessibility to banking credit and export promotion, of these firms. Consequently greater economic, commercial, and financial support of the Indian authorities to small and medium sized agro-industries and allied, individually or in clusters, will be indispensable to generate massive employment and exports in the SSI sector.

In relation to the big public industrial firms, the so-called dis-investment process should continue, although gaining in intensity. Note that to privatise profitable public firms in a non-open market way—as it was done in the early-2000s—may increase the monopolistic degree in some activities, with non-significant budgetary advantages. Conversely, subsequent to fiscal reform to gain sufficiency and after negotiations with the Trade Unions, to get rid of non-strategic public firms, particularly those in heavy losses, should be an urgent and sustained policy.

Concerning the external protection of the Indian industry, we do believe that, with some exceptions (called "irritants" in the West), past disarmament of industrial tariff and non-tariff barriers could be considered as sufficient after the intensive efforts carried out by India in this field along the 90s and first years of 2000.

Also in relation with industrial matters, we do believe that the Indian treatment of FDI should significantly change, eliminating misgivings and last traces of negative discrimination in fiscal and prices issues; and above all, FDI legislation should be sustained to create certainty, against the well entrenched habit of the Indian administration to change its mind during procedures. In this regard, ordered creation or consolidation of SEZ could be a good way, for the moment not enough exploited by India, to gather significant FDI.

The currently deficient fiscal system should also be modified to enable increase of tax revenues at all administrative levels. The current volume of tax revenues of Union and states is clearly insufficient to adequately improve the volume and quality of the provided public services (let us remember the existence of an almost incipient Social Security system), and to finance the dis-investment process of the non-strategic public firms in red. At the same time, this fiscal situation generates high total public deficits, nowadays of the tune of 9-10 per cent in GDP terms, which through successive accumulation of internal indebtedness may induce at mid-term a resumption of inflation.

Indeed the current taxation system, which could have been justifiable at the time of Independence, is today far from updated. In this regard, the indirect taxation should be homogenised (finally implementing a VAT) in order to reach a unique market across all

India. In parallel, fiscal autonomy of the states should be shifted towards income tax, according to considerations of the theory of Fiscal Federalism. Additionally, and accordingly, objective and stable rules could be established for the development of a Grants-in-Aid system to efficiently improve inter-states solidarity and to eliminate states-Union misgivings.

Although the financial system is more developed in India than the Indian economy as a whole, and works significantly better than that of China, segmented financing induced by a compulsory "statutory investment ratio" (over-fulfilled by Indian bankers) and creation of lines of banking credits for different purposes—easy to be bypassed by multi-activity industrial groups—should be progressively built down. And this, while public subsidies related to interest rates for certain preferential investments of SSI and farmers could be positively enhanced. On the other hand, licensing and branching of foreign banks should be cheaper and facilitated in order to improve the average efficiency of the banking system. Throughout all the banking activity, deposit and credit, interest rates should be additionally liberalised to enable a better matching of profitability and risks.

To finalise this list of main problems of the Indian economy, we will refer to its ongoing quasi-population explosion. The recent level of the annual Indian population growth rate (1.9 per cent), though it may present advantages to India in the very long term through protracting the duration of the high speed expected growth process, is today a clear hindrance for a quicker development of the per capita GDP of the country. Logically it averts the increase of private and public savings, thus limiting the necessary increase of the domestic investment ratio.

We do believe that a primary, more protracted, and modern education system for children, in particular for girls, as a key-mechanism to deactivate population explosion, should be the greatest priority for the Union and state governments of India. Indeed, higher public expenditure in primary and secondary education is the most profitable business that any public sector may undertake in developing countries. *Ad hoc* arguments to continue subsidising higher education in India in detriment of a universal access to primary education is pure demagogy against creation of equal opportunities for all, boys and girls, and for achieving a quicker de-activation of the current rapid population growth.

7.4. Advantageous Characteristics of China and India in the World Today

Notwithstanding the commented functional deficiencies and unfavourable basic economic indicators that these two Asian giants have, one should not forget their current high speed of economic progress, and other indicators which significantly favour them.

For instance, in comparison to the rest of the countries analysed in this essay, the expenditure in GDP terms realised by China in essential issues for accelerating the economic growth, such as the expenditure in ITC (Information Technology and Communications) and R&D (basic research and development) is remarkable. Let us remember the direct incidence of these special expenditures in the growth process, as suggested by the endogenous growth theory, explained in Chapter 2. Note however that against expectations, the case of India has not been so positive in 2002, in particular in expenditures realised in IT.

As a consequence of their past rapid population rises—much quicker in the case of India in the last two decades—China and India will for long have, *ceteris paribus*, higher growth rates of their labour force. This will be an advantage in the long run for both countries, because it will make longer periods of rapid economic growth possible. This positive trait will be additionally supported in these two countries by the huge deposits of transferable people attached to agricultural activities with nil marginal productivity.

Concerning the speed of industrialisation and the contribution of this sector to the GDP, the case of China is simply amazing. Although this rapid industrialisation has been recently criticised by some economists (even by Chinese ones), the reality is that past (and current) circumstances of complex accessibility in Western markets of agriculture and services coming from the South, left few options to the Chinese government for implementing a rapid "outward looking" growth, as then recommended by mainstream economists. One should not forget either that the astonishing industrialisation process of China in the last two decades has had a lot to do with the SEZ policy implementation and the FDI there installed.

The case of the Indian industrialisation has been very different from that of China, not spectacular at all in quantitative terms, with scant intervention of FDI, and without a dramatic growth of its exports share. Certainly a very different model of industrialisation, full of misgivings towards FDI, that nevertheless in the last years is changing, thus progressively adjusting to mainstream economics.

Changing the subject, we have to underline the re-orientation of these two countries in relation to their external sectors, particularly that of China. In this regard the success of the Chinese exports has been outstanding. Its share in total world exports has currently (2003) reached a figure of 5.9 per cent from 0.8 per cent in 1978, when the reforms process started. In the same period the Indian gain in world exports share has only been moderate, shifting from 0.5 per cent in 1980 to a 0.7 per cent in 2003. Thirteen years of advantage in the initiation of the process of liberalisation (1978 *versus* 1991), early creation of SEZ and other privileged areas, and real facilitation of FDI, have made the difference between the share in total world exports of these two countries.

Although in relation with FDI and SEZ the Chinese and Indian policies have for long been diametrically opposed, both countries have significantly opened their economies in the 90s. In this regard, relative dismantling of tariffs of China and India along the 90s has been spectacular. Notwithstanding these significant reductions, the current levels of Indian tariffs are higher than those of China, due to the fact that the departure position in 1991 of the Indian ones was simply overwhelming, as a result of its previous super-autarkic policies. Anyway the indicator "growth rate of exports less GDP growth rate" places these two countries—unexpectedly for many in the case of India—among the leaders of external trade opening in the last decade.

Even more, facing the future we have to underline that the commercial success of China and India will be facilitated by (and also facilitate) the rapid growth rates of neighbouring countries, some of them much more developed than the two Asian giants. Recent statistics of the 90s (1992-2002) prove that intra-regional trade of developing countries of the East Asia-Pacific and South Asia regions is shooting up, while relative penetration of Western exports of goods in these regions is relatively fading.

Indeed, although in international trade related issues no country can easily survive in closed circuits and closed areas, the rapid growth rates of GDP and intra-regional trade of relevant Asian developing countries and regions, commanded by China and India, will progressively make this continent economically and politically less dependent from the West, thus in future leaving Western countries less and less room of manoeuvre to practise unreasonable trade policies.

7.5. Perspectives and Difficulties in the Future and Reactions

Despite the fact that the political profile of the world today is not very prone to international justice, or even to a "fairer" distribution of income simply by means of leaving "all" markets work, many developing Asian countries have reaped economic success in last decades. GDP growth rates of China and India are just proofs of this.

According to the recent trends in trade of goods, it is not difficult to anticipate that while the volume of total exports of the "high income countries" will diminish in next 16 years (in 2020) to 55-60 per cent of total international trade from its current 70-75 per cent, the volume of exports of the more dynamic Asian developing countries—those included in the East Asia-Pacific and South Asian regions—will shoot up, reaching 28-30 per cent of total world exports, from the current 13-15 per cent.

As a consequence of the current and expected growing shift of the Western demand of manufactured products to Asia, the ongoing and perhaps sustained dislocation policy of Western MNC towards Asia, and the maintenance of wages of industrial workers in Asia at a comparatively lower level, the continuation of a rapid increase of Asian industrial exports to the West is *ceteris paribus* guaranteed.

If this expectation becomes real, one could deduce that in the next 16 years (up to 2020) the volume of total industrial jobs probably will not grow at all in the West. Conversely, if things roll as they currently do, the sole continent in which a massive creation of industrial jobs is guaranteed is Asia. In particular, if some necessary economic corrections—as those mentioned lines above—were introduced in China and India, it is possible that in the period

2005-2020 the absolute industrial employment growth in China and India altogether, reach a joint amount of around 125 million jobs. An almost galactic figure for a short period of 16 years, which is over the current joint volume of industrial employment in the US and the Euro-zone. As a consequence, the industrial structure of the West will necessary change towards activities with the highest technological components and with a super-skilled human factor.

Concurrently, in trying to become less dependent on Western markets and countries, whose expected comparative growth rhythms are low, it is possible that the main Asian developing countries, particularly China and India, stress their levels of mutual economic cooperation. For instance, the creation of a great Free Trade Zone (FTZ) led by China and India is something which is nowadays already in grounding. If such a FTZ creation was successful, it would not come as a surprise if some years later, a Customs Union between these two countries and others of their hinterland would be set up. In this context, a treaty for conditioned but freer movements of capital between these two countries could also be expected, since the induced improvement in the allocation of common financial resources would not jeopardise the external financial balances of these two countries. As a complement, a joint cooperation agreement for oil searching in Asian or African countries, or the establishment of longer term contracts for guaranteed provision of oil, in consistency with significant "premiums" in the oil "futures" market, could also become a reality.

7.5.1. *Possible Economic Strategies of the West to Defend Current Positions*

Among the possible economic strategies that the West could deploy to avoid own economic and political dwindling, the most elemental one could consist of "doing nothing", just waiting for the Asian giants to simmer in their own sauce, as a consequence of the appearance of "predictable" internal or external difficulties. Troubles that, being of economic or political character, would engulf the current favourable expectations of the two Asian giants.

In our view, if the West adopted this strategy, current economic trends would *sine die* continue. This means that, conversely to what is imagined by some commentators, if China, India, and neighbouring countries continue with their velocity of economic and commercial progress (perhaps with some deceleration in the Chinese case), and Western MNC go on with their current process of industrial dislocation towards Asia—while EU-US continue with growing imports of goods and services from Asia, and with comparative low rhythms of growth—there will be no net creation of industrial jobs in the West.

Note that in this case and, in exchange of dislocation, Western GNP will significantly overcome own GDP. Of course Western citizens will for long continue being rich but with less and less jobs creation and declining relative population, thus progressively losing international political influence in a more democratic and open world.

Nevertheless, we doubt that this "non-reaction" attitude will be adopted by all rich countries. Looking back in history, it seems likely that the hegemonic power and some allies will not accept its economic decline although it comes as a derivative of the biased economic rules that, to a great extent, they themselves masterminded along last half a century.

Conversely, some ways of commercial castling seems to us more probable. These could adopt two different profiles. The first, a smooth and internationally more acceptable approach, would pursue the slowdown of the growth of imports coming from Asia, by means of lifting certain trade barriers. A second one could consist of decidedly entering into a process of commercial restrictions, which at the end of the day would be more prejudicial for the West than the former alternative. Consequently, this second alternative seems less likely.

Note for example, that under both strategies more exigent rules on post-sale services of certain industrial goods could become compulsory. Observe that the fulfilment of these rules would force Asian countries to additionally export capital to the West, thus relatively discouraging growing exports.

Alleged "social or environmental dumping"— until now part of the WTO-Singapore issues, recently "parked" after the WTO-Geneva meeting in 2004—could also be used in the future as a pretext to set up or rise *ad hoc* special barriers or rules to scrap comparative advantages of the Asian industry (not to mention obstruction devises related to agricultural exports).

It is true that the non-existence, or the underdevelopment, of Social Security systems in relevant Asian exporting countries, in particular in China and India, counts as a cost advantage for them. We do believe however that the per unit higher costs of production brought in by this concept in Western countries is something democratically chosen, and it has an equivalence to higher paid wages to Western workers used to collectively consume current or future health or security. One could wonder if poor countries should be penalised just for not being able of financing something that they would like to have: "comprehensive social security systems". Note additionally that these systems have been enhanced or grown deeper in the West, mainly along the period 1950-75 and largely because their implementation was affordable, due to the higher GDP growth rates in the "golden age of capitalism" (1950-1973).

The same could be said in relation to labour standards. In particular to the so-called problem of child labour in developing countries, interpreted in the West as a non-acceptable additional comparative advantage. Poverty is normally the cause of this behaviour by deprived families—as it happened in the West until the second half of the 20th century—and if the former argument was used to avert exports of poor countries, putting special barriers against them, their poverty would intentionally or unintentionally be aggravated by the West. Indeed, the rights of children in poor families would be better served if the West bothered to effectively bridge the poverty gap by other means.

The former argument could also be applied to other labour standards as for instance the number of annually worked hours. Note that this issue would be particularly hypocritical, given the fact that two of the Western countries that recently have grown quicker —US and UK—are countries that along the last quarter of the 20th century have significantly protracted the annual worked hours of their labourers, in order to gain comparative advantage (labour productivity), and no other rich country has protested against that. The same arguments and contra-arguments could be repeated in relation to environment standards.

We do believe that helping the poor countries to fight against these nasty situations (lack of social security, deficient labour conditions, child labour etc.) by means of providing them with growing and phased financing coming from specialised UN agencies for bridging the gap in a reasonable period of time, would be the right way to deal with these issues. Nonetheless, reading the recent history, it is possible that instead of opting for increasing development co-operation, the West regrettably take a revenge against pure market automatism, by means of linking mentioned "assumed and multifaceted foul play" of the poor, to lesser accessibility to Western markets.

Indeed, if this last strategy became real—something clearly undesirable—it would pervert the concept of comparative advantage. In such a way that even David Ricardo, if he was alive, would blush in shame.[434]

7.5.2. Reactions of China and India

In current times of full information, widespread economic and technological knowledge, and consciousness on their economic and political relevance, the effectiveness of any "foul play" against China and India does not seem to be guaranteed.

On the contrary if, in the next years or decades, aggressive economic or political initiatives were implemented by the West in order to significantly trouble the Asian (China and India) economic development, a process of bifurcation of the UN would be likely.

In other words, if economic or political initiatives taken by the West were considered as seriously damaging for the main developing

---

434. According to the theory of Ricardo, comparative advantages have to do with the relative costs of production of the different goods and services in different countries, disregarding the causes (natural or institutional) of these relative costs. The differences in the unit cost of goods or services, have to do with the different qualities and prices (or wages) of the used inputs (land, capital, labour and technology) in every country. For instance, if the land is economically more productive in a country, thus making cheaper a certain production, this activity will have a comparative advantage and its products will be exported. Note however that this advantage could always be "interpreted as unfair" by the producers of the importing countries because the exporter country has access to a (more productive) "privileged land." The same could be said in relation to "privileged (with lower wages) labour force" in comparison to the ruling wages in the importing countries when the salaries in the latter are precisely higher because it has been so decided politically at the time of creating or enhancing Social Security systems. We do believe that spurious arguments, as that of differentiated Social Security systems or different working conditions, have always been used - as it today occurs - to pervert the principle of comparative advantage. Indeed if there were no privileged factors in quality or price, there would be neither comparative advantages nor interchange.

countries, it could occur that, under the leadership of China and India, a majority of developing countries would establish an alternative to the current UN: an United Developing Nations Organisation (UDN).

If, on the other hand, China and India enhanced their current growing involvement in aid to poorest countries by establishing significant funds for the Development Financing of LDC, the conditions for mentioned bifurcation would be even less remote.

We recognise that such a process of international political and economic bifurcation would be bad news for the world as a whole. But we also acknowledge that the biased and reiterated behaviour of the West over the past decades, could in the future call this upon us. In fact, to politically control the multilateral rulers and to establish the (biased) rules of the game, to afterwards change the rules in the middle of the match because its results are inconvenient for the organisers of the party, is simply not-acceptable.

7.6. Towards a Better Solution: Changing the International Order

Consequently a better strategy for the world as a whole would be to politically reorganise the UN by means of democratising it. This would enable that the democratic movement surpass the ancient and narrow nationalistic spaces in which it has traditionally evolved, to finally reach a universal level.

Additionally, to reschedule multilateral economic institutions and to restate the current international economic order, following the principles and corollaries of the neoclassical economic model, but formulated in an international and social tenable approach, would be the best solution for the world, and consequently for China and India, and also for the West.

In this context, a reformulation of international policies in order to overcome long lasting political deprivation of some countries, and to bridge the growing economic gap, seems to be indispensable to attain international public goods, as peace and security are, necessary for avoiding future tensions in a more populated and composite world.

Restatement for reaching fairer and freer commercial rules in WTO, and above all to construct a new system of international public transfers from the UN to the "low and middle-low income" countries, to sufficiently bridge their economic gap in a reasonable period of time, are urgent needs for all and a "convenient and profitable investment in security and certainty" for rich countries.

Unfortunately, as described in the text, mentioned redistribution of economic or political power by means of international democratisation, and acceptance by rich countries of the new economic realities stemming from the divergent evolution of the economic parameters of Asia and the West in a context of growing economic freedom and solidarity obligations, do not seem very likely at short-mid term.

Note in this regard that practically the only successful method that the poor or deprived have historically found for getting justice in political and economic fields has been to put pressure in a coordinated way against powerful minorities. Observe in this respect, that current times of full information and easier co-operation (also among NGO's), arrival to adulthood of big economic and populated nations as China and India, and existence of an unequivocal trend towards democratisation all over the world, are circumstances that never have existed and that may make easier and successful the mentioned co-ordinated pressure.

Finally, we will add that although China and India—as described lines above—currently have intrinsic potentialities as to become powerful and developed countries in some decades, they should not forget that these potentialities are just some of the "necessary economic conditions" they have to fulfil for gaining the future they may reach.

Besides solving the internal challenges they face, in our world today as always in history, the additional and dominant "necessary condition" they will have to accomplish for reaching the top global levels they aspire to, is the attainment of a sufficient political clout in order to counterbalance unfair impositions that others may try to bring in. Consequently an upgrading of the international profiles of these two countries, looking for coalitions to modify current UN, could be also crucial for their definite success and for the achievement of the international public goods, which the world urgently needs at this crucial moment of history.

STATISTICAL ANNEXES

Table 1

Poverty and Social Indicators

	International Poverty Line		*Gini Index (several Years)*	*Pub. Exp. on Health 2001 (% GDP)*	*Tot. Exp. on Health 2001 (% GDP)*	*Pub. Exp. on Education 2001 (% GDP)*	*Male Adult Illiter.rate 2002 (%)*	*Pub. Exp. on Pensions (% GDP) Sev.*	*Military Exp. 2002 (% GDP)*	*Life Expect. 2002 (Number of Years)*	*Exp. on IT 2002 (% GDP)*	*Exp. on R&D 1996-2002 (% GDP)*
	Below 1$ (%)	*Below 2$(%)*										
China	16.6	46.7	44.7	2.0	5.5	2.2	7	2.7	2.5	71	5.8	1.09
India	34.7	79.9	32.5	0.9	5.1	4.1	31	(..)	2.6	63	2.8	1.23
France	(..)	(..)	32.7	7.3	9.6	5.8	(..)	13.4	2.5	79	5.2	2.20
Germany	(..)	(..)	38.3	8.1	10.8	4.5	(..)	12.1	1.5	78	5.2	2.50
Italy	(..)	(..)	36.0	6.3	8.4	4.6	1	17.6	1.9	78	4.4	1.07
UK	(..)	(..)	36.0	6.3	7.6	4.4	(..)	10.3	2.4	77	6.1	1.90
Brazil	8.2	22.4	59.1	3.2	7.6	4.0	13	9.8	1.6	69	8.3	1.05
Japan	(..)	(..)	24.9	6.2	8.0	3.6	(..)	6.9	1.0	82	5.3	3.09
Russian Fed.	6.1	23.8	45.6	3.7	5.4	3.1	(..)	5.7	4.0	66	3.7	1.16
US	(..)	(..)	40.8	6.3	13.9	4.4	(..)	7.5	3.4	77	6.1	2.80
Indonesia	7.2	52.4	34.3	0.6	2.4	1.3	8	(..)	1.1	67	1.5	(..)
South Korea	2.0	0.5	31.6	2.6	6.0	3.6	1	1.3	2.7	74	6.5	(..)
Malaysia	2.0	9.3	49.2	2.0	3.8	7.9	8	6.5	2.1	73	7.3	(..)
Phillipines	14.6	46.4	46.1	1.5	3.3	3.2	5	1.0	1.0	70	4.2	(..)
Singapore	(..)	(..)	32.8	1.3	3.9	3.7	4	1.4	5.2	78	6.5	2.11
Thailand	2.0	32.5	33.8	2.1	3.7	5.0	3	(..)	1.4	69	3.7	0.10
Vietnam	17.7	63.7	29.9	1.5	5.1	2.8	5	1.6	(..)	70	3.4	(..)

Source: World Bank (2004). World Development Indicators.

Table 2
Population

	Total Population (millions)			*Average Population Growth (%)*		*Population Age Composit. (%)*		*Crude Birth*	*Dependency Ratios Over*	*Rural Population*	
	1980	*2002*	*2015*	*1980-02*	*2002-2015*	*0-14 (2002)*	*15-64 (2002)*	*Rate (%)*	*Working People*	*2002 (%)*	*Growth Rate*
China	981	1280	1390	1.2	0.6	24.2	68.6	1.5	0.5	62	0.1
India	687	1049	1231	1.9	1.2	32.8	62.2	2.4	0.6	72	1.6
France	53	59	62	0.4	0.3	18.7	65.2	1.3	0.5	24	0.0
Germany	78	82	80	0.2	–0.2	15.1	68.1	0.9	0.4	12	–1.4
Italy	56	58	55	0.1	0.3	14.1	67.2	0.9	0.5	33	0.0
UK	56	59	59	0.2	0.0	18.4	65.6	1.1	0.5	10	–0.1
Brazil	121	174	201	1.6	1.1	27.9	66.8	1.9	0.5	18	–1.2
Japan	116	127	124	0.4	–0.2	14.3	67.6	0.9	0.5	21	–0.2
Russian Fed.	139	144	134	0.2	–0.5	16.9	70.2	0.9	0.4	27	–0.3
US	227	288	320	1.1	0.8	21.7	66.4	1.4	0.5	22	0.3
Indonesia	148	212	245	1.6	1.1	29.8	65.4	2.0	0.6	57	0.2
South Korea	38	48	50	1.0	0.4	21.0	71.8	1.2	0.4	17	-3.2
Malaysia	14	24	30	2.6	1.5	33.3	62.4	2.2	0.6	41	1.0
Phillipines	48	80	98	2.3	1.6	36.5	59.6	2.6	0.7	40	0.3
Singapore	3	4	5	2.6	1.1	21.1	71.4	1.1	0.4	0	0.0
Thailand	47	62	66	1.3	0.6	23.2	70.3	1.5	0.4	80	1.1
Vietnam	58	80	92	1.8	1.1	31.4	63.3	1.9	0.6	75	1.5

Source: World Bank (2004). World Development Indicators.

Table 3

Labour Force Structure

	Population Aged 15-64 2001 (Millions)	*Labour Force*			*% Female in Labour Force*	*Pension Contributors % of Labour Force*
		2002 (Millions)	*Growt. 1980-02 Rate*	*Growt. 2002-10 Rate*	*2002*	*Several Years*
China	**865**	**769**	**1.6**	**0.8**	**47**	**17.6**
India	**637**	**470**	**2.0**	**1.8**	**32**	**10.6**
France	38	27	0.6	0.3	45	88.4
Germany	56	41	0.4	0.0	42	94.2
Italy	39	26	0.6	–0.4	38	87.0
U.K	**38**	**29**	**0.4**	**–0.1**	**44**	**89.7**
Brazil	114	81	2.5	1.2	35	36.0
Japan	86	68	0.8	–0.4	42	97.5
Russian Fed.	101	77	0.1	–0.1	49	(..)
US	**188**	**148**	**1.4**	**0.9**	**46**	**94.0**
Indonesia	136	104	2.6	2.0	41	8.0
South Korea	34	24	2.1	1.0	42	58.0
Malaysia	15	10	3.0	2.8	38	48.7
Phillipines	46	34	2.7	2.4	38	31.0
Singapore	3	2	2.8	0.9	39	73.0
Thailand	43	37	2.0	0.7	46	18.0
Vietnam	49	42	2.2	1.7	49	8.4

Source: World Bank (2004). World Development Indicators.

Table 4

GDP and Per Capita GDP

	GDP 2002 US bn $	Average GDP Growth Rate (%)			Structure of Output (% GDP) 2002			P.ca. GDP 2002 (US$)	2002 P.ca.GDP PPP Terms	GDP 2002 PPP US$ bn.
		1980-90	1990-02	1980-02	Agriculture	Indust (Man.)	Services			
China	1.234	10.3	9.7	10.0	15	51 (35)	34	960	4.521	5.972
India	**495**	**5.7**	**5.8**	**5.8**	**23**	**27 (16)**	**51**	**470**	**2.651**	**2.778**
France	1.362	2.4	1.9	2.2	3	25 (18)	72	22.241	27.041	1.609
Germany	1.876	2.3	1.6	1.9	1	30 (28)	69	22.741	26.981	2.226
Italy	1.101	2.5	1.7	2.1	3	29 (21)	68	19.081	26.171	1.511
UK	**1.511**	**3.2**	**2.6**	**2.9**	**1**	**26 (17)**	**73**	**25.511**	**26.581**	**1.574**
Brazil	494	2.7	2.7	2.7	6	21 (13)	73	2,831	7.451	1.301
Japan	4.323	4.1	1.3	2.7	1	31 (21)	68	34.011	27.381	3.841
Russian Fed.	306	(..)	(2.7)	(..)	6	34 (..)	60	2.13	8.081	1.165
US	**9.629**	**3.5**	**3.3**	**3.4**	**2**	**25 (17)**	**73**	**35.401**	**36.111**	**10.414**
Indonesia	149	6.1	3.6	4.8	17	44 (25)	38	710	3.071	650
South Korea	473	8.9	5.6	7.2	4	41 (29)	55	9.931	16.961	808
Malaysia	86	5.3	6.2	5.7	9	47 (31)	44	3.541	8.501	207
Phillipines	82	1.0	3.5	2.3	15	33 (23)	53	1.031	4.451	130
Singapore	86	6.7	6.7	6.7	0	36 (28)	64	20.691	23.731	99
Thailand	123	7.6	3.7	5.7	9	43 (34)	48	2.001	6.981	425
Vietnam	35	4.6	7.6	6.2	23	39 (21)	38	430	2.301	185

Source: World Bank (2004). World Development Indicators.

Table 5

Nominal Growth of Trade Per Annum (% Δ) 1992-2002

Export Areas	*Import Areas (Industrialised and "High Income" Countries)*					*Import Areas (Low and Middle Income Countries)*							*World*
	EU	*Japan*	*US*	*All Industrial*	*All High Income*	*East. As-Pac.*	*Eur-Ctr.Asia*	*LatAmer. Cari*	*Md-Est-N.Afr*	*South Asia*	*SubSah. Afric*	*All Low & Mid.*	
All High income	3.3	2.4	6.1	3.9	**4.0**	8.7	7.6	2.9	0.9	5.1	1.3	6.5	**4.5**
EU	**3.5**	**3.3**	8.3	4.0	4.0	7.2	**8.6**	3.1	1.5	4.6	1.5	6.5	**4.4**
Japan	–0.9		2.2	0.9	1.4	7.1	4.0	–0.1	–3.2	–0.4	–3.5	4.0	**2.1**
US	2.9	0.7		3.8	3.8	8.2	1.8	3.9	–2.0	5.4	1.1	6.0	**4.5**
All Low and Middle inc.	7.0	6.9	11.7	8.7	8.6	14.9	3.2	7.1	6.3	10.2	9.0	**9.2**	**8.7**
East Asia-Pacific	**12.1**	9.3	**14.4**	12.0	10.5	**16.5**	10.7	16.7	10.0	**14.7**	15.8	14.3	**11.2**
Europ-Central Asia	11.2	0.2	12.7	11.0	11.0	6.3	**8.7**	7.0	5.7	8.3	10.9	7.8	**9.9**
Latin Amer-Caribe	2.4	–0.5	12.3	9.4	9.4	12.9	6.1	**7.0**	4.8	14.8	5.3	8.1	**9.1**
Middle East-North Africa	**2.7**	**3.0**	**3.7**	**3.0**	**3.3**	16.1	2.9	**–2.1**	**6.0**	**4.6**	8.7	6.7	**4.1**
South Asia	6.1	0.0	10.9	7.4	7.8	**15.5**	5.2	19.0	4.6	**9.8**	11.5	9.7	**8.3**
Sub-Saharan Africa	6.6	17.6	5.6	6.7	7.3	27.6	17.5	10.0	5.7	8.7	**11.4**	13.5	**8.8**
World	**3.9**	**3.9**	**7.7**	**4.9**	**5.0**	**9.7**	**6.0**	**4.2**	**2.1**	**6.7**	**3.3**	**7.1**	**5.4**

Source: World Bank (2004). World Development Indicators.

Table 6

Structure of External Trade of Goods and Commercial Traits

	Exports 2002 (%)			Imports 2002 (%)			Exp.of Goods & Serv./GDP	Imp.of Goods &Serv./GDP	Rate Growt.in Trade Less GDP Gr. Rate 1990-2002	Base 1995=100 Real Eff.Exch. Rate. 2002
	Food	Agri. & Raw M.	Manufactures	Food	Fuels	Manufactures				
China	5	1	90	3	7	80	29	26	4.5	121.4
India	**12**	**1**	**75**	**6**	**33**	**52**	**15**	**16**	**5.6**	**(..)**
France	11	1	81	9	9	78	27	25	**4.0**	**89.8**
Germany	4	1	86	7	8	71	35	32	**4.0**	**86.6**
Italy	7	1	88	9	9	70	27	26	**3.5**	**110.0**
UK	5	0	79	8	4	79	26	28	3.9	130.4
Brazil	28	4	54	7	15	73	16	14	**4.8**	**(..)**
Japan	1	1	93	13	19	58	10	10	**2.6**	**78.9**
Russian Fed.	2	4	22	23	2	70	35	24	**2.6**	**109.0**
US	8	2	81	5	10	78	10	14	4.5	133.6
Indonesia	12	4	54	11	21	59	35	29	**0.8**	**(..)**
South Korea	2	1	92	6	21	64	48	40	**6.9**	**(..)**
Malaysia	8	2	79	5	5	83	114	97	**(2.1)**	**115.0**
Phillipines	5	0	50	8	9	56	49	49	**3.1**	**85.6**
Singapore	2	0	85	4	13	80	174	152	**(..)**	**93.7**
Thailand	15	3	74	5	12	76	65	57	**2.9**	**(..)**
Vietnam	(..)	(..)	(..)	(..)	(..)	(..)	56	60	**(..)**	**(..)**

Source: World Bank (2004). World Development Indicators.

Table 7

Financing, Investment and Central Government Finances

	2002 Investing & Saving Process (% GDP)			2001 Central Expend., Interests and Social Sec. (%)				FDI on Gross	FDI in GDP	Dom. Gredit	Capitalisation Stock Exch.	Turnover Stock
	Gross Natio. Savings	Adjusted Net Savings	Gross Capit. Formation	Exp. Central Government om GDP	Interest on Current Revenue	Interest on Expenditure	S.Secu.Taxes on Current Revenue	Capital Form. 2001 (%)	Terms 2002 (%)	to Priv.Sector on GDP 2001 (%)	on GDP 2002 (%)	Exchange 2002 (%)
China	43.7	30.7	40	10.9	(..)	(..)	0	10.1	3.9	136.5	36.6	11.5
India	**22.3**	**9.8**	**23**	**13.0**	**37.0**	**28.1**	**0**	**3.2**	**0.6**	**32.6**	**25.7**	**14.1**
France	21.1	14.0	19	(..)	(..)	(..)	(..)	19.9	3.6	87.2	67.6	88.1
Germany	20.4	9.5	18	32.7	7.3	(..)	48	8.5	1.9	118.9	34.6	140.5
Italy	19.8	10.3	20	41.3	15.5	15.0	30	6.9	1.2	82.3	40.3	109.1
UK	14.4	7.5	16	36.0	7.7	8.0	17	25.8	1.8	142.6	119.9	135.4
Brazil	19.7	9.0	20	26.8	15.4	14.0	34	25.1	3.7	35.5	27.4	3.4
Japan	27.2	14.4	26	(..)	(..)	(..)	0	0.6	0.2	175.3	53.2	71.1
Russian Fed.	30.6	–5.7	21	26.8	9.5	10.1	26	13.7	0.9	17.6	35.8	3.0
US	**14.4**	**6.4**	**18**	**20.8**	**10.8**	**11.1**	**33**	**15.1**	**0.4**	**140.6**	**106.4**	**202.5**
Indonesia	18.2	2.1	14	24.8	21.6	19.1	2	–13.2	–0.9	22.3	17.3	3.8
South Korea	27.3	17.5	26	(..)	(..)	(..)	(..)	2.8	0.4	115.6	52.2	17.8
Malaysia	34.5	16.8	24	(..)	(..)	(..)	(..)	2.2	3.4	146.1	130.7	3.3
Phillipines	24.5	18.0	19	19.2	31.2	25.1	0	13.9	1.4	36.4	50.1	0.9
Singapore	42.7	29.6	21	22.2	1.3	1.1	0	41.4	7.0	115.5	117.2	39.3
Thailand	30.4	16.5	24	19.7	7.1	6.1	3	13.9	0.7	102.5	36.3	18.2
Vietnam	33.6	19.3	32	24.3	4.3	4.1	0	12.9	4.0	43.1	—	—

Source: World Bank (2004). World Development Indicators.

Table 8

Reserves and Outstanding External Debt

	International Reserves Bn.US$ 2002	*Imports (Goods+Services)*		*Total Exter. Debt 2002 Bn. US $*	*(%) Total Debt Serv./Imports of Go.&Ser.*	*Total Debt on GDP in 2001*
		Bn.US$ Year 2002	*Ratio Interna. Res./Imports*			
China	297	328	0.905	168	4.2	2.1
India	**72**	**83**	**0.867**	**104**	**12.6**	**2.0**
France	61	365	0.167	(..)	(..)	(..)
Germany	89	643	0.138	(..)	(..)	(..)
Italy	55	300	0.183	(..)	(..)	(..)
UK	**42**	**436**	**0.096**	**(..)**	**(..)**	**(..)**
Brazil	37	61	0.686	227	28.6	11.3
Japan	469	408	1,141	(..)	(..)	(..)
Russian Fed.	48	85	0.564	147	12.0	5.8
US	**157**	**1392**	**0.112**	**(..)**	**(..)**	**(..)**
Indonesia	32	52	0.615	132	13.8	11.1
South Korea	121	183	0.661	(..)	7.1	6.2
Malaysia	34	91	0.373	48	3.6	7.8
Phillipines	16	38	0.421	61	13.3	10.3
Singapore	82	137	0.598	(..)	(..)	(..)
Thailand	38	73	0.520	59	7.9	18.0
Vietnam	4	21	0.190	13	6.5	3.7

Source: World Bank.(2004). World Development Indicators.

Table 9

Tax Structure and Tax Policies

	Tax Revenue % on GDP 2002	*Taxes on Income Profit & Capit. Gains on Total Taxes 2002 (%)*	*Dom. Taxes on Goods & Serv. on Add Value 2002 (%)*	*Import Duties on Tax Revenue in %*	*Highest Marginal Tax Rate*	
					Individual Rate	*Corporate Rate*
China	6.8	(..)	13.0	(..)	40	17
India	**9.9**	**37.4**	**5.5**	**24.1**	**30**	**37**
France	(..)	(..)	(..)	(..)	(..)	33
Germany	(..)	(..)	8.9	6.1	49	27
Italy	38.5	38.8	11.6	0.0	45	34
UK	**34.3**	**41.8**	**12.8**	**0.0**	**40**	**30**
Brazil	(..)	(..)	(..)	(..)	28	15
Japan	(..)	(..)	(..)	(..)	37	30
Russian Fed.	22.5	10.8	11.3	5.1	13	24
US	**17.7**	**55.5**	**0.7**	**1.0**	**39**	**35**
Indonesia	13.6	48.0	6.5	4.6	35	30
South Korea	(..)	(..)	(..)	(..)	36	27
Malaysia	(..)	(..)	(..)	(..)	28	28
Phillipines	13.3	45.6	4.7	19.6	32	32
Singapore	15.4	52.7	5.1	2.6	22	22
Thailand	14.4	34.3	7.8	12.3	37	30
Vietnam	16.4	32.0	9.0	22.8	(..)	32

Source: World Bank (2004). World Development Indicators.

Table 10

Rural and Urban Environment

	Rural Population		Urban Population		Rural Population	Arable & Irrigated Land		% Irrig. Land	Per Cap.Used
	% Over Total Population	Aver. Growth Rate1980-02 in %	% Over Total Population	Popul. in Cities Over 1 Million % on Total	Density per sq.Km.2001	Arable Land on Land Area 2001%	% Permanent Cropland on Land Ar.2001	Cropland 1999-2001	Comm.Energy 2001.Kg.of Equiv.Oil
China	**62**	**0.1**	**38**	**14**	**561**	**15.4**	**1.2**	**36.3**	**896**
India	**72**	**1.6**	**28**	**10**	**460**	**54.4**	**2.7**	**32.2**	**515**
France	24	0.0	76	21	78	33.5	2.1	13.4	4.487
Germany	12	-1.4	88	41	86	33.9	0.6	4.0	4.264
Italy	33	0.1	67	19	232	27.8	9.5	24.2	2.981
UK	**10**	**-0.**	**90**	**23**	**109**	**23.5**	**0.2**	**1.8**	**3.982**
Brazil	18	-1.2	82	34	54	7.0	0.9	4.4	1.074
Japan	21	-0.2	79	38	603	12.2	1.0	54.7	4.099
Russian Fed.	27	-0.3	73	(..)	32	7.3	0.1	3.6	4.293
US	**22**	**0.3**	**78**	**38**	**37**	**19.1**	**0.2**	**12.6**	**7.996**
Indonesia	57	0.2	43	10	591	11.3	7.2	14.4	729
South Korea	17	-3.2	83	14	491	20.8	2.5	60.4	4.114
Malaysia	41	1.0	59	6	554	5.5	17.6	4.8	2.168
Phillipines	40	0.3	60	16	564	18.9	16.8	14.6	538
Singapore	0	0.0	100	89	0	1.6	0.0	(..)	7.058
Thailand	80	1.1	20	12	326	29.4	6.5	27.1	1.235
Vietnam	75	1.5	25	13	923	20.0	6.0	37.6	495

Source: World Bank (2004). World Development Indicators.